Rhetorical Criticism

Rhetorical Criticism

Context, Method, and the Book of Jonah

by
PHYLLIS TRIBLE

FORTRESS PRESS
Minneapolis

In Memoriam

Ralph E. McLain

RHETORICAL CRITICISM

Library of Congress Cataloging-in-Publication Data
Trible, Phyllis.
   Rhetorical criticism : context, method, and the book of Jonah / by Phyllis Trible.
      p.   cm—(Guides to biblical scholarship. Old Testament guides)
   Includes bibliographical references.
   ISBN 0-8006-2798-9 (alk. paper) :
   1. Bible.   O.T.   Jonah—Criticism, interpretation, etc.
   2. Rhetoric in the Bible.   I. Title.   II. Series: Guides to
   Biblical scholarship.   Old Testament series.
   BS1605.2.T75   1994
   220.6'6—dc20   94-34616
                                                                          CIP

The paper used in this publication meets the minimum requirements of American National Standard for Information Sciences—Permanence of Paper for Printed Library Materials, ANSI Z329.48-1984.   ∞™

Manufactured in the U.S.A.   AF 1-2798
98   97   96   95   94   1   2   3   4   5   6   7   8   9   10

Contents

Editor's Foreword

This book continues a series of volumes designed to introduce and demonstrate the various methods of biblical criticism. Rhetorical criticism, the focus of this volume, often in our time has been associated with the work of the late James Muilenburg, but, as Phyllis Trible shows, it is neither a new approach nor limited to a narrow school. Rather, a great many scholars identify their work as such, and virtually all interpreters of the Bible are concerned with its rhetoric, understood in one way or another.

In accounting for the broad context of rhetorical criticism, Trible considers its roots in Greek civilization in the fifth century B.C.E. She discusses the history of literary critical theory and of the literary study of the Bible, from ancient times into the contemporary period. What originated as legal persuasion became the art of persuasive speech, and oratory became literature. Since the time of Aristotle, two understandings of rhetoric (and of rhetorical criticism) have emerged. Narrowly, rhetoric is viewed as discovering the means of persuasion (Aristotle). More broadly, rhetoric is the art of speech and composition. These two views—of rhetoric as the art of persuasion and of rhetoric as the art of composition—persist into contemporary biblical scholarship.

James Muilenburg is the modern ancestor of this enterprise, and his presidential address to the Society of Biblical Literature in 1968 was a decisive turning point. But those who followed his lead have done so by cutting new trails as well. The rhetorical criticism unfolded in this volume is not the same as it was in 1968, although the genetic links are both strong and clear. A great deal has taken place in biblical studies in the last three decades, especially in the literary study of the Bible. So Trible is careful to set out rhetorical criticism in relation to such developments, and to show how it has grown in interaction with other approaches. In locating rhetorical criticism in its contemporary matrix, Trible presents a perceptive analysis of the flood of literary critical theory that has emerged in recent years. And in the process she addresses many of the highly debated issues about the status of text, reader, and interpretation in the contemporary biblical (as well as the literary and philosophical) scenes.

Broadly speaking, rhetorical criticism is a literary method—in contrast with, for example, the historical investigation of the background of the Bible, or the history of the biblical literature. It is a literary approach in that it is text-centered. What Trible sees as distinctive about rhetorical criticism is its insistence upon the organic unity of form and content. Although she knows they are not the same, Trible refuses to drive a wedge between form and content, arguing that "proper articulation of form-content yields proper articulation of meaning."

This book was written on several levels and will engage a range of readers to their benefit. On the one hand, it is for the student just beginning to explore the Bible critically. So it introduces a way of reading and interpreting biblical literature. On the other hand, it is for the seasoned scholar, addressing issues of importance at the cutting edge of the discipline of biblical studies, and presenting for the first time a comprehensive statement of rhetorical criticism.

The work is didactic both directly and indirectly. In addition to describing the·approach in its context and giving practical guidelines, the rhetorical features frequently recognized in biblical literature are woven into the warp and woof of the book itself. Thus chapters are constructed chiastically and Part Two is designed as an *inclusio*. But we should refrain from further comment on this point lest we spoil the surprise (and delight) for the reader. Suffice it to say that the book itself is an example of rhetoric, and Trible frequently explains what she is doing in terms of the classical categories of rhetoric. Moreover, concise summaries conclude both small and large sections.

Part One introduces the method in context and Part Two is a demonstration of the approach. It is not accurate to say that in Part Two the method is applied to the Book of Jonah. Rather, rhetorical criticism is presented as it works through a single piece of biblical literature. Jonah is read through the lens of this approach, but not without attention to other angles of vision. Along the way Trible calls the reader's attention to interpretive moves as they are made. The demonstration enables one to learn the method by seeing it at work on a text and—as Trible points out—by seeing the biblical text at work on the method.

Gene M. Tucker
Emory University

Preface

When I was a child, the wondrous story of Jonah fascinated, frightened, and filled me full. When I became a college student, I did not put away childish interests but began to transpose them into critical reflection. Instrumental in the transposition was Ralph E. McLain, then head of the Department of Religion at Meredith College. His insightful teaching, which included an unforgettable assignment and lecture on Jonah, introduced me to biblical scholarship. On his recommendation I undertook further study at Union Theological Seminary. There I fell under the spell of James Muilenburg, whose sensitivities to the literary and theological dimensions of scripture changed my life. When I became a doctoral student in search of a dissertation topic, he welcomed the choice of Jonah. At that juncture, scholars paid little attention to the book. Their lack of interest provided me a niche for research that joined childhood fascination and critical learning. Yielding to the method that Professor Muilenburg would later call "rhetorical criticism," the story began to reveal its treasures.

In the years since I completed the dissertation, Jonah studies have become an industry. Monographs of all sorts continue to pour forth. They exploit the riches of the book without diminishing its resilience. Despite great waves of words stirring up storms on the sea of scholarship, Jonah refuses to be drowned. It survives for yet other readers and other seasons. So when the opportunity came to prepare a guidebook on rhetorical criticism, Jonah surfaced as the text best suited for my didactic efforts. The return to serious study of the narrative has disclosed once again unexpected treasures. But it has also brought unrelenting toil. Given the expanding world in which biblical studies now reside, no explication of rhetorical criticism, on whatever text, can be done apart from an acknowledged context. Unlike the ephemeral plant that became Jonah's setting, this context continues to grow, seemingly without end. And it does not always give shade—nor deliver one from evil.

If no single author can control all that is involved, she can call upon friends, colleagues, and students. Professor David Lotz read the historical overview in chapter 1 with the same perspicacity he brings to bear on students' papers. Professor Barry Ulanov lent his vast knowledge of literary history, theory, and practice to the editing of chapters 1 through 4. Professor George Landes, who after serving on my doctoral committee developed his own interest in Jonah, listened with patience to my rhetorical ramblings. Ms. Kay Chalmers, Scottish Fellow in Old Testament at Union Theological Seminary during 1992–93, performed bibliographical and editorial services with enthusiasm and alacrity. Ms. Yeong-Mee Lee, doctoral student in Old Testament, delivered the text from many errors by her close attention to detail.

Three people have tended the manuscript in its entirety. Julie Galas, faculty secretary, prepared numerous drafts with skill and verve. She nurtured the project through its early stages. Dr. Angela Bauer, having just completed a doctoral dissertation in the biblical field, used the intricacies of the computer to tame the complexities of the text. In the process, she feared not to hold me to the high standards to which she had been held. Sarah Ryan, with sensitivity and sense developed over years of teaching, made sure that the words could reach an audience beyond the biblical guild. She read them many times, from the beginnings long ago through countless versions to the very end. Each of these women has cheerfully endorsed the refrain that "we have to get it right."

In dedicating this book to the memory of Ralph McLain, I honor Meredith College. For over a century it has upheld standards of excellence in the education of women. There I first beheld a host of women who had earned doctorates. Exceptional in their day, they encouraged by example and precept the love of learning. They taught me that I too might pursue scholarly delights. Let the record show the names of Professors Julia Hamlet Harris, Norma Rose, and Maxine Garner.

Phyllis Trible

Abbreviations

AB	Anchor Bible
ABD	*Anchor Bible Dictionary*
BBR	*Bulletin for Biblical Research*
BDB	F. Brown, S. R. Driver, and C. A. Briggs, *A Hebrew and English Lexicon of the Old Testament*
BSOAS	*Bulletin of the School of Oriental and African Studies*
BZ	*Biblische Zeitschrift*
CBQ	*Catholic Biblical Quarterly*
CHB	Cambridge History of the Bible
FOTL	Forms of Old Testament Literature
HAR	*Hebrew Annual Review*
HBT	*Horizons in Biblical Theology*
HKAT	Handkommentar zum Alten Testament
HTR	*Harvard Theological Review*
HUCA	*Hebrew Union College Annual*
IB	*The Interpreter's Bible*
ICC	International Critical Commentary
IDBS	Interpreter's Dictionary of the Bible Supplement
Int	*Interpretation*
JAAR	*Journal of the American Academy of Religion*
JB	Jerusalem Bible
JBL	*Journal of Biblical Literature*
JQR	*Jewish Quarterly Review*
JSOT	*Journal for the Study of the Old Testament*
LCL	Loeb Classical Library
NAB	New American Bible
NEB	New English Bible
NJV	New Jewish Version

NPEPP	*The New Princeton Encyclopedia of Poetry and Poetics*
NRSV	New Revised Standard Version
RSV	Revised Standard Version
SBL	Society of Biblical Literature
VT	*Vetus Testamentum*
ZAW	*Zeitschrift für die alttestamentliche Wissenschaft*

Prologue

In the making of rhetoric there are tongues and the confusion of tongues. From the ancient to the contemporary world, the concept elicits disparate meanings: the trivial and the profound, the ugly and the sublime, the pejorative and the adulatory, the popular and the scholarly. Amid the confusion, this study explicates one kind of rhetorical criticism used in biblical studies.

The two parts of the book bear different tasks. Part One sets the context. Chapter 1 sketches the background; chapter 2 introduces biblical rhetorical criticism; chapter 3 expands the background. The discussion invites readers to join an enormous conversation not by feigning knowledge through facile acquaintance but by choosing a few topics for detailed study. Part Two presents the method. Chapter 4 offers guidelines for beginning. Chapters 5 through 9 show rhetorical criticism at work on the book of Jonah. Chapter 10 offers guidelines for continuing use of the method. The discussion invites readers to learn rhetorical criticism and begin to practice it.

As a whole, the book adds yet another tongue to the perennial making of rhetoric—without confusion, one hopes.

PART ONE
CONTEXT

1
Sketching the Background

In December 1968 James Muilenburg delivered to the Society of Biblical Literature his presidential address entitled "Form Criticism and Beyond."[1] He named the "beyond" rhetorical criticism, thereby bringing a time-honored rubric to the attention of the Society. Though he presented the endeavor as a supplement to form criticism, it has since become a full-fledged discipline evoking a rich heritage and enjoying a vital presence.

This chapter begins to set the context for rhetorical criticism as proposed by Muilenburg and expanded by his successors. It sketches four components that form the background of the discipline: classical rhetoric, literary critical theory, literary study of the Bible, and form criticism.

A. CLASSICAL RHETORIC

In ancient Greece a professor or public speaker known as "rhetor" (ῥήτωρ) taught a subject called "rhetoric" (ῥητορική). It signified the "art" (τέχνη) of discourse that in time became a complex system of communication.[2]

---

1. James Muilenburg, "Form Criticism and Beyond," JBL 88 (1969): 1–18.
2. For the primary texts, translated and edited, see the Loeb Classical Library Series (Cambridge: Mass. and London)[LCL]. Secondary sources helpful in compiling this sketch include Renato Barilli, *Rhetoric*, trans. Guiliana Menozzi, *Theory and History of Literature*, vol. 63 (Minneapolis: University of Minnesota Press, 1989); George A. Kennedy, *Classical Rhetoric and Its Christian and Secular Tradition from Ancient to Modern Times* (Chapel Hill: The University of North Carolina Press, 1980); Peter Dixon, *Rhetoric* (London: Methuen, 1971); Ernst Robert Curtius, *European Literature and the Latin Middle Ages*, Bollingen Series 36, trans. Willard R. Trask (New York: Pantheon Books, 1953), 62–72. For a

1. Historical Overview

Although the antecedents of classical rhetoric belong to the Homeric traditions of the ninth century B.C.E., the concept emerged in the fifth century.[3] Greeks in Sicily devised persuasive ways to defend themselves in legal disputes. When these oral skills reached Athens, they underwent significant changes as rhetoric expanded beyond legal persuasion. Four developments mark the early history of the subject. First, the Sophists (fifth century B.C.E.) emphasized the verbal acumen of a public speaker apart from the truth or morality of the speech. Isocrates (436–338 B.C.E.) countered this view, insisting that ethics and philosophy join structure and style to constitute the art of discourse.[4] Further, by writing rather than delivering his speeches, he turned oratory into literature. Second, Socrates (469–399 B.C.E.) and Plato (428–348 B.C.E.) extended the criticism made by Isocrates. In the dialogues, Socrates attacked rhetoricians for their irresponsible disregard of truth or logic (dialectic).[5] He deemed their art invalid unless eloquence served wisdom. On compositional matters he advanced the concept of organic unity as fundamental to proper speech: the need to define the subject and make certain that the parts fit the whole.[6] Third, Aristotle (384–322 B.C.E.) in *The "Art" of Rhetoric* provided the first comprehensive treatment of the discipline as art, science, theory, and practice.[7] In contrast with Plato, he defined it as a counterpart of logic (dialectic). It was not verbal ornamentation but a technique of argument. Rather than simply to persuade, rhetoric sought to discover "the possible means of persuasion in reference to any subject

---

standard textbook, see Edward P. J. Corbett, *Classical Rhetoric for the Modern Student,* 3rd ed. (New York: Oxford University Press, 1990).

    3. For another view, see Thomas Cole, who argues that "the word *rhetoric* itself bears every indication of being a Platonic invention." In other words, rhetoric originates in the fourth century. See *The Origins of Rhetoric in Ancient Greece* (Baltimore: The Johns Hopkins University Press, 1991), 2.

    4. Isocrates, 3 vols., trans. George Norlin and Larue van Hook, LCL (1980–82). See esp. "Against the Sophists," and "Antiodosis," vol. 2, 160–77; 179–365. The ancient debate between philosophy and rhetoric continues to the present; see Stanley Fish, "Rhetoric," *Critical Terms for Literary Study,* eds. Frank Lentricchia and Thomas McLaughlin (Chicago: University of Chicago Press, 1990), 203–22.

    5. See, e.g., Plato, "Gorgias," vol. 3, trans. W. R. M. Lamb, LCL (1975), 249–535.

    6. See Plato, "Phaedrus," vol. 1, trans. Harold North Fowler, LCL (1982), 407–579.

    7. See Aristotle, *The "Art" of Rhetoric,* vol. 22, trans. John Henry Freese, LCL (1982); Aristotle, *On Rhetoric,* trans., with notes by George A. Kennedy (New York: Oxford University Press, 1991). Kennedy helpfully eliminates sexist language found in older translations but absent in the original; cf. xii.

whatever."[8] Fourth, the anonymous author of the treatise *On the Sublime* (first century C.E.) moved away from the Aristotelian formulation.[9] He developed a literary (written) rhetoric whose effect "is not to persuade the audience but rather to transport them out of themselves."[10] Balancing technique with the inspiration of the author, he advocated the power of the sublime.

From the Greeks rhetoric passed to the Romans. The principal figure Cicero (106–43 B.C.E.) recorded the history of the subject and made his own substantial contribution. Indeed, his *De Inventione* became the primary authority for more than a millennium.[11] *De Oratore*, his greatest work, held a triumphal view of rhetoric as "art of arts."[12] It organized and unified the world, bringing together form and content, theory and practice, thinking and speaking, ethics and style. This stance recalled the perspective of Isocrates and presaged the work of the orator and teacher Quintilian (40–95 C.E.). Though the latter departed from Cicero by positing a relationship instead of a unity between words and thoughts, he shared the view of rhetoric as a comprehensive whole.[13] It included ethics and eloquence. Describing rhetoric as the discipline of speaking well (*bene dicendi scientia*), Quintilian stressed the persuasive and moral power of public speech. His *Institutio Oratoria* conceived the subject as the center of a complete educational system.

2. Representative Features

Elements, types, and goals constituted major categories of classical rhetoric.[14] Each came in sets of three. The elements involved in

---

8. See Aristotle, *Rhetoric*, LCL, I.ii 2.

9. "Longinus" *On the Sublime* in Aristotle, *The Poetics*, trans. W. Hamilton Fyfe, LCL (1982), 119–254.

10. Ibid., 1.4.

11. Cicero, *De Inventione*, vol. 2, trans. H. M. Hubbell, LCL (1976). Cf. *Rhetorica ad Herennium*, trans. Harry Caplan, LCL (1989). Though long attributed to Cicero, this textbook on civil and moral rhetoric, with an extended treatment on memory, was perhaps written by an associate. See Harry Caplan, *Of Eloquence: Studies in Ancient and Mediaeval Rhetoric*, eds. and intro., by Anne King and Helen North (Ithaca: Cornell University Press, 1970), 1–25.

12. Cicero, *De Oratore*, Books 1 and 2, trans. E. W. Sutton and H. Rackham, LCL (1988); Book 3, trans. H. Rackham, LCL (1982). Cf. Barilli, *Rhetoric*, 26–33.

13. Quintilian, *Institutio Oratoria*, trans. H. E. Butler, LCL (1980).

14. On the elements and the types, see Aristotle, *Rhetoric* 1.3; on the goals, see Cicero, *De Oratore*, 2.114–29.

communication were speaker, speech, and audience (or author, text, and reader). The types of communication were judicial, deliberative, and demonstrative. Each had a particular focus, setting, purpose, time, and emphasis. Judicial rhetoric, focused on justice, belonged to the law court. Through artful words the speaker sought to persuade the audience (the judge) to make a right decision about past events. Speech received the emphasis. Deliberative rhetoric, focused on expediency, belonged to public assembly. Through artful words the speaker sought to persuade the audience about future events. The audience as "judge of things to come" (Aristotle) received the emphasis. Demonstrative rhetoric, focused on adulation, belonged to public ceremony. Through artful words the speaker sought to move the audience to praise for individuals in the present. The speaker as orator received the emphasis. The goals of communication were directed to the audience: the intellectual goal of teaching, the emotional goal of touching the feelings, and the aesthetic goal of pleasing so as to hold attention.

Besides delineating elements, types, and goals, ancient rhetoricians divided their subject into five parts, called "canons" or "faculties."[15] Invention (*inventio*) concerned the discovery of material suitable to the occasion. Arrangement or structure (*dispositio*) organized material into an ordered whole from introduction through conclusion. Style (*elocutio*), whether grand, moderate, or simple, sought appropriate words for content. It investigated figures and tropes. Memory (*memoria*) devised mnemonic systems as preparation for oral delivery. It signaled the firm grasp of content and form. Delivery (*pronunciatio* or *actio*) concentrated on aspects of oral presentation appropriate to the subject and the style. Within each part subdivisions abounded to produce an elaborate system of rules for rhetoric.

The chart on the following page encapsulates major features of classical rhetoric.[16]

Summary. Heterogeneous viewpoints lent flexibility to the development of classical rhetoric.[17] Alongside the narrow definition of discovering the means of persuasion stood the broad concept of the art of speech and composition. Debates about words (*verba*) and things (*res*), about form

---

15. See Cicero, *De Inventione* 1.9; also *De Oratore*, Books 2 and 3. Though the nomenclature for the five parts appeared first in Greek, the Latin terms are more familiar.
16. Sarah Ryan prepared the chart.
17. See H. I. Marrou, *A History of Education in Antiquity* (New York: Sheed and Ward, 1956), 52–54, 84–91, 284–91.

THREE ELEMENTS OF COMMUNICATION
speaker or author
speech or text
audience or reader

THREE TYPES OF COMMUNICATION

	judicial (forensic)	deliberative (hortatory)	demonstrative (*epideictic*)
focus:	justice	expediency	adulation/denunciation
setting:	law court	public assembly	public ceremony
purpose:	to persuade	to persuade	to please or inspire
time:	past	future	present
emphasis:	speech	audience	speaker

THREE GOALS OF COMMUNICATION
intellectual goal of teaching
emotional goal of touching the feelings
aesthetic goal of pleasing so as to hold attention

FIVE PARTS OF RHETORIC

Invention (*inventio*):	discovery of material suitable to the occasion
Structure (*dispositio*):	arrangement of material in an organized whole
Style (*elocutio*):	choice of appropriate words; use of figures and tropes
Memory (*memoria*):	formulation of mnemonic systems as preparation for oral delivery
Delivery (*pronunciatio/actio*):	features of oral presentation

and content, about theory and practice, also resulted in diverse formulations. Yet insistence upon the inseparability of these pairs countered any interpretation of style (*elocutio*) as mere embellishment.[18] Tropes and figures of speech illuminated substance. In addition, the Socratic concept of organic unity, the relation of parts to the whole, shaped the nature of communication. Such features provide the first component in the background of biblical rhetorical criticism.

18. *De Oratore* argues this case forcefully.

B. LITERARY CRITICAL THEORY

With affinities to classical rhetoric, literary critical theory forms the second component.[19] A model devised by the twentieth century American critic M. H. Abrams presents an overview of the subject.[20] Four elements constitute the total situation of a literary artifact: the work, the artist, the universe, and the audience. Abrams orders them in a triangle with the work of art at the center.

Universe
↑
Work
↙   ↘
Artist   Audience

The particular emphasis assigned each element gives rise to four sets of theories about the nature of literature: mimetic, pragmatic, expressive, and objective.

1. Mimetic Theories

The most ancient and persistent approach holds that literature mirrors a world external to itself. The Greek word *mimesis* (imitation) denotes the concept. Aristotle held that *mimesis* is characteristic of all art but differs according to the means it uses, the objects it considers, and the manner it exhibits.[21] Using these criteria, he separated literature from such artistic endeavors as flute and lyre playing. In identifying major genres, notably epic, tragedy, and comedy, he asserted that a single orientation controls

---

19. For a useful collection that spans classical rhetoric and literary theory, see D. A. Russell and M. Winterbottom, eds., *Ancient Literary Criticism: The Principal Texts in New Translations* (Oxford: Oxford University Press, 1972). For a standard textbook on the history of Western literary criticism, see Hazard Adams, ed., *Critical Theory Since Plato* (New York: Harcourt Brace Jovanovich, 1971); cf. "General Introduction," 1–10.

20. M. H. Abrams, *The Mirror and the Lamp: Romantic Theory and the Critical Tradition* (London: Oxford University Press, 1953), esp. 3–29. Though quite helpful, this model simplifies a rich subject made even more complex by multicultural sensitivities.

21. See *Aristotle's Poetics: A Translation and Commentary for Students of Literature*, trans. Leon Golden, commentary by O. B. Hardison, Jr. (Englewood Cliffs, N.J.: Prentice-Hall, 1968); cf. also the introduction and selections in Adams, *Critical Theory*, 47–66.

them all. "The capacity to produce an imitation is the essential characteristic of the poet."[22]

The mimetic perspective concentrates on the universe, a comprehensive term that refers to existing things: people, ideas, images, materials, or actions. It evaluates literature by how well it imitates, represents, or copies the external world. Various formulations of the concept dominate literary theory from the fourth century B.C.E. through the eighteenth century C.E.[23] The orientation persists to this day.

2. Pragmatic Theories

In the late sixteenth century, the Englishman Sir Philip Sidney (1554–86) drew attention to the second orientation, namely the audience whom literature addresses. While assenting to Aristotle's maxim that "poesy therefore is an art of imitation," he shifted emphasis from representation to effect as he concluded, "with this end, to teach and delight."[24] His words echoed the Latin poet Horace (65–8 B.C.E.) who had written that "the aim of the poet is either to benefit, or to amuse, or to make his words at once please and give lessons of life."[25]

The emphasis produces pragmatic or affective theories. They evaluate literature according to its effect upon the audience, an endeavor that aligns literary discourse with classical rhetoric. Though present in the ancient and medieval worlds, the pragmatic orientation gained prominence in later times.

3. Expressive Theories

The third orientation centers on the artist. In his "Preface to the Second Edition of *Lyrical Ballads*," William Wordsworth (1770–1850)

---

22. *Aristotle's Poetics*, 4. For a helpful discussion, with the relevant texts from the *Poetics* and the *Rhetoric*, see Aristotle, *On Poetry and Style*, trans., with an introduction, G. M. A. Grube (Indianapolis: Hackett Publishing, 1989). In contrast with Aristotle, Plato disparaged mimesis, claiming that art is twice removed from reality. It imitates the world of sense (appearance), which in turn imitates the external world of ideas. See esp. the selections from the *Republic* and the *Laws* in Adams, *Critical Theory*, 11–46.

23. For a major study, extending into the twentieth century, see Erich Auerbach, *Mimesis: The Representation of Reality in Western Literature* (Princeton, N.J.: Princeton University Press, 1953).

24. See Sir Philip Sidney, "An Apology for Poetry," in Adams, *Critical Theory*, 154–77, esp. 158.

25. See Horace, "Art of Poetry," in Adams, *Critical Theory*, 67–75, esp. 73.

described poetry as "the spontaneous overflow of powerful feelings; it takes its origin from emotion recollected in tranquility."[26] A work of art primarily expresses the author's own mind, heart, and soul rather than reflecting the universe or affecting the audience. The view thus evaluates literature by how well it manifests the particular experience of the artist.

Though expressive theories governed literary criticism in the nineteenth century, their roots belonged to the ancient world. Writing about the sources of elevated language, the anonymous author of *On the Sublime* held it "impossible that those whose thoughts and habits all their lives long are petty and servile should flash out anything wonderful, worthy of immortal life. No, a great style is the natural outcome of weighty thoughts, and sublime sayings naturally fall to men of spirit." He concluded that "sublimity is the true ring of a noble mind."[27] The sentiment presaged Wordsworth's description of poetry to forge another link between classical rhetoric and literary theory.

4. Objective Theories

What Wordsworth avowed, T. S. Eliot disavowed. For him, "poetry is not a turning loose of emotion, but an escape from emotion; it is not the expression of personality, but an escape from personality."[28] Eliot insisted upon the text as "something made" (*poiesis*) in and of itself. "When we are considering poetry," he said, "we must consider it primarily as poetry and not another thing."[29]

This fourth orientation, centering on the literary artifact, has brought forth objective theories with names such as formalism, aesthetics, and New Criticism. They all reject the concept of literature as a means to an end, whether mimetic, pragmatic, or expressive. Instead, they deem each text a self-subsisting aesthetic object. As a unique configuration of form and content, a text constitutes an intrinsic world of interrelated elements that work together to produce an organic whole. The familiar aphorism of Archibald MacLeish (1892–1982) captures the point: "A poem should

---

26. See William Wordsworth, "Preface to the Second Edition of *Lyrical Ballads*," in Adams, *Critical Theory*, 432–43, esp. 441.

27. See "Longinus" *On the Sublime* 9.1–4.

28. T. S. Eliot, "Tradition and the Individual Talent," in Adams, *Critical Theory*, 783–87.

29. Cf. the use of this quotation by Abrams, *The Mirror and the Lamp*, 27.

not mean / But be."[30] The perspective evaluates literature according to its internal coherence.

Even though antecedents for objective theories run through Coleridge (1772–1834) all the way back to Aristotle, not until the twentieth century has attention focused on the work itself as the sine qua non for literary criticism. In 1949 René Wellek and Austin Warren presented a definitive statement of the orientation.[31] Some years later, Northrop Frye tempered objective theories by situating individual texts within a community of literature. The critical significance of his contribution awaits analysis.[32]

    ✿   ✿   ✿   ✿   ✿   ✿   ✿

Summary. Mimetic, affective, expressive, and objective orientations have appeared in literary-critical theory from Aristotle on, though each has held sway at different times. Throughout the long history, well into the twentieth century, critics have concentrated on the question of value.[33] Assuming the meaning of literature, they have asked whether a text is good and what makes it so. They have answered from the perspectives of the universe, the audience, the artist, and the work. In the latter half of the twentieth century, however, critics have concentrated on the question of interpretation. Assuming the value of literature, they have asked what it means. In answering from the perspectives of the universe, the audience, the artist, and the work, they have viewed the interpretive task as endless.[34] Among other results, the shift from evaluation to interpretation has aligned the study of secular and sacred texts. Biblical scholars, assuming the value of the text they study, have always sought its meaning(s) and in the process have used (often unwittingly) the four orientations of secular literary theory. Accordingly, these perspectives play major roles in shaping the background of biblical rhetorical criticism.

C. LITERARY STUDY OF THE BIBLE

The third component consists of innumerable contributions over millennia to literary study of the Bible. Like classical rhetoric and literary

---

30. Archibald MacLeish, "Ars Poetica," in *Contemporary Trends: American Literature Since 1900*, eds. John Herbert Nelson and Oscar Cargill (New York: The Macmillan Co., 1949), 357–58.

31. René Wellek and Austin Warren, *Theory of Literature* (New York: Harcourt, Brace & World, 1949).

32. See Northrop Frye, *Anatomy of Criticism* (Princeton: Princeton University Press, 1957). On Frye, see chapter 3.

33. This discussion draws upon E. D. Hirsch, Jr., "Carnal Knowledge," *New York Review of Books* 26 (14 June 1979): 18–20.

34. Hirsch himself reduces norms for interpretation to the reader and the author.

theory, it constitutes a history; unlike them, it does not constitute a discipline. A sampling hints at the story.[35]

1. Ancient Times

At the turn of the Common Era the Jewish philosopher Philo (c. 20 B.C.E.–50 C.E.) claimed that Moses learned from the Egyptians the lore of Greek meter, rhythm, and harmony, all of which he used to compose Hebrew poetry.[36] The Jewish historian Josephus (37–100 C.E.) similarly declared that Moses used hexameter verse to compose a song to God (Exod. 15) and to recite a poem to the people (Deut. 32) and that David, when free from fighting wars, fashioned "songs and hymns to God in varied meters—some he made in trimeters, and others in pentameters."[37] Among the early church fathers, Jerome (331–420) emerged as a consummate stylist, having studied Latin grammar and rhetoric.[38] Comparing Roman and biblical literature, he judged the latter superior. Who needs Horace, he asked, when one has the Psalter? Who needs Virgil when one has the Gospels? Who needs Cicero when one has Paul? Augustine (354–430) also compared the two literatures. To this task he brought an education comparable to Jerome's and, beyond that, a professorship in rhetoric.[39] At first Augustine found the Bible inferior to the "sublimity of Cicero" and so appealed instead to the deep mysteries of scripture that delighted the mind.[40] But later he conceived a Christian rhetoric that judged the Bible

---

35. For an overview, see *The Cambridge History of the Bible (CHB)*, 3 vols. (Cambridge, Eng.: The University Press, 1963–70); for a compendium of literary commentary, see Alex Preminger and Edward L. Greenstein, eds., *The Hebrew Bible in Literary Criticism* (New York: Ungar, 1986).

36. Philo, *De Vita Mosis*, vol. 6, trans. F. H. Colson, LCL (1966), 1.23.

37. Josephus, *Jewish Antiquities*, vol. 4, Books 1–4, trans. H. St. J. Thackeray, LCL (1978), 2.345–46 and 4.302–3; ibid., vol. 5, Book 7, trans. Thackeray and Ralph Marcus, LCL (1977), 7.305.

38. See, e.g., J. N. D. Kelley, *Jerome: His Life, Writings, and Controversies* (London: Duckworth, 1975), esp. 10–17, 141–67; Curtius, *European Literature*, 39–40, 72–73, 446–48; H. F. D. Sparks, "Jerome As Biblical Scholar," in *CHB*, vol. 1: *From the Beginnings to Jerome*, ed. P. R. Ackroyd and C. F. Evans (1970), 510–41; E. F. Sutcliffe, S.J., "Jerome," in *CHB*, vol. 2: *The West from the Fathers to the Reformation*, ed. G. W. H. Lampe (1969), 80–101.

39. See Peter Brown, *Augustine of Hippo* (Berkeley: University of California Press, 1969), esp. 35–39, 65–72.

40. Augustine, *The Confessions of Saint Augustine*, trans. E. M. Blaiklock (New York: Thomas Nelson Publishers, 1983), 611–13. Cf. Brown, *Augustine*, 40–45.

no less worthy than the works of the best classical authors.[41] Of the five parts of rhetoric, he concentrated on style (*elocutio*), asserting that its system of tropes and figures enhanced the understanding of scripture. Of the three goals, he considered teaching the most important. Of the three types of speech, he found each, judicial, deliberative, and demonstrative, to have an appropriate place. Using classical categories, he analyzed the eloquence of Paul and the prophets to conclude that in their compositions form and content blended perfectly.

2. The Middle Ages

Christian exegetes of the Middle Ages continued literary and rhetorical studies.[42] Cassiodorus of Italy (c. 487–580) upheld the Augustinian view that scripture partakes of classical learning, even though he developed it in a different way.[43] His Psalms commentary overflowed with stylistic identifications; his analysis of Job led to the assertion that the art of rhetoric began in the Bible. The Venerable Bede of Britain (673–735) likewise claimed that Greek rhetorical devices originated from the Hebrew.[44] Working within the Augustinian tradition, he classified biblical books according to their poetic structure, and he catalogued figures and tropes. In France the Victorines studied the letter of scripture, extolling its translucency and sensuousness.[45] Hugh (c. 1096–1141) joined to the study of the Bible the liberal arts, especially grammar. Richard (c. 1123–73) delighted in metaphors. Andrew (c. 1110–75) followed Hugh and Jerome in the study of grammar and rhetoric. For all of them, aesthetic features enhanced the spiritual meanings of scripture. From the patristic through

---

41. See Saint Augustine, Book 4, *On Christian Doctrine*, trans. with introduction D. W. Robertson, Jr., The Library of Liberal Arts (Indianapolis: Bobbs-Merrill, 1958), 117–69; cf. Brown, *Augustine*, 259–69; Curtius, *European Literature*, 40–41, 73–74; Gerald Bonner, "Augustine As Biblical Scholar," in *CHB*, vol. 1, 541–63.

42. For an overview, see G. W. H. Lampe, et al., "The Exposition and Exegesis of Scripture," in *CHB*, vol. 2, 155–252.

43. Cassiodorus, *De Rhetorica*, ed. C. Halm, *Rhetores Latini minores* (Lipsiae, 1863). Cf. Curtius, *European Literature*, 41, 74–75, 448–50.

44. Bede, *Liber de schematibus et tropis*, ed. C. Halm, *Rhetores Latini minores* (Lipsiae, 1863). See M. L. W. Laistner, *Thought and Letters in Western Europe A.D. 500 to 900* (London: Methuen and Co., 1957), 158–64; cf. 298–306 for a discussion of biblical exegesis in the eighth and ninth centuries.

45. On the Victorines as biblical exegetes with a literary bent, see Beryl Smalley, *The Study of the Bible in the Middle Ages* (South Bend, Ind.: University of Notre Dame Press, 1978), 83–195.

the medieval period, these and other Christian scholars analyzed the Bible word by word and phrase by phrase. They performed what secular literary critics call a "close-textured treatment."[46]

This type of treatment did not, however, begin with Christians. Jewish commentators had long pursued verse by verse explications of the sacred text.[47] For instance, the scholar Saadya Gaon (882–942) of Babylonia prepared a dictionary of Hebrew poetics that emphasized grammar, style, and rhetoric. Rather than recognizing the presence of poetry in the Bible, he seemed to have worked with the concept of eloquent prose. More than a century later, Moses ibn Ezra (c. 1055–1140) of Spain declared the sacred text a prose document, with the exceptions of Psalms, Job, and Proverbs, and even them he found lacking in meter and rhyme. His study of Hebrew poetics explored metaphors and tropes such as antithesis, paronomasia, anaphora, and *inclusio* to conclude that the Bible exhibited rhetorical excellence second to none.[48] The contemporary Judah Halevi (c. 1075–1141), also living in Spain, praised Hebrew as the language that God spoke. He held that wordplays on proper names such as Adam and Eve made sense only in that language; that prophecy required elevated speech; that Moses, David, Joshua, and Solomon composed in a variety of genres such as exhortations, songs, and hymns; and that the Hebrews eschewed metrical poetry, with its stress on sound, in favor of the more excellent value of meaning.[49] Not unlike their Christian counterparts, Jewish medieval exegetes plumbed the literary treasures of scriptures, analyzing form, style, tropes, and related features to explicate meanings.

---

46. See G. R. Evans, *The Language and Logic of the Bible: The Earlier Middle Ages* (Cambridge, Eng.: Cambridge University Press, 1991), 128 and *passim*. The insistence upon "close-textured treatment" resonates, *mutatis mutandis*, with rhetorical study of the Bible.
47. See Tzvee Zahavy, "Biblical Theory and Criticism: Midrash and Medieval Commentary," in *The Johns Hopkins Guide to Literary Theory & Criticism*, eds. Michael Groden and Martin Kreiswirth (Baltimore: The Johns Hopkins University Press, 1994), 81–84; Shaye J. D. Cohen, *From the Maccabees to the Mishnah* (Philadelphia: Westminster Press, 1987), esp. 201–13; James L. Kugel and Rowan A. Greer, *Early Biblical Interpretation* (Philadelphia: Westminster Press, 1986), esp. 73–102; Erwin I. J. Rosenthal, "The Study of the Bible in Medieval Judaism," in *CHB*, vol. 2, 252–79. Cf. James L. Kugel, *The Idea of Biblical Poetry: Parallelism and Its History* (New Haven: Yale University Press, 1981), 172–200; Adele Berlin, *Biblical Poetry Through Medieval Jewish Eyes* (Bloomington and Indianapolis, Ind.: Indiana University Press, 1991). Despite its title, Berlin's study includes the Renaissance.
48. On these and other literary terms, see ensuing chapters.
49. Berlin, *Biblical Poetry*, 61–66.

3. The Renaissance

Although the Renaissance marked a rebirth of classical learning, sustained interest in the Bible, specifically in its literary features, did not go wanting. The story begins in Italy. The fourteenth century humanist Petrarch (1304–1374) wrote of the power, beauty, and superiority of scriptural poetry even as he embraced the classical literary tradition.[50] A century later the Jewish scholar Judah Messer Leon (c. 1420–c. 1498) produced a major study on rhetoric entitled *Sēpher Nōpheth Ṣūphīm* (*The Book of the Honeycomb's Flow*).[51] Versed in Aristotle, Cicero, and Quintilian, he not only cataloged biblical literary devices by classical terms but appropriated the entire system of ancient rhetoric for the scriptures. Yet he maintained, as had the Christian exegetes Cassiodorus and Bede, that the Bible, not the classics, constituted the source of rhetoric. "[I]t is the Torah which was the giver."[52] Scripture became then the primary textbook for the art of discourse and persuasion. In the following century, the Jewish scholar Azariah de Rossi (c. 1511–c. 1578) analyzed biblical poetry by drawing upon classical, Christian, and Jewish sources.[53] Aware that Philo, Josephus, Jerome, and other ancients had found classical meter in Hebrew poetry but that Judah Halevi and other rabbis had not, de Rossi sought to resolve these conflicting views. His scholarly work *Me'or 'Ēnayim* (1573) advanced the concept of meter as ideas (or thought units), rather than as sound, and so proposed that counting ideas would disclose structure. This innovative approach laid the groundwork for later studies.[54]

As the Renaissance moved northward from Italy, other scholars contributed to literary study of the Bible.[55] Johannes Reuchlin (1455–1522)

---

50. Cf. E. Harris Harbison, *The Christian Scholar in the Age of the Reformation* (New York: Charles Scribner's Sons, 1956), 38–43.

51. Judah Messer Leon, *The Book of the Honeycomb's Flow* (*Sēpher Nōpheth Ṣūphīm*), first published at Mantua 1475/76. See the critical edition and translation by Isaac Rabinowitz (Ithaca: Cornell University Press, 1983).

52. Messer Leon, *ibid.*, Book I.13.13 (p. 145).

53. Cf. Kugel, *Idea of Biblical Poetry*, 200–202; Berlin, *Biblical Poetry*, 141–53.

54. Cf. de Rossi's work with Robert Lowth, *De Sacra Poesi Hebraeorum* (Oxford, 1753); see below note 63. On other Jewish Italian contributions in the sixteenth and seventeenth centuries, see Berlin, *Biblical Poetry*, 154–72.

55. For an overview, see *CHB*, vol. 3, *The West from the Reformation to the Present Day*, ed. S. L. Greenslade (1963); esp. Roland H. Bainton, "The Bible in the Reformation," 1–17.

became the first non-Jewish scholar in Germany to master Hebrew, subsequently publishing a grammar and lexicon to introduce Christian students to the Old Testament in its original language.[56] The Dutch humanist Erasmus (c. 1466–1536), whose influence extended throughout Europe and England, judged the study of rhetoric to be an essential tool for sound biblical exegesis. His publication of the New Testament in Greek (for the first time ever), together with a new Latin translation (1516), and his subsequent *Paraphrases of the New Testament* attest his linguistic, textual, and rhetorical interests.[57] In the English Renaissance, Sir Philip Sidney (1554–86) declared biblical poesy representative of the chief kind of mimesis, with the intention "to teach and delight." Claiming that the Bible imitated "the inconceivable excellencies of God," he named in particular "David in his Psalms; Solomon in his Song of Songs, in his Ecclesiastes, and Proverbs; Moses and Deborah in their Hymns; and the writer of Job." He counseled, "Against these none will speak that hath the Holy Ghost in due holy reverence."[58]

4. The Modern Period

In the modern period literary study of the Bible absorbed rationalistic and historical interests.[59] The seventeenth century Englishman Thomas Hobbes (1588–1679) denied Mosaic authorship to the entire Pentateuch, proposed a chronological arrangement of biblical literature,

---

56. Johannes Reuchlin, *De Rudimentis Hebraicis* (Pforzheim: Thomas Anshelm, 1506); Reuchlin, *De Accentibus, et Orthographia, Linguae Hebraicae* (Hagenau: Thomas Anshelm, 1518). Cf. Lewis W. Spitz, *The Religious Renaissance of the Great Humanists* (Cambridge, Mass.: Harvard University Press, 1963), 61–80.

57. These interests were shared by Protestant reformers in Germany and Switzerland: Luther, Melanchthon (Reuchlin's grandnephew), Bucer, Zwingli, and Calvin. All of them except Luther had received humanistic educations (*studia humanitatis*) that stressed rhetoric among other liberal arts. See *Collected Works of Erasmus: New Testament Scholarship*, ed. Robert D. Sider (Toronto: University of Toronto Press), vol. 42 (1984), vol. 46 (1991), vol. 49 (1988). Cf. Louis Bouyer, "Erasmus in Relation to the Medieval Biblical Tradition," in *CHB*, vol. 2, 492–505; Harbison, *The Christian Scholar*, 69–102; Jerry H. Bentley, *Humanists and Holy Writ: New Testament Scholarship in the Renaissance* (Princeton, N. J.: Princeton University Press, 1983), 112–93.

58. Sir Philip Sidney, "An Apology for Poetry," in Adams, *Critical Theory*, 158.

59. For an overview, see W. Neil, "The Criticism and Theological Use of the Bible, 1700–1950," in *CHB*, vol. 3, 238–93.

and challenged scriptural authority.[60] Adopting a comparable approach, the Dutch philosopher Baruch Spinoza (1632–77) stressed the need to understand the rhetorical nature of biblical discourse for proper interpretation.[61] His hermeneutical principles inspired the French Catholic Richard Simon (1638–1712), who argued for the right to examine the Bible in the same way as any other document from the ancient world.[62] His research laid the groundwork for source and redaction criticism, each representing a type of literary criticism.

The eighteenth century witnessed the influential study *De Sacra Poesi Hebraeorum* (1753) by Robert Lowth, professor of poetry at Oxford University.[63] Heir to centuries of study,[64] this work systematized biblical poetry under the principle *parallelismus membrorum* (parallelism of members). It identified three main types of parallelism: synonymous, antithetic, and synthetic. Shortly thereafter (1782–83), the German romanticist Johann Gottfried von Herder advanced a contrasting approach. It sought to convey the "spirit" of Hebrew poetry as the spontaneous and natural expression of a people in relation to their history.[65]

60. Thomas Hobbes of Malmesburg, *Leviathan, or The Matter, Forme, & Power of a Common-wealth Ecclesiasticall and Civill* (London: Printed for Andrew Crooke, at the Green Dragon in St. Paul's Church-yard, 1651); cf. esp. chapter 33, "Of the Number, Antiquity, Scope, Authority, and Interpreters of the Books of Holy Scripture," 199–206. For a critical edition, see C. B. Macpherson, ed., *Leviathan* (Harmondswork, Middlesex, Eng.: Penguin, 1968). Cf. David Johnston, *The Rhetoric of Leviathan* (Princeton, N. J.: Princeton University Press, 1986).

61. See Benedict [Baruch] De Spinoza, "Theologico-Political Treatise," in *The Chief Works of Benedict De Spinoza*, trans. with introduction by R. H. M. Elwes, vol. 1 (New York: Dover Publications, 1951), chapters 7–11.

62. See Norman Sykes, "The Religion of Protestants," in *CHB*, vol. 3, esp. 193–98; F. J. Crehan, S. J., "The Bible in the Roman Catholic Church from Trent to the Present Day," ibid., 218–22.

63. Robert Lowth, *De Sacra Poesi Hebraeorum* (Oxford, 1753). Cf. John Drury, ed., *Critics of the Bible 1724–1873* (Cambridge, Eng.: Cambridge University Press, 1989), 69–102; Ruth apRoberts, "Robert Lowth and Biblical Criticism," *The Biblical Web* (Ann Arbor: University of Michigan Press, 1994), 107–34.

64. On Jewish precursors of Lowth, see Kugel, *Idea of Biblical Poetry, passim*, esp. 274–82; Berlin, *Biblical Poetry*, 142–44.

65. Johann Gottfried von Herder, *The Spirit of Hebrew Poetry*, trans. James Marsh (Burlington, Vt.: Edward Smith, 1833; reprint Naperville, Ill.: Aleph Press, Alec R. Allenson, 1971); von Herder, *Against Pure Reason: Writings on Religion, Language, and History*, trans. and ed. with introduction by Marcia Bunge (Minneapolis, Minn.: Fortress Press, 1993), 141–200. Cf. Hans W. Frei, *The Eclipse of Biblical Narrative: A Study in Eighteenth and Nineteenth Century Hermeneutics* (New Haven: Yale University Press, 1974), 183–201.

Matthew Arnold, professor of poetry at Oxford in the nineteenth century, explored the content of the Bible as "criticism of life."[66] In the same era the English critic Richard Moulton published a major work on the foundational forms of biblical literature, which he identified as lyric poetry, history, epic, rhetoric, wisdom, and prophecy.[67] Having become a professor at the University of Chicago, Moulton stimulated literary study of the Bible in the United States. Meanwhile, in Germany Julius Ley developed a new approach to Hebrew metrics, and Karl Budde made a definitive study of the Hebrew dirge.[68]

From the first half of the twentieth century come four representative contributions. In Germany Eduard König produced a comprehensive analysis of biblical figures and tropes.[69] Eduard Sievers conceived a multivolume work outlining Hebrew meter and rhythm and then applied the results to Genesis and Samuel.[70] In the United States John Genung prepared a guidebook that viewed scripture as a library developing from Hebrew literary fragments to the apocalypse of John.[71] In Jerusalem Umberto Cassuto filled two commentaries with literary observations about Genesis 1–11.[72] He analyzed syntactic forms, stylistic features, verse

---

66. Matthew Arnold, *Literature and Dogma* (New York: Macmillan, 1883); cf. John Drury, *Critics of the Bible,* 152–92. See Arnold, *God and the Bible: A Review of Objections to 'Literature & Dogma'* (New York: Macmillan, 1875); cf. *Culture and Anarchy,* ed. Samuel Lipman (New Haven: Yale University Press, 1994), esp. the chapter entitled "Hebraism and Hellenism," 86–96.

67. Richard G. Moulton, *The Literary Study of the Bible* (Boston: D. C. Heath, 1895).

68. Julius Ley, *Grundzüge des Rhythmus, des Vers- und Strophenbaues in der hebräischen Poesis* (Halle, 1875); Karl Budde, "Das Hebräische Klagelied," *ZAW* 2 (1882): 1–52.

69. E. König, *Stilistik, Rhetorik, Poetik in Bezug auf die biblische Literatur* (Leipzig, 1900).

70. Eduard Sievers, *Metrische Studien,* 3 vols. (Leipzig: B. G. Teuber, 1901, 1904, 1907).

71. See John Franklin Genung, *A Guidebook to the Biblical Literature* (Boston: Ginn, 1916). Cf. his earlier work: Genung, *The Epic of the Inner Life: Being the Book of Job* (Boston: Houghton Mifflin, 1891).

72. See U. Cassuto, *A Commentary on the Book of Genesis: Part One: From Adam to Noah,* trans. Israel Abrahams (Jerusalem: Magnes Press, 1961); *Part Two: From Noah to Abraham* (with an Appendix, a fragment of Part Three), trans. Israel Abrahams (Jerusalem: Magnes Press, 1964). These commentaries, written in Hebrew, were first published respectively in 1944 and 1949 in Jerusalem. Cf. also Cassuto, *A Commentary on the Book of Exodus,* trans. Israel Abrahams (Jerusalem: Magnes Press, 1967), first published in Hebrew in Jerusalem, 1951.

structures, plays on words, and grammatical niceties. The details of his work as well as his point of view foreshadowed rhetorical criticism. "For to gain an exact understanding of a Biblical passage," he wrote, "it is very important to observe the way in which literary expression is given to the thought."[73]

D. FORM CRITICISM

Form criticism constitutes the fourth component in the background. More than any other, the German scholar Hermann Gunkel (1862–1932) shaped this discipline. He called it *Gattungsforschung*, the investigation of types of literature.[74] In time, the rubric form criticism (*Formgeschichte*) emerged, primarily through New Testament studies.[75] The principal topics are oral tradition, genre, setting in life, and extra-biblical parallels.[76] They form a literary-sociological inquiry. Of the two emphases, the literary contributes more directly to rhetorical analysis.

1. Oral Tradition

Gunkel posited a long and complicated history of oral traditions behind the written sources that compose scripture.[77] Believing that these

---

73. Cassuto, *Commentary on Genesis*, Part 1, 2.

74. See, e.g., Hermann Gunkel, *Genesis*, HKAT I/1 (Göttingen: Vandenhoek & Ruprecht, 1901); Gunkel, *Die Psalmen*, HKAT II/2 (Göttingen: Vandenhoek & Ruprecht, 1926). For introductions to Gunkel and his work, see *inter alia* James Muilenburg, "Introduction" to Gunkel, *The Psalms: A Form-Critical Introduction* (Philadelphia: Fortress Press, 1967), ii–ix; Martin J. Buss, "The Study of Forms" in *Old Testament Form Criticism*, ed. John H. Hayes (San Antonio: Trinity University Press, 1974), 47–52; John W. Rogerson, "Introduction" to Gunkel, *The Folktale in the Old Testament*, trans. Michael D. Rutter (Sheffield: Almond Press, 1987), 13–18, a work first published in 1921.

75. See Martin Noth, "Developing Lines of Theological Thought in Germany," trans. John Bright (Fourth Annual Bibliographical Lecture, Union Theological Seminary in Virginia, 1963), 8.

76. For expositions of traditional form criticism, see Klaus Koch, *The Growth of the Biblical Tradition: The Form-Critical Method*, trans. S. M. Cupitt (New York: Charles Scribner's Sons, 1969); Gene M. Tucker, *Form Criticism of the Old Testament* (Philadelphia: Fortress Press, 1971); Tucker, "Form Criticism, OT," *IDBS*, 342–45; Gerhard Lohfink, *The Bible: Now I Get It!: A Form-Criticism Handbook*, trans. Daniel Coogan (Garden City, N.Y.: Doubleday, 1979); John Barton, "Form Criticism (OT)," *ABD*, vol. 2 (New York: Doubleday, 1992) 838–41.

77. See, e.g., Hermann Gunkel, *The Legends of Genesis*, trans. W. H. Carruth with introduction by William F. Albright (New York: Schocken Books, 1964), a work first published in 1901.

traditions were originally quite brief, he used the criteria of content and structure to identify them. Examples from Genesis included Noah's drunkenness, the tower of Babel, and Jacob at the Jabbok. The next stage of the process yielded more detailed stories such as Eden, the flood, and the betrothal of Rebekah. Linkage of stories resulted in cycles of tradition that over time became a large narrative. For instance, the four cycles of Jacob-Esau, Jacob-Laban, the birth of twelve sons, and theophanies combined to form the extensive Jacob narrative. Eventually it and other oral narratives were incorporated in written sources that became the book of Genesis.[78]

2. Genre

After isolating independent units of oral tradition, Gunkel classified them according to *Gattungen,* the German word for literary types or genres. Content, mood, and linguistic form provided the criteria for identification. In the Psalms, for example, he designated five main types: Hymns, Communal Laments, Individual Songs of Thanksgiving, Individual Laments, and Royal Psalms.[79] In Genesis he specified Legend (*Sage*) as the dominant genre, with subtypes such as aetiological, ethnological, etymological, and ceremonial.[80] Recognition of genres disclosed the conventions of biblical literature.

3. Setting in Life

Conventions belonged to particular settings. On given occasions people spoke in certain ways. Thus Gunkel sought to ascertain the *Sitz im Leben* (setting in life) to which each genre originally belonged.[81] The phrase intended a sociological rather than a historical situation: how a

---

78. On these sources, see, e.g., Richard Elliott Friedman, *Who Wrote the Bible?* (New York: Harper and Row, 1987); Bernhard W. Anderson, *Understanding the Old Testament,* 4th ed. (Englewood Cliffs, N.J.: Prentice-Hall, 1986), 19–23, and the references cited therein; Edgar Krentz, *The Historical-Critical Method* (Philadelphia: Fortress Press, 1975); Norman Habel, *Literary Criticism of the Old Testament* (Philadelphia: Fortress Press, 1971).

79. See, e.g., Hermann Gunkel, *Psalms,* 30–39.

80. Gunkel, *Legends of Genesis,* 13–36. Cf. the study of *Märchen* (folktale) in Gunkel, *Folktale in the Old Testament.*

81. Cf. Hermann Gunkel, "Fundamental Problems of Hebrew Literary History," in *What Remains of the Old Testament,* trans. A. K. Dallas (New York: Macmillan, 1928), 57–68.

literary convention functioned in ancient Israel, including the particular institution to which it was attached. For instance, people sang Hymns in worship, women sang Victory Songs for returning warriors, prophets delivered Oracles in the outer court of the Temple, and the elders of Israel spoke words of Wisdom at the village gates. The total setting of a *Gattung* involved speaker, listener, occasion, use, and effect.

4. Extra-biblical Parallels

In exploring oral traditions, genres, and settings in life, Gunkel developed comparisons between the Bible and literature scattered over time and place. With attention to Genesis,[82] he wrote about Egyptian influence in the Joseph romance, Moabite influence in the Lot legends, and Babylonian influence in the stories of creation, flood, and tower of Babel. He found Greek parallels to narratives such as the three visitors to Abraham, the curse upon Reuben, and the quarrel between the brothers Esau and Jacob. He even cited a Buddhist parallel to the story of Sodom. In every case he showed how Israel adapted foreign themes and content for its own religious interests. The pursuit of parallels dislodged provincial interpretation to show that, far from being an isolated document, the Bible belonged to world literature.

✿ ✿ ✿ ✿ ✿ ✿ ✿

Biblical rhetorical criticism lives in an expanding context that stretches from ancient times to the present. Classical rhetoric, literary critical theory, literary study of the Bible, and form criticism are the major components in the background. This chapter has sketched them as they lead to Muilenburg's 1968 presidential address. The next chapter reports on the address and on subsequent biblical studies that exemplify rhetorical method and practice. It introduces the foreground.

---

82. Gunkel, *Legends of Genesis*, 88–122.

2
Introducing the Foreground

To introduce biblical rhetorical criticism[1] this chapter, like the first, employs the classical faculties of invention and arrangement. Gathering materials for the occasion (*inventio*), it orders them (*dispositio*). The particular order is a chiasm.[2] Section A reports on the Muilenburg program; section B examines rhetoric as the art of composition; section B' examines rhetoric as the art of persuasion; section A' evaluates the Muilenburg legacy.

A. THE MUILENBURG PROGRAM: PROPOSAL AND PRACTICE

1. Proposal

In his presidential address on rhetorical criticism Muilenburg first affirmed the necessity of form criticism. "[M]y allegiance is completely on the side of the form critics, among whom, in any case, I should wish to be counted."[3] He proposed, however, that "the circumspect scholar will not fail to supplement . . . form-critical analysis with a careful inspection of the literary unit in its precise and unique formulation."[4] This double stance explained the syntactic subtlety in his carefully worded title "Form Criticism and Beyond." Its meaning differed from the concept "beyond

---

1. The adjective "biblical" will not continue to appear except where needed for emphasis, clarity, or contrast with the classical discipline.
2. For an explanation of the term "chiasm," see the extended note at the end of the chapter.
3. Muilenburg, "Form Criticism and Beyond," 4.
4. Ibid., 7.

form criticism."[5] For Muilenburg, Gunkel endured—and there was more. The "more" represented not the rejection of form criticism but its supplementation with rhetorical criticism.

Supplementation signals deficiencies. According to Muilenburg, traditional form criticism tends to fixate on conventions, slight historical commentary, separate form from content, isolate small units, and resist psychological and biographical interpretation. These criticisms pertain to the generalizing nature of the discipline. It neglects the individual, personal, unique, particular, distinctive, precise, versatile, and fluid features of the text. Muilenburg used all these adjectives to set the stage for his proposed supplement. It lifts up the words "artistry," "aesthetics," and "stylistics." Aware of resistance to such ideas, he reminded his colleagues that scripture has literary merit, as indeed a host of their predecessors understood. Further, he held that the high quality of Hebrew literature bespeaks an intentional achievement, even though ancient Israel did not cultivate aesthetics per se. Next he identified his particular interest in Hebrew composition: discerning structural patterns, verbal sequences, and stylistic devices that make a coherent whole. He named this endeavor rhetoric and its methodology rhetorical criticism. His canon stated that "a responsible and proper articulation of the words in their linguistic patterns and in their precise formulations will reveal to us the texture and fabric of the writer's thought, not only what it is that he thinks, but as he thinks it."[6]

Three emphases characterize the canon: rhetoric signifies the art of composition; the method involves close reading of texts; the purpose is to discover authorial intent. The emphases recall classical rhetoric and literary-critical theory. First, rhetoric as the art of composition echoes the Socratic concept of organic unity. It also resonates with objective theories that view the text as an integral whole. Second, the method of close

---

5. The syntactic and semantic difference between these two formulations has been lost on scholars who claim that Muilenburg wants to go "beyond form criticism." The difference is likewise obscured by those who give his presidential address a title it does not have: "After Form Criticism What?" See, e.g., Wilhelm Wuellner, "Where Is Rhetorical Criticism Taking Us?" *CBQ* 49 (1987): 451; Wuellner, "Rhetorical Criticism and Its Theory in Culture-Critical Perspective: The Narrative Rhetoric of John 11," *Texts and Interpretation*, eds. P. J. Hartin and J. H. Petzer (Leiden: E. J. Brill, 1991), 184; Burton L. Mack, *Rhetoric and the New Testament* (Minneapolis: Fortress Press, 1990), 12.

6. Muilenburg, "Form Criticism and Beyond," 7. Use of masculine pronouns to identify "the writer" attests the convention of earlier times. It appears in many quotations throughout the book but will not be noted each time. Contemporary convention strives for non-sexist language.

reading evokes the classical interest in content (*inventio*), structure (*dispositio*), and style (*elocutio*). The method also corresponds to objective procedures that show how the parts of a unit work together to produce the whole. Third, the purpose to discover authorial intent suggests the accent placed upon the speaker in demonstrative rhetoric. But this purpose diverges from objective theories to align with expressive orientations. What Abrams designated "insights into the mind and heart of the poet himself," Muilenburg transposed to "the writer's intent and meaning."[7]

Outside the presidential address Muilenburg varied the formulation of his canon. Another rendition proposed that "a proper articulation of form yields a proper articulation of meaning."[8] Like the preceding, this version highlights artistic composition and involves the method of close reading. But rather than specifying authorial intent, it evokes only the general concept of meaning. By analogy with classical rhetoric, meaning may center in the text (the judicial genre) or in the reader (the deliberative), as well as in the author (the demonstrative). By analogy with literary theory, meaning may center in the world (mimetic theories) or in the audience (pragmatic theories), or in the text (objective theories), as well as in the author (expressive theories). Whichever orientation prevails, meaning always contains a theological dimension. Scripture as artistic composition engages the ultimate questions of life. Art serves faith.[9]

Muilenburg assigned the rhetorical critic two tasks.[10] The first is to define the limits of a literary unit by using the criteria of form and content. Devices such as climax, *inclusio*, and chiasm set the boundaries.[11] Major motifs, usually given at the beginning of a unit, come to resolution at the end. Yet defining limits can be difficult because a single text may contain several climactic points. To mistake an internal break for the conclusion disavows artistic integrity and skews authorial intent. The second task is to discern structure: to delineate overall design and individual parts, show how they work together, identify literary devices and explicate their

---

7. Abrams, *The Mirror and the Lamp*, 23; Muilenburg, "Form Criticism and Beyond," 9.

8. Muilenburg used this version in oral tradition: classroom and lecture settings.

9. Cf. Muilenburg, "Form Criticism and Beyond," 18.

10. Ibid., 8–18.

11. The word "climax" derives from the Greek meaning "ladder." It designates a series of parallel items in ascending order of intensity. The word *inclusio* derives from the Latin. It designates parallelism of words, phrases, or sentences between the beginning and ending of a unit. Chiasm may be viewed as a series of *inclusios*.

functions in marking sequences and shifts within units. In this formulation structure (*dispositio*) subsumes style (*elocutio*). Attention to both features discloses the art of Hebrew composition.

2. Practice

Appearing late in Muilenburg's career, the designation rhetorical criticism collects intuitions, insights, and procedures that evolved over decades. But it does not identify a comprehensive system. Instead, the method lives where it came to birth, in the exegesis of texts. Practice precedes proposal. A report on selected writings by Muilenburg suggests the issues he addressed and the way he worked.[12]

a. Literary and Rhetorical Devices throughout Texts

In 1953 a study on repetition "as a prominent feature of Hebrew rhetoric and style"[13] reviewed the contributions of Lowth and Gunkel and then summarized the diverse roles that this phenomenon plays in scripture. It centers thought, gives a sense of totality, provides continuity, signals the structure and limits of units, and so discloses the character of biblical thinking. For example, the fourfold occurrence of the verb "awake" in the Song of Deborah expresses the urgency of the call to war (Judg. 5:12). The formula "for three . . . and for four . . ." in Amos 1–2 determines its sevenfold structure. The verb *šûb* (repent) and the noun *mešûbâ* (apostate) run throughout Jeremiah 3:1—4:4, along with other repetitions, to give the poem unity, chart progress, and accent key pronouncements. In developing his thesis, Muilenburg cited authorities from the history of the literary study of the Bible, quoted from ancient Near Eastern literature, and employed the discipline of form criticism. He drew explicitly upon the background in which rhetorical analysis unfolds.

In 1961 a definitive article on the Hebrew word *kî* located this morpheme among other particles that perform as signals of language.[14] Many

---

12. For a collection and a bibliography, see Thomas F. Best, ed., *Hearing and Speaking the Word: Selections from the Works of James Muilenburg* (Chico, Calif.: Scholars Press, 1984). On his interest in form criticism, see, e.g., Muilenburg, "Literary Forms," *A Companion to the Bible*, ed. H. H. Rowley (Edinburgh: T. & T. Clark, 2d ed. 1963), 123–43.

13. James Muilenburg, "A Study in Hebrew Rhetoric: Repetition and Style," *VT*, Suppl. 1 (Leiden: E. J. Brill, 1953), 97–111.

14. James Muilenburg, "The Linguistic and Rhetorical Usages of the Particle כִּי in the Old Testament," *HUCA* 32 (1961) 135–60.

occurrences testify to its emphatic and deictic functions. *Kî* introduces a climactic affirmation (Job 7:12), shapes an emphatic negative (Josh. 5:14), sets both emphatic and climactic contrast to a preceding affirmation (Num. 24:22), performs as the demonstrative (Ps. 41:12), introduces a direct quotation (Exod. 3:12), concludes a parable to interpret its meaning (Isa. 5:7), and gives motivation for a curse (Gen. 3:14) and for an oracle of assurance (Isa. 60:5). The motivating function of the particle also relates to types of literature (*Gattungen*): law, oath, lamentation, hymn, petition, and wisdom saying. The versatility of *kî* shows how Hebrew poets often broke with conventional patterns of speech. Understanding this rhetorical device contributes to theological interpretation.

b. Rhetorical Exegesis of Particular Texts

(1) Second and Third Isaiah

In 1956 Muilenburg published a commentary on Isaiah 40–66 that used rhetorical analysis extensively.[15] A lengthy discussion entitled "Poetic Form, Structure, and Style" covered such features as parallelism, meter, assonance, and dramatic style. The exegesis of the first poem, Isaiah 40:1-11, identified it as the prologue to the entire prophecy. The setting moves from decrees in the heavenly council of Yhwh to their fulfillment on earth. A proem (preface), three strophes, and a coda form the overall structure:[16]

> **Proem**
> Comfort, comfort my people,
> says your God.
> Speak tenderly to Jerusalem,
> and cry to her
> that her warfare is ended,
> that her iniquity is pardoned,
> that she has received from the LORD's hand
> double for all her sins. (40:1-2)

15. James Muilenburg, "The Book of Isaiah: Chapters 40–66," *IB* 5, ed. George Arthur Buttrick, et al. (New York: Abingdon Press, 1956), 381–419; 422–773.
16. Though Muilenburg worked directly from the Hebrew, for the English translation he used the Revised Standard Version, in keeping with the format of *The Interpreter's Bible*. On the proper translation of Hebrew for rhetorical analysis, see below chapter 4.

Strophe One

A voice cries:
"In the wilderness prepare the way of the LORD,
    make straight in the desert a highway for our God.
Every valley shall be lifted up,
    and every mountain and hill be made low;
the uneven ground shall become level,
    and the rough places a plain.
And the glory of the LORD shall be revealed,
    and all flesh shall see it together,
for the mouth of the LORD has spoken." (40:3-5)

Strophe Two

A voice says, "Cry!"
    And I said, "What shall I cry?"
All flesh is grass
    and all its beauty is like the flower of the field.
The grass withers, the flower fades,
    when the breath of the LORD blows upon it;
    surely the people is grass.
The grass withers, the flower fades,
    but the word of our God will stand forever. (40:6-8)

Strophe Three

Get you up to a high mountain,
    O Zion, herald of good tidings,
lift up your voice with strength,
    O Jerusalem, herald of good tidings,
    lift it up, fear not;
say to the cities of Judah,
    "Behold your God!"
Behold, the Lord God comes with might,
    and his arm rules for him;
behold, his reward is with him,
    and his recompense before him. (40:9-10)

Coda

He will feed his flock like a shepherd,
    he will gather the lambs in his arms,
he will carry them in his bosom,
    and gently lead those that are with young. (40:11)

The proem (40:1-2) consists of a triad of stichs (half lines) with the imperatives "comfort," "speak," "cry" and with their objects "people," "Jerusalem," "her." The climactic last verb "cry" leads to three disclosures that give the framework for the three strophes. Each strophe begins with a clear marker: in 40:3a "a voice cries"; in 40:6a "a voice says, 'Cry'"; in 40:9a the scene shifts from heaven to earth with a vocative address, "O Zion." Correspondingly, each strophe ends with a clear marker: in 40:5c the proclamation "for the mouth of the Lord has spoken"; in 40:8b the affirmation "the word of our God will stand for ever"; in 40:9c-10 the climactic triad "behold" announcing the imminent coming of God. This culminating theophany yields in 40:11 to the coda that describes God as shepherd.

Throughout his exegesis Muilenburg stressed the interrelationship of style, grammar, and content as the poem develops a triumphal message. The imperative "comfort," used twice at the beginning, emphasizes "the note of compassion and urgency." The object "my people" connotes covenant language. Together verb and object bind God and people. The climactic force of the third imperative at the beginning, "cry," receives further stress when it introduces the grand theophanic ending: "cry to the cities of Judah, 'Behold, your God!'" (40:9). The particle *hinnēh* (behold) opens each of the three concluding exclamations. They portray God as conqueror and king, his arm raised to win victory for the people. Yet this military imagery halts when the coda presents the contrasting portrait of God the shepherd feeding the flock, gathering the lambs in the divine arms, and leading them (40:11). Commented Muilenburg, "The arm raised in triumph is lowered in compassion."[17] Though he did not use the word *inclusio*, he observed that the comforting theme of the coda returns to the comforting theme of the proem. The correspondence helps to define the limits of the unit.

(2) Exodus 15:1-18

By 1966, in an article on the Song of the Sea (Exod. 15:1-18), Muilenburg was using the words "rhetorical analysis" to describe his exegetical method.[18] After situating this poem in ancient Near Eastern literature, identifying the genre as liturgy, and speculating about the cultic setting, he turned primary attention to the structure and the style. A highly

---

17. Ibid., 433–34.
18. James Muilenburg, "A Liturgy on the Triumphs of Yahweh," *Studia Biblica et Semitica*, ed. W. C. van Unnik and A. B. van der Woude (Wageningen, Netherlands: H. Veenman en Zonen, 1966), 233–51.

detailed explication followed.[19] It observed that corresponding motifs of divine exaltation set the boundaries of the unit (15:1b and 15:17-18) and sound its theological orientation. Within the boundaries, hymnic refrains to Yhwh (15:6, 11, 16cd) provide clear markers for three major divisions. Each division falls into two strophes, one hymnic confession and the other epic narrative. Throughout the poem, key words, meter, images, literary devices, and parallelism of lines offer ample evidence for the inseparability of form and content in shaping meaning. Thereby Muilenburg showed that, contrary to some scholarly judgments, the third division (15:12-16) not only coheres internally but also belongs with the other two. His exegesis disclosed the integrity of the text.

A closing paragraph cautioned that rhetorical analysis should not be regarded "merely as an aesthetic exercise."[20] Two tests establish its validity, the auditory and the visual. Reading the Song of the Sea aloud highlights assonance to show the effect of repeated sounds. Transcribing the poem on paper to identify various parts, underline repetitions, and mark key words demonstrates intentional patterns. Though Muilenburg himself did not make the connection, these tests correspond to facets of classical rhetoric: the auditory to oral persuasion and the visual to literary discourse.

o   o   o   o   o   o   o

Summary. The presidential address to the Society of Biblical Literature, along with other publications by Muilenburg, inaugurated a new interest in the subject of rhetoric. Even though he assigned his methodology a modest status as a supplement to form criticism, it has become a full-fledged biblical discipline practiced in different ways.[21] The differences relate to two distinct, though not incompatible, understandings of rhetoric: the art of composition and the art of persuasion.

B. ART OF COMPOSITION

Rhetoric as the art of composition derived from the Sophists, especially Isocrates, and continued with Quintilian and the church fathers. Interest lay in artful speech, particularly in structure (*dispositio*) and style

---

19. Generalized descriptions of rhetorical analysis obscure the specificities that constitute the life of texts and of the discipline. Muilenburg's study works its way through the *ipsissima verba* of the Song. This summary only suggests the direction.

20. Muilenburg, "A Liturgy on the Triumphs of Yahweh," 250.

21. See Duane F. Watson and Alan J. Hauser, *Rhetorical Criticism of the Bible: A Comprehensive Bibliography with Notes on History and Method* (Leiden: E. J. Brill, 1994).

(*elocutio*).[22] Three samples from contemporary biblical scholars illustrate the application of this understanding.[23]

1. Lundbom on Jeremiah

While a student of Muilenburg, Jack Lundbom wrote a dissertation on rhetoric in Jeremiah.[24] Pursuing the two tasks of defining limits and delineating structures, he proposed that *inclusio* and chiasmus are controlling figures in the book. They develop the argumentation.

Inclusio signifies deliberate continuity between the beginning and the end of a unit. It occurs at three levels: the book itself, the poems within the book, and the stanzas within the poems. The book opens and closes with "the words of Jeremiah" (1:1; 51:64). Chapters 1–20 constitute a distinct section, even as source critics have recognized. At the beginning, God's words "you came forth from the womb" (1:5) answer the question Jeremiah poses at the end: "why from the womb did I come forth . . . ?" (20:18). Discerning this connection, an attentive reader finds not despair in the prophet's question but hope in the divine answer. Yet in the single poem to which the question belongs (20:14-18), the opposite meaning obtains through another *inclusio*. The first stanza begins "cursed be *the day*"; the last concludes "to see toil and sorrow and end in shame all *my days*?" In a single stanza of another poem (8:4-9), the word "repent" appears at the opening in a divine rhetorical question that expects an affirmative answer: "If one turns away, does he not *return*?" (8:4). It reappears at the close of the stanza in a divine negative declaration about the people: "they refuse *to return*" (8:5). The *inclusio* locks in an analogy of incongruity between the one who returns and those who do not.

Chiasmus signifies a syntactic structure that inverts normal word order. As with *inclusio*, it occurs at three levels: stanzas within the poems, the poems, and the book itself. (By inverting here the order of the levels, Lundbom fashions his own chiasmus.) The first level includes reversals

---

22. Describing rhetoric in antiquity, Curtius says that it "signifies 'the craft of speech'; hence, according to its basic meaning, it teaches how to construct a discourse artistically." Curtius, *European Literature and the Latin Middle Ages*, 64.

23. Again, to do justice to rhetoric as the art of composition is difficult through the use of samples. Specificities of texts defy efforts to condense analysis. One needs to see the whole cloth—a view that awaits Part Two.

24. Jack R. Lundbom, *Jeremiah: A Study in Ancient Hebrew Rhetoric*, Dissertation Series, Number 18 (Missoula, Mont.: SBL and Scholars Press, 1975). The translations of the Hebrew are his own.

of verbs and subjects: e.g., in 2:19a, the verb "chasten" and the subject "wickedness" followed by the subject "apostasy" and the verb "reprove." Contrasting terms also appear: e.g., in 20:14, the sequence "cursed," "day," "day," "blessed." The second level is amply illustrated by the poem in 8:13-17:[25]

> **A** 'Gathering I will end them,'
>   oracle of Yhwh,
>   'there is *nothing* on the grapevine
>   And *nothing* on the fig tree
>   even the leaves are withered
>   and what I gave them has passed away from them.' (8:13)
>
> **B** Why do we sit still?
>   gather together
> And let us *enter* the fortified *cities*
>   and be silent there.
> For Yhwh our God has silenced us
>   given us poisoned water to drink
>   because we have sinned against Yhwh. (8:14)
>
> **C** We looked for peace, but *nothing* good came,
>   for a time of healing, but, behold, terror. (8:15)
>
> **B′** From Dan is heard
>   the snorting of their horses.
> At the sound of their neighing stallions
>   the whole land quakes.
> *They enter* to devour the land and all that fills it,
>   the *city* and those who dwell in it. (8:16)
>
> **A′** For behold I am sending you
>   poisonous serpents.
> *Nothing* you do can charm them
>   and they shall bite you,
>   oracle of Yhwh. (8:17)

Key words and speakers balance inversely. Verses 13 (A) and 17 (A′) present Yhwh speaking and repeat the particle "nothing." Verses 14 (B) and 16 (B′) have the people speaking (or Jeremiah for the people) and repeat the words "enter" and "city." The center verse 15 (C) relates all the parts: the people speak, as in B and B′, and the particle "nothing" occurs, as in

---

25. Ibid., 82–84.

34

A and A'. The arrangement and the content underscore the message of despair. At the beginning (A) Yhwh finds nothing to harvest from the crop for the people who are referred to as "them"; at the end (A') Yhwh addresses the people directly, declaring that nothing "you do" can save "you." The people urge entry into the city even while noting that Yhwh has given them poisoned water (B); correspondingly, they make clear that armies enter the city to devour it and the inhabitants (B'). The center clinches the dreadful message: nothing good comes (C). Overall, chiastic structure aids memory, enhances argumentation, and shapes totality of thought.

The third level of chiasmus pertains to collections of poetry and prose that no longer appear intact. For instance, Lundbom isolated a group of texts known as the Zedekiah Cluster.[26]

> A   Chapter 24 — after the exile of Jeconiah
> B   Chapter 27 — beginning of Zedekiah's reign (fourth year)
> B'   Chapter 28 — beginning of Zedekiah's reign (fourth year)
> A'   Chapter 29 — after the exile of Jeconiah

By identifying such clusters,[27] Lundbom recovered the prehistory of the text, thereby leading the reader to ponder why ordered material ever became disordered.

This study of *inclusio* and chiasmus showed how Jeremiah prepared his message and how editors molded it into the larger whole. The analysis also illuminated the argumentative character of the discourse to expose a resistant audience. Thereby the art of composition incorporated the art of persuasion. In asserting that "structure is a key to meaning and interpretation," Lundbom followed the rhetorical program of his mentor Muilenburg.[28]

---

26. Ibid., 109–12.

27. E.g., the Jehoiakim Cluster of Jer. 25, 26, 35, 36; ibid., 107–9; cf. the poetic collection in Jer. 8:22—9:10; ibid., 99–100.

28. Ibid., 114. Cf. further Lundbom, *Jeremiah*, AB (New York: Doubleday, forthcoming). In addition to Muilenburg, Lundbom acknowledged a debt to his teacher William L. Holladay. Cf. Holladay, *Jeremiah 1* (Philadelphia: Fortress Press, 1986) and *Jeremiah 2* (Minneapolis: Fortress Press, 1989). In its analysis of each literary unit this commentary contains a distinctive section called "Structure." It discusses the limits of passages and their inner makeup, both concerns of rhetorical criticism. Holladay dedicated his two volumes to Saint Jerome and James Muilenburg.

2. Craven on Judith

Toni Craven prepared as her dissertation a rhetorical reading of the book of Judith.[29] She credited Lowth with introducing her to the phenomenon of Hebrew repetition and Muilenburg with teaching her its significance in literary composition. But unlike Muilenburg, Craven rejected form criticism and minimized authorial intent. She called her study "compositional analysis" with description as the goal. By use of a musical analogy, she distinguished the goal from performance, the interpretation of a text. Though rhetorical criticism undertakes both endeavors, they constitute separate critical tasks. The descriptive explicates the interconnection of structure and content; the interpretive follows to elucidate meaning.

Judith divides into two major parts.[30] Chapters 1–7 narrate Assyrian military aggression, led by the general Holofernes, and the resultant fear in Israel; chapters 8–16 report the deeds of the Jewish woman Judith in response to the threat. The formal symmetries that bind these parts appear as expressed identities, expressed antitheses, implied antitheses, and artificial identities. (So Craven fashioned her own chiastic arrangement.) Expressed identities and expressed antitheses require at least one set of equivalent or identical terms. Examples of the former include: the first act of the leading characters Nebuchadnezzar and Judith is to "send" for another (1:7; 8:10); both claim to work by "my hand" (2:12; 8:33); both urge their people to "call" upon their respective deities (3:8; 8:17). Examples of expressed antitheses include: the contrasting characters Holofernes (2:2) and Judith (8:16) execute opposing "plans"; for different reasons "fear and trembling . . . fall" upon rebel nations (2:28) and upon the Assyrian troops (15:2); a pledge of honesty to Holofernes is one time "true" (5:5) and another "false" (11:5). Implied antitheses contrast parallel elements. Holofernes is male and Judith female. He uses military might to win victories; she uses beauty and wisdom. Artificial identities exhibit grammatical or functional correspondences. A temporal phrase opens each part of the narrative (1:1 and 8:1), and the numeral thirty-four figures in the plans of each side (7:20 and 12:10, 15:11).

---

29. Toni Craven, *Artistry and Faith in the Book of Judith* (Chico, Calif.: Scholars Press, 1983). No Hebrew original exists for the book of Judith, and so rhetorical analysis was done on the Greek text. Craven noted that it "is structured along the lines of a classical Hebrew narrative with repetition serving as the cornerstone of its composition" (6). She used her own translations of the Greek.

30. Ibid., 53–64.

These many symmetries led Craven to the discovery of chiastic structures in each of the two parts. The first structure appears as follows:

A Assyria campaigns against its enemies (2:14—3:10).
 B The Israelite leader Joachim orders preparations for war (4:1-15).
  C Achior is expelled from the Assyrian camp (5:1—6:11).
  C′ Achior is received into the Israelite city (6:12-21).
 B′ The Assyrian general Holofernes orders preparations for war (7:1-5).
A′ Assyria campaigns against its enemies (7:6-32).

The chiasm of the second part focuses on Judith:

A Judith is introduced (8:1-8).
 B Judith conceives a plan to save Israel (8:9—10:9a).
  C Judith and her maid leave the Israelite city (10:9b-10).
   D Judith kills Holofernes (10:11—13:10a).
  C′ Judith and her maid return to the Israelite city (13:10b-11).
 B′ Judith conceives a plan to destroy Israel's enemy (13:12—16:20).
A′ Judith is praised in life and death (16:21-25).

In contrast to the first chiasm, this one has a center: Judith killing Holofernes (D). Structure and content make her deed the heart of the story.[31] From analysis of external design, Craven turned to internal structure.[32] She identified literary devices and offered close readings, line by line if not word by word. For example, concatenation, the formal interlocking of units by repeated words or phrases, appears with the numeral one hundred twenty in 1:16 and 2:5 and continues in 2:15 with the numeral one hundred twenty thousand.[33] Chiasms occur repeatedly, as illustrated in 9:11a.[34]

---

31. By showing how artfully the book is crafted, how balanced it is in form and content, Craven undercut scholarly judgments that demean the first part as lengthy, dull, and defective.
    32. Craven used the word "structure" in two ways. The phrase "internal structure" indicates the narrow use; the broad use encompasses "external design" and "internal structure."
    33. Craven, *Artistry and Faith*, 75.
    34. Ibid., 91. Using a standard procedure in rhetorical criticism, Craven employed a series of markings under words, phrases, and clauses to indicate various connections. The markings were arbitrarily chosen, but their use was consistent and purposeful. For further comments on the procedure, see the discussion in chapter 4.

> For not in numbers is your power
> nor is your might in men of strength.

Many interlocking devices characterize the Introit to Judith's hymn of praise:[35]

> Strike up a song to my God on timbrels,
> Sing unto the Lord with cymbals,
> Raise for him a psalm and a tale of praise,
>   +++
> Honor and invoke his name. (Jdt. 16:1)
>   +++

Five imperatives structure the unit.[36] Each of the four lines begins with one: "strike," "sing," "raise," and "honor." The last verb "invoke" follows "honor" to achieve end stress. Divine references also appear in each line: "to my God," " unto the Lord," "for him," and "his name." Parallel words and phrases in lines one and two secure their symmetry. One imperative with two objects in line three balances two imperatives with one object in line four to secure their symmetry. In addition, line one interlocks with line three as the word "song" parallels "a psalm" and "a tale of praise."

Using the method of close reading, Craven examined the whole and the parts of Judith. She highlighted the principle of repetition to show the artistic and theological integrity of the story. Her compositional analysis resonated with the Muilenburg mode even though she rejected form criticism, minimized authorial intent, and attempted to separate description from interpretation.

3. Ceresko on Samuel

Citing Muilenburg's address as "an almost classic definition" of rhetorical criticism, Anthony Ceresko applied the method to 1 Samuel 17:34-37, David's boast to Saul in the Goliath story.[37] First he presented the narrative text translated in a poetic structure.[38]

---

35. Ibid., 106.
36. Though Craven herself did not make all of the following observations, they fit her rhetorical analysis.
37. Anthony R. Ceresko, O.S.F.S., "A Rhetorical Analysis of David's 'Boast' (1 Samuel 17:34–37): Some Reflections on Method," *CBQ* 47 (1985): 58–74.
38. Ibid., 59–60. Ceresko does not explain why he attempted to make a poetic structure.

Then David said to Saul,
"Your servant used to be shepherd
for his father's flock.
Whenever a lion came
or a bear attacked
and carried off a sheep from the herd, (17:34)
I would take off after it
and bash it and rescue (the sheep)
    from its mouth.
If it rose against me,
I would seize it by the scruff
and bash it and kill it (17:35)
Lion and bear alike
your servant struck down.
So this uncircumcised Philistine
will be like one of them,
since he has defied the ranks
of the Living God." (17:36)
And David continued,
"Yahweh who rescued me
from the claw of the lion
and from the paw of the bear
himself will rescue me from the grasp
of this Philistine." (17:37)

Ceresko set these verses within the wider context of 1 Samuel 17:31-40. He showed that it forms a chiasm (ABCB'A') with David's boast (17:34-37) at the center. Having defined the limits of the text, he charted its overall structure and then turned to a close reading. Content and syllable counting disclose two major sections: David's description of rescuing sheep from a lion or a bear (17:34-35) and David's use of this experience as evidence that he can kill Goliath (17:36-37). These sections share key words, including "strike," "rescue," "lion," "bear," and "David said."[39] They also share sound patterns, notably the frequency of the Hebrew consonants *qōp* (q), *kap* (k), and *gîmel* (g). Parallel pairs such as "a lion"/"a bear" and "I

---

39. Regrettably, Ceresko's translation obscures the appearance of key words by using different English terms for the same Hebrew terms. E.g., the Hebrew verb *'mr* he translated in 17:34 as "said" but in 17:37 as "continued"; the verb *nkh* in 17:35 as "bash" but in 17:36 as "struck." Though such variations may enhance English composition, they inhibit rhetorical analysis. By not acknowledging the problem, Ceresko undercut the repetition he deemed so valuable for interpreting the text. Cf. the discussion of this problem in chapters 4 and 6.

would strike it"/"I would kill it" further link the sections. Within the second section, repetition of key words forms a concentric structure:[40]

> "the lion" . . . "the bear" (17:36a)
> "this uncircumcised Philistine" (17:36b)
> "the Living God" (17:36c)
> "David" [continued] (17:37a)
> "Yahweh" (17:37b)
> "the lion" . . . "the bear" (17:37c)
> "this Philistine" (17:37d)

Divine names surround David to protect him from the outer circles of his enemies: the lion, the bear, and the Philistine.

Upon completing his rhetorical analysis, Ceresko considered its implication for other methods.[41] First, he argued that the demonstrated artistry of the passage counters text-critical judgments that it is corrupt. For example, the phrase "and David continued" (17:37a) is central and thus not to be deleted as superfluous. Second, he found that his work supports source critical observations about 1 Samuel 16 and 17 as contrasting accounts that juxtapose divine guidance and human resourcefulness. Explicating "David's way with words" illuminates the stress on the human side (1 Sam. 17). Third, he claimed that his analysis aids socio-cultural investigation. The portrayal of David as soldier-poet parallels similar depictions of heroes in ancient Greece and medieval Japan. Fourth, he suggested that the rhetorical power uncovered in this passage may help the search for the historical David. However one evaluates these proposals, they show a conversation between rhetorical criticism and other disciplines.

¤   ¤   ¤   ¤   ¤   ¤   ¤

Summary. Though the studies by Lundbom, Craven, and Ceresko build on the Muilenburg program, they exhibit different styles, emphases, and goals in analyzing diverse texts. The samples hardly exhaust the subject, but they suffice for introducing rhetoric as the art of composition.[42]

---

40. Ceresko, "A Rhetorical Analysis of David's 'Boast,'" 66.

41. Ibid., 67–74.

42. Studies of this kind continue to appear. For a technical analysis that integrates textual criticism, see Leslie C. Allen, "Ezekiel 24:3-14: A Rhetorical Perspective," *CBQ* 49 (1987): 404–14. For an extensive application of Muilenburg's method to Third Isaiah, see Gregory J. Polan, O. S. B., *In the Ways of Justice toward Salvation: A Rhetorical Analysis of Isaiah 56–59*, American University Studies, Series VII, Vol. 13 (New York: Peter Lang, 1986); cf., e.g., Robert H. O'Connell, "Deuteronomy VIII 1–20: Asymmetrical Concentricity and the Rhetoric of Providence," *VT* 40 (1990): 437–51.

B'. ART OF PERSUASION

The second understanding defines rhetoric as the art of persuasion. Beginning with Aristotle, it has prevailed throughout the centuries.[43] How a speaker or writer shapes discourse to affect an audience sets the interest. Although Muilenburg accented a different aspect of rhetoric, some biblical scholars of persuasion cite his direct influence upon their work. Others contrast his approach to theirs. Five samples demonstrate the application of this understanding.

1. Gitay on Second Isaiah

In 1978, ten years after Muilenburg's address, Yehoshua Gitay completed a dissertation on Isaiah 40–48 that later became a book.[44] Using Aristotelian rhetoric, he separated his approach from both the Muilenburg mode and form criticism. Though he acknowledged that Second Isaiah "did not follow any classical conventional school of rhetoric," he held that this system *mutatis mutandis* can explicate the biblical text.[45] He described the system as exploring the act of communication among speaker, speech, and audience. Hence, he proposed that Second Isaiah made a public address to Jewish exiles in Babylon, seeking to persuade them of divine activity on the international scene and so alter their religious attitude. To accomplish this goal, the prophet used various arguments, arranged them in effective ways, and employed numerous stylistic devices. Of the three kinds of persuasive discourse, the judicial best characterized his speech. Its setting suggested a court of law where the issue of justice involved prosecution and defense. The prophet urged his audience to make a right decision. Gitay analyzed the prophecy according to a fourfold pattern. Its application to Isaiah 40:1-11 typifies the approach[46] and invites comparison with Muilenburg's study of the same passage.

43. Cf. the comments by Mack, *Rhetoric and the New Testament,* 12–13; C. Clifton Black II, "Keeping Up with Recent Studies: xvi. Rhetorical Criticism and Biblical Interpretation," *Expository Times* 100 (1989): 252–58.

44. Yehoshua Gitay, *Prophecy and Persuasion: A Study of Isaiah 40–48* (Bonn: Linguistica Biblica, 1981).

45. Ibid., 36, 62. Cf. Michael V. Fox, who says that "in Israel we have a well-documented major rhetorical movement entirely independent of the classical tradition from which Western rhetoric and rhetorical criticism descend" ("The Rhetoric of Ezekiel's Vision of the Valley of the Bones," *HUCA* 51 [1980]: 1–15). Gitay and Fox echo different viewpoints present in the history of literary study of the Bible; see chapter 1.

46. Gitay, *Prophecy and Persuasion,* 63–80.

First, under the rubric Rhetorical Unit appeared a summary of content. It proclaims a new situation between Israel and God, a divine announcement motivated by the people's sense of hopelessness. The time of punishment is over; God again cares. The message comes in parts designated topic (40:1), thesis (40:2), confirmation (40:3-8), and epilogue (40:9-11). For Gitay classical categories supersede the internal markers that led Muilenburg to divide the content into proem (40:1-2), three strophes (40:3-4, 6-8, 9-10), and coda (40:11).

Second, under the rubric Invention (*inventio*) appeared a consideration of the ways that Isaiah tries to reach his audience. The rational appeal uses divine authority and the covenant concept; the emotional "speaks to the heart" (40:2), describing "your God" as a tender shepherd caring for the sheep (40:11); the ethical identifies the "I" of the prophet with the people (40:6) to gain their confidence. Though Muilenburg did not use these categories, his observations are not incompatible with them.

Third, under the rubric Organization (*dispositio*) appeared commentary on the parts of the Rhetorical Unit. The topic is comfort. The thesis states that the punishment is over and so prepares the people for change. The confirmation seeks to prove the case by using God's revelation through nature to show that divine power fulfills its word. The epilogue reports the conclusion that follows from demonstration of the thesis. It places the redemption of Israel in both a political and cosmological framework. For the most part, Muilenburg's exegetical comments harmonize with this presentation.

Fourth, under the rubric Style (*elocutio*) appeared commentary on literary devices. For example, the repetition of the word "comfort" (40:1) signals anadiplosis, a device whereby the last word of one clause begins the following clause. Its use stresses a point and impresses the hearer. The association of sounds in the words *nḥmû* (comfort, 40:1) and *dbrû* (speak, 40:2) indicates assonance, a device that repeats similar or identical vowel sounds within nearby words to attract attention. The repetition of *kî* at the beginning of several cola (e.g., three times in 40:2) identifies anaphora, a device whereby the same word or group of words is repeated at the beginning of successive clauses. Its use embellishes, amplifies, and emphasizes. Such stylistic observations resonate with the Muilenburg approach.

Throughout his exegesis, Gitay quoted classical rhetoricians, particularly Cicero and the authors of *Rhetorica Ad Herennium* and *On the Sublime*. He also drew upon contemporary rhetoricians who follow the Aristotelian system. The explicit appropriation of these sources and the omission of form-critical insights separated his analysis from that of Muilenburg.[47]

2. Clifford on Second Isaiah

In an analysis different from Gitay's, Richard Clifford also argued for a rhetoric of persuasion in Second Isaiah. Though acknowledging a debt to Muilenburg, he viewed the prophet not as a lyric poet but as an orator who is both eloquent and persuading. The latter adjective he defined as "practical, given to sustained argument to move people to specific action."[48] Part One of his study considered the context and message of Second Isaiah. His world, his audience, and the tradition to which he belonged set the context; the limits of the literary units set the message. Clifford followed Muilenburg, against form critics, in concentrating upon techniques that produce long units: strophic patterning, parallelism, wordplay, repetition, rhyme, and coherent argument. Expression (style) and argument (content) unite to present five contrasting concepts: the first and last things, Babylon and Zion, Israel and the nations, Yhwh and the gods, the servant and Israel.

Part Two consisted of translation and commentary. Examination of Isaiah 40:1-11 illustrates the approach.[49] Like Muilenburg, Clifford interpreted the genre and setting as a heavenly council scene with parallels in ancient Near Eastern literature. Departing from Muilenburg (and from Gitay), he divided the poem into four strophes (40:1-2, 3-5, 6-8, 9-11). A decree announces the forgiveness of "my people" Israel (40:1-2). A court official interprets its meaning (40:3-5) when he orders Israel to prepare a way in the desert for Yhwh so that the divine glory will be revealed to all flesh. The heavenly dialogue continues (40:6-8) as a courtier tells the

---

47. Gitay used this approach only for prophets; he did not claim that the classical system is applicable to all scripture. See, e.g., Y. Gitay, "A Study of Amos's Art of Speech: A Rhetorical Analysis of Amos 3:1-15," *CBQ* 42 (1980): 293–309; Gitay, "Reflections on the Study of the Prophetic Discourse: The Question of Isaiah 1:2-20," *VT* 33 (1983): 207–21 (with comments on the Muilenburg approach); Gitay, *Isaiah and His Audience: The Structure and Meaning of Isaiah 1–12* (Assen/Maastricht, The Netherlands: Van Gorcum, 1991); Gitay, "Rhetorical Criticism," in *To Each Its Own Meaning: An Introduction to Biblical Criticisms and their Application*, eds. Steven L. McKenzie and Stephen R. Haynes (Louisville, Ky.: Westminster/ John Knox Press, 1993), 135–49.

48. Richard J. Clifford, *Fair Spoken and Persuading: An Interpretation of Second Isaiah* (New York: Paulist Press, 1984), 4.

49. Ibid., 71–76. Note that Muilenburg, Gitay, and Clifford agreed on the limits of this unit.

prophet to declare what he has heard. But the prophet responds with a conventional lament on human frailty that includes the line, "The grass is withered, the flower is dead." The courtier seems to agree, even repeating the line verbatim. Then he undercuts the lament by countering, "but the word of our God stands forever." At the end (40:9-11) the prophet speaks to Zion, thereby fulfilling the divine decree of the initial strophe (40:1-2). He orders Zion to "say to the cities of Judah, 'Behold your God.'" As the courtier commissioned the prophet, so the prophet commissions Zion to proclaim the good news of divine deliverance. Clifford concluded that in the opening drama and in those to follow "the prophet is to show his people how they are to respond."[50] In other words, the large poetic units of Second Isaiah develop the argument of a prophet who is an orator. Their purpose embodies a theological journey: to persuade the people to return to Zion. Though the accent on persuasion aligned this approach with Gitay's, Clifford never invoked the classical system.

3. Barton on the Prophets

An essay by John Barton held that the prophets sought to justify to their hearers the ways of God with the world.[51] That goal required rhetorical acumen because the correlations between historical events and divine ordering were neither obvious nor necessary. To demonstrate his thesis, Barton identified four techniques of persuasion. First, rhetorical questions expecting the answer "no" legitimated divine punishment. Jeremiah employed the artifice: "Has a nation changed its gods, even though they are no gods? But my people have changed their glory for that which does not profit" (2:11).[52] Second, structure produced the desired rhetorical twist. In a series of oracles Amos indicted foreign nations for war crimes and so announced divine punishment upon them (1:3—2:5). Both the ordering and the content of this material would have elicited approval from the Israelite people. But then Amos turned the argument against Israel, even though its own offenses did not involve war crimes (2:6-16). Continued use of the same literary structure would have led the nation to overlook the differences in content while persuading it of the justice of divine punishment. Third, poetic justice served as a rhetorical device.

50. Ibid., 76.
51. John Barton, "History and Rhetoric in the Prophets," in *The Bible As Rhetoric*, ed. Martin Warner (London: Routledge, 1990), 51–64.
52. Cf. Walter A. Brueggemann, "Jeremiah's Use of Rhetorical Questions," *JBL* 92 (1973): 358–74.

Isaiah consigned those who neglected Yhwh for desires of the appetite to the appetite of Sheol (5:11-14). The crafting of his argument persuaded by matching crime and punishment. Fourth, analogies to nature constituted a technique. To convict Judah of pride, of being high and lifted up, Isaiah evoked the high cedars of Lebanon (2:12-17). As tall trees were felled, so Yhwh would bring low Judah. The analogy convinced the people that they deserved divine punishment. In various ways prophets practiced the art of persuasion to achieve theological ends.

Though Barton's essay did not include a discussion of theory, the details of his exegesis reflect the Aristotelian understanding of rhetoric as discovering "the possible means of persuasion in reference to any subject whatever."[53] Indeed, the volume to which his work belongs uses this definition extensively for the exploration of biblical texts.

4. Clines on Job

The same volume contains a deconstructionist essay on Job in which David Clines argued that the book undermines itself in two arenas.[54] First, chapter after chapter works mightily to demolish the dogma of moral retribution only to have the epilogue triumphantly restore it. Despite the emphatic denial throughout, in the end piety brings rewards. Second, the book purports to probe the universal issue of human suffering, and yet Job's predicament is in fact unique. He suffers to vindicate God. Despite appearances, the book does not account for human suffering. Clines remarked, "It looks as though this book of Job is another self-deconstructing artifact."[55] But then he observed that, to the contrary, the book endures. What sustains it? Rhetoric, the power to persuade, was the answer. Generations of readers have embraced the book, savoring its poetry, aligning themselves with Job, and rejoicing in his vindication. Contradictions and mistakes within the story do not deter identification with it. Most eloquently, rhetoric triumphs over logic and fact.

Whatever the merits of a deconstructionist reading, this appeal to persuasive rhetoric illustrates a general use of the concept. Though some scholars explore rhetoric in the close reading of texts, Clines sought it in the overarching effect.

---

53. See chapter 1.
54. David Clines, "Deconstructing the Book of Job," in *The Bible as Rhetoric*, 65–80. On deconstruction, see chapter 3.
55. Ibid., 77.

5. Patrick and Scult on Job

The preceding studies on persuasion contrasted with the Muilenburg emphasis on composition. Gitay separated the two approaches. Clifford stated indebtedness but stressed difference. Though Barton and Clines did not comment, their expositions showed the divergence. By contrast, Dale Patrick and Allen Scult evoked Muilenburg's vision in their effort to construct a biblical rhetoric of persuasion.[56] Their stated intention was to fulfill his charge to "move beyond the mere identification of forms and genres towards reconstituting the text as a piece of living discourse."[57] Their plan involved an appeal to the full range of the classical tradition. Interpreting the extant text rather than reconstructed sources, they shifted concern from authorial intentionality to reader response.[58] They proposed a broad notion of rhetoric: an act of communication designed to achieve a particular effect upon its audience, past or present. So the Bible seeks to persuade readers of its worldview.

To argue their case (and thus persuade their own readers), Patrick and Scult converted a description from the philosopher Ronald Dworkin into a dictum: "Interpret a text as the best text (aesthetically, intellectually, and affectively) the text can be."[59] Five criteria guide interpretation: comprehensiveness accounts for the whole work; consistency pertains to internal coherence; cogency seeks the public sense or rightness of the text; plenitude allows for fullness of meanings; and profundity seeks itself, eschewing shallow renditions. If the interpreter (a spiritual seeker) meets these criteria, then the resultant interpretation satisfies the test of the best. It is persuasive.

Unlike Gitay, Patrick and Scult did not adapt the classical system of rhetoric. Unlike Clifford, they did not comment on the biblical text in verse sequence. Unlike Barton, they did not dwell on specific techniques. Somewhat like Clines, though with greater specificity and without a deconstructionist stance, they presented a rhetorical overview. Their essay on the book of Job offered point and counterpoint.[60] The title, "Finding the Best Job," conformed to their dictum. They first applied it to choosing the text to be studied, but the results remained uncertain. In its final form Job discloses tensions and incongruities: the relationship between the prose

---

56. See Dale Patrick and Allen Scult, *Rhetoric and Biblical Interpretation* (Sheffield: Almond Press, 1990). The book is dedicated to James Muilenburg and E. A. Speiser.
57. Ibid., 13.
58. Ibid., 12f. On reader-response criticism, see chapter 3.
59. Ibid., 85.
60. Ibid., 81–102.

and poetic sections, the interruption of the Elihu speeches in chapters 33–37, and the confusions within chapters 23–28 about speakers and length of speeches. To honor the extant text sacrifices coherence, eloquence, and profundity; to honor a reconstructed text sacrifices comprehensiveness. Patrick and Scult acknowledged that their dictum yielded no clear choice, even though they preferred the final form of the book. When they next applied the dictum to identifying Job generically, they concluded that it best models classical laments. Accusations against God constitute right speech (42:7). Yet the lament teems with problems and ambiguities. Rather than arguing, as Clines did, that the poetic speeches and the prosaic epilogue undermine each other, these scholars viewed them as mutually enhancing. They saw the epilogue, much as the prologue, effecting distance for the reader in contrast to the reader's intimate involvement with the speeches. Further, they regarded the ambiguities in Job's final speech (40:2-6) as a deft move by the author that forces the reader to complete meaning. The engaging of the reader becomes the rhetorical act of persuasion.

In addition to the philosophical base derived from Dworkin, the reader-centered rhetoric of Patrick and Scult had theological motivation and purpose. They claimed that the canonizers intentionally shaped scripture as a unified teaching.[61] Accordingly, the ideal reader is willing to interpret the text as one communication from God, even in the presence of its acknowledged diversities. Indeed, the reader as spiritual seeker makes a dialectic synthesis of diversity. Such interpretation becomes "a rhetorical exchange between a text and its audience."[62]

Whether Patrick and Scult fulfilled their purpose of outlining a method that fittingly responds to Muilenburg's charge remains a moot question. The switch from his interest in authorial intent to theirs in reader response; from his line by line, even word by word, analysis to their more general study of a text; from his accent on structure and style to theirs on persuasion—these and other features suggest that as they "moved beyond," so they moved away. They composed a different model of rhetorical criticism.

◦ ◦ ◦ ◦ ◦ ◦ ◦

Summary. Much like the samples of rhetoric as the art of composition, these as the art of persuasion exhibit different styles and emphases.[63]

61. Ibid., 130.
62. Ibid., 135.
63. For a recent study that adheres to the Aristotelian tradition, see Rodney K. Duke, *The Persuasive Appeal of the Chronicler* (Sheffield, Eng.: The Almond Press, 1990); for another that focuses on persuasion, drawing its definition from Fox (see note 45 above),

Some invoke general concepts; others offer close readings. In the latter case they resonate with the art of composition. Thus, many of Muilenburg's concerns persist, though less prominently.

A'. CRITICAL ANALYSIS OF THE MUILENBURG PROGRAM

To credit or criticize Muilenburg for the entire program of biblical rhetorical criticism since 1968 would be fallacious. Nevertheless, his contribution remains the pivot around which studies continue to cluster. Given its importance, the conclusion of this chapter returns to the enterprise. Section A' corresponds in subject matter to section A but differs in purpose. The beginning describes and explains; the end evaluates and reflects. It examines five issues that biblical scholars have raised about the Muilenburg mode.

First, the definition of the enterprise invites challenges. Muilenburg identified rhetoric as "understanding the nature of Hebrew literary composition" and rhetorical criticism as the accompanying methodology.[64] Michael Fox declares that this characterization misses the main point as it "has been understood by the great majority of rhetorical theorists from Aristotle on," namely the point of suasion (persuasion).[65] Studying "stylistic-aesthetic" features of a text apart from their suasive force does not qualify as rhetorical criticism.[66] Gitay likewise criticizes the characterization because it diverges from the classical meaning of persuasion to focus on style.[67] Wilhelm Wuellner indicts Muilenburg and his successors for becoming "victims of the fateful reduction of rhetoric to stylistics, and of stylistics in turn to the rhetorical tropes or figures."[68] C. Clifton Black

---

see Charles S. Shaw, *The Speeches of Micah: A Rhetorical-Historical Analysis* (Sheffield: JSOT Press, 1993), esp. 22–23.

64. Muilenburg, "Form Criticism and Beyond," 8.

65. Fox, "The Rhetoric of Ezekiel's Vision of the Valley of the Bones," 1–2.

66. In a footnote critical of Muilenburg, Fox charged that "a word [i.e., "rhetoric"] loses value through inflation of its meaning." Yet in another footnote supportive of rhetorical theory he acknowledged without protest that the discipline "is currently expanding its scope to include epistemology" and that thereby "the meaning of 'suasion' is reinterpreted and broadened." Ibid., 1, note 1; 3, note 5. On the inflation of rhetorical theory, far beyond the strictures that Fox would impose, see chapter 3 A.

67. See Gitay, *Prophecy and Persuasion*, 27; "Rhetorical Criticism," *To Each Its Own Meaning*, 136. Cf. M. O'Connor, *Hebrew Verse Structure* (Winona Lake, Ind.: Eisenbrauns, 1980), 10.

68. See Wuellner, "Where Is Rhetorical Criticism Taking Us?" 451. He viewed literary structure (the Muilenburg mode) as yielding the static concept of architecture but

depicts the mode as "virtually synonymous with 'literary artistry,'" and deems it too narrow, tending toward distortion by placing literature in a vacuum.[69] It wavers between being a program and an approach, a method and a perspective. While thanking Muilenburg for teaching him methodology, Isaac M. Kikawada would broaden the process of composition from the mind of the author to a hierarchy of diagrams and charts.[70] Computer programming provides the conceptual parallel for a revised definition.

According to Martin Kessler, the debate over definition but reflects literary critical discussions at large.[71] He sketches a spectrum of ideas about rhetoric from Aristotle's statement of discovering the best means of persuasion to Frye's view of rhetorical criticism as the "theory of genres." The secular scholar David Goodwin subsumes the varieties of ideas under two accepted definitions: analysis of rhetorical discourse and rhetorical analysis of all discourse.[72] The former works on intentionally persuasive texts and basically follows neo-Aristotelian criticism. (That is not the Muilenburg mode.) The latter investigates a wide range of communication and works beyond the narrow strictures of persuasion.[73] In the flexibility of this definition the Muilenburg mode comfortably resides.

Kessler also directs attention to the second issue, the concept of diachronic and synchronic readings. The former interprets a text through the history of its composition and the latter exclusively in its final form. Though he hints that rhetorical criticism may link the two approaches, he himself promotes it as "the leading candidate for synchronic criticism."[74] Kikawada too declares rhetorical criticism a synchronic study.[75] Brevard

---

rhetorical structure as yielding the dynamic concept of strategy or reinvention. One wonders what an architect would think of this idea; cf. Ellen Eve Frank, *Literary Architecture* (Berkeley: University of California Press, 1979), 3–13. Cf. Wuellner, "Rhetorical Criticism and Its Theory in Culture-Critical Perspective," 171–85.

69. Black, "Keeping up with Recent Studies," 252–58.

70. Isaac M. Kikawada, "Some Proposals for the Definition of Rhetorical Criticism," *Semitics* 5 (1977): 67–91.

71. Martin Kessler, "A Methodological Setting for Rhetorical Criticism," *Semitics* 4 (1974): 22–36. Reprinted in David J. A. Clines, David M. Gunn, and Alan J. Hauser, eds., *Art and Meaning: Rhetoric in Biblical Literature*, Suppl. Ser. 19 (Sheffield: JSOT, 1982), 1–19.

72. David Goodwin, "Rhetorical Criticism," *Encyclopedia of Contemporary Literary Theory*, ed. Irena R. Makaryk (Toronto: University of Toronto Press, 1993), 174–78.

73. On broad and narrow understandings of rhetoric, see Corbett, *Classical Rhetoric for the Modern Student*, 3–5.

74. Kessler in *Art and Meaning*, 9, 14.

75. Kikawada, "Some Proposals," 69.

Childs approvingly situates it among methods concerned "to do justice to the integrity of the text itself apart from diachronistic reconstruction."[76] In contrast, Roy Melugin faults the discipline for showing too little interest in the growth of the text.[77] Patrick and Scult weigh the two approaches, allowing their rhetorical criticism to operate, where possible, at both levels.[78] Muilenburg himself never addressed the issue. In theory he embraced historical criticism alongside rhetorical criticism.[79] In practice he sometimes joined the methods, though he showed a preference for synchronic interpretation.[80]

The third issue concerns the relationship between form criticism and rhetorical criticism. Muilenburg sought to supplement the former with the latter. Yet Rolf Knierim asserts that Muilenburg stayed totally within form criticism even when he described rhetorical criticism.[81] In other words, there is form criticism and no beyond. From the opposite side, Melugin writes that by stressing individual creativity to the neglect of traditional forms Muilenburg tended to "an almost exclusive use of 'rhetorical criticism.'"[82] In other words, there is little form criticism and much beyond. These evaluations cancel each other.[83] For certain, critics differ about the use and relationship of the disciplines. Lundbom integrates

76. Brevard S. Childs, *Introduction to the Old Testament as Scripture* (Philadelphia: Fortress Press, 1979), 74.

77. Melugin, "Muilenburg, Form Criticism, and Theological Exegesis," *Encounter with the Text*, ed. Martin J. Buss (Philadelphia: Fortress Press, 1979), 92–96.

78. Their analysis of Job admitted the difficulty of compromise between diachronic and synchronic approaches. Yet their analysis of Genesis 1–3 treated separately the P and J sources and then brought them together compatibly. See Patrick and Scult, *Rhetoric and Biblical Interpretation*, 88–92; 105–19.

79. Cf., e.g., his historical critical comments on the book of Jeremiah: James Muilenburg, "Baruch the Scribe," in *Proclamation and Presence*, ed. John I. Durham and J. R. Porter (Richmond: John Knox Press, 1970), 215–38.

80. Cf. Muilenburg, "A Liturgy on the Triumphs of Yahweh," 168f. "Such an approach [i.e., rhetorical criticism] does not question the importance of historical or literary criticism, or *Gattungskritik*, or of tradition-historical criticism, but attempts, rather, to understand the composition of the passage in its present form."

81. See Rolf Knierim, "Old Testament Form Criticism Reconsidered," *Int* 27 (1973): 435–68. The assertion appears to rest on a redefinition of form criticism and a restricted reading of Muilenburg's presidential address; cf. 458, note 91.

82. Roy F. Melguin, "The Typical versus the Unique among the Hebrew Prophets," in *Book of Seminar Papers*, vol. 2 (SBL: 1972), 341.

83. Cf. David Greenwood, "Rhetorical Criticism and Formgeschichte: Some Methodological Considerations," *JBL* 89 (1970): 418–26.

them in his study of Jeremiah; Craven divorces them in her reading of Judith; Ceresko ignores form criticism even when setting up an interdisciplinary conversation for his rhetorical analysis of 1 Samuel 17:34-37. Yet all three scholars cite Muilenburg as their model. The debate remains flexible and fluid.

Aesthetics is the fourth issue. While recognizing that the Bible has no concept of belles lettres, Muilenburg nevertheless affirmed its high literary quality. Some scholars have criticized him for this emphasis. Childs complains that in the commentary on Isaiah 40–66 aesthetic interests replaced rather than promoted theological interpretation.[84] Clifford fears that what was "only a tendency in Muilenburg, a tendency generally in dialogue with other approaches, can become in less skilled hands a genuine flight into aestheticism."[85] Wuellner frets that aesthetic interest turned rhetorical criticism into an outmoded version of literary criticism.[86] Muilenburg himself understood the point. He worried about the aesthetic leanings of Gunkel and took pains to present rhetorical analysis as an exegetical tool.[87] "It would be a mistake," he said, "to regard it merely as an aesthetic exercise."[88] With this judgment Black agrees. "The contribution of this approach is more than aesthetic; there are exegetical gains."[89]

Criticism about an aesthetic orientation relates to the fifth issue of sociological, historical, and political concerns. Clifford writes that Muilenburg's commentary on Isaiah 40–66 separates text from context to slight both literary tradition and historical events.[90] Melugin makes a similar observation, noting a lack of interest in social setting and function.[91] And

---

84. Brevard S. Childs, *Old Testament Books for Pastor and Teacher* (Philadelphia: Westminster, 1977), 73.

85. Clifford, *Fair Spoken and Persuading*, 35.

86. Wuellner, "Where Is Rhetorical Criticism Taking Us?" 451f. Cf. Eagleton, *Literary Theory*, 20f, 205f.

87. But on Gunkel's view of aesthetics and exegesis, cf. Stephen A. Geller, "Through Windows and Mirrors into the Bible: History, Literature and Language in the Study of Text," *A Sense of Text: The Art of Language in the Study of Biblical Literature*, JQR Suppl. (1982): 7–13, and *passim*.

88. See Muilenburg, "A Liturgy on the Triumphs of Yahweh," 168.

89. See Black, "Keeping Up with Recent Studies," 254. Note that the criticism of aesthetics over against the praise of theology is a variation on the ancient debate between rhetoric and philosophy; see chapter 1, note 4.

90. Clifford, *Fair Spoken and Persuading*, 35.

91. Melugin, "Muilenburg, Form Criticism, and Theological Exegesis," 93.

Walter Brueggemann finds rhetorical criticism "too enamored of style to notice speech as a means and source of power."[92] He faults Muilenburg for neglecting the inevitable political power of all rhetoric.[93] Such comments mirror the ever-changing terrain of biblical studies.

Summary. The Muilenburg program and responses to it elicit five reflections. First, the attention given the subject from its inception in 1968 to the present attests its pivotal importance in biblical studies. Scholars value the enterprise for opening a new frontier, for marking a decisive methodological turn.[94] Second, its importance bears the burden of unfulfilled expectations. Unlike his mentor Gunkel, who offered a full exposition of *Gattungskritik,* Muilenburg never developed a comprehensive statement of rhetorical criticism. He worked by intuition; he shared evolving perceptions; he did not construct a system. Third, expectations foster a tendency to fault the discipline for not being what it is not: for not being, for instance, classical rhetoric or form criticism or tradition-history or sociological analysis or political praxis. Fourth, the slighting of such concerns brings the general criticism of narrowness. A corollary observation wishes for more sophisticated analysis.[95] Fifth, certain criticisms promote issues that postdate Muilenburg. Since his time form criticism has changed and sociological analysis blossomed; literary theories have mushroomed and political agendas sought to dominate. These developments alter both the discipline and the components in its background. Accordingly, the latter require further attention before the former can again be considered.

92. Walter Brueggemann, "At the Mercy of Babylon: A Subversive Rereading of the Empire," *JBL* 101 (1991): 17–19.

93. This observation helps to situate Muilenburg's program between two periods in biblical scholarship. For comments, see the extended note at the end of the chapter.

94. Brueggemann, "At the Mercy of Babylon," 17; Bernhard W. Anderson, "The New Frontier of Rhetorical Criticism," in *Rhetorical Criticism,* ed. Jared J. Jackson and Martin Kessler (Pittsburgh, Pa.: The Pickwick Press, 1974), ix–xviii.

95. The adjective "sophisticated" seems to be popular among critics who seek to move "beyond" Muilenburg. Among others, Brueggemann, Melugin, Patrick and Scult, and Wuellner resort to it.

EXTENDED NOTES

Note 2 on page 25

The term "chiasm" derives from the shape of the Greek letter chi (X). The two diagonal lines in this letter crisscross to yield four points with a center. From left to right, first at the top and then at the bottom, the points correspond inversely, as the following diagram demonstrates.

This basic pattern of inversion, with or without a center, can be extended beyond four items: for example, a b c d d' c' b' a'. The mark (') to the right of the second set of letters (d' c' b' a') is called a prime; its use distinguishes different sections of the same variable. Chiasm (or the Latin spelling, chiasmus) designates inverted correspondences between words, phrases, sentences, or larger units. The arrangement for this chapter yields a skewed chiasm. The four elements balance in the inversion of their topics; they diverge in the length of their discussions. Cf. John W. Welch, ed., *Chiasmus in Antiquity: Structures, Analyses, Exegesis* (Hildesheim: Gerstenberg Verlag, 1981).

Note 93 on page 52

The generation to which Muilenburg belonged pursued historical criticism to the neglect of literary analysis. Though he accepted the emphasis, he chafed under it and departed from it. The current generation is more diffuse in its pursuits. Some scholars adhere to historical concerns, though from new perspectives. They study the text to discern power politics and sociological milieu. Cf., e.g., the return to source-critical study of the Pentateuch through the lens of power politics in Robert B. Coote and David Robert Ord, *The Bible's First History* (Philadelphia: Fortress Press, 1989); Robert B. Coote, *In Defense of Revolution* (Minneapolis: Fortress Press, 1991); Robert B. Coote and David Robert Ord, *In the*

Beginning (Minneapolis: Fortress Press, 1991); cf. also David Jobling, Peggy L. Day, and Gerald T. Sheppard, eds., *The Bible and the Politics of Exegesis* (Cleveland, Ohio: The Pilgrim Press, 1991). Other scholars have turned to literary and rhetorical analyses, often identifying themselves as heirs of Muilenburg; see chapter 3. Still others propose combining all these interests to yield a metadiscipline. Cf., e.g., Norman K. Gottwald, *The Hebrew Bible: A Socio-Literary Introduction* (Philadelphia: Fortress Press, 1985), 6–34.

3
Expanding the Background

Classical rhetoric, literary critical theory, literary study of the Bible, and form criticism: even as these components constituted the background for the Muilenburg proposal, so they continue to provide the context in which biblical rhetorical criticism takes place. By returning to the subject, this chapter joins the first to fashion an *inclusio*. It surrounds the discussion of the foreground (ABA').[1] But an explosion of ideas in each component now renders the background vastly more complex, indeed uncontrollable. Tongues and the confusion of tongues heighten the babel.[2]

A. CLASSICAL RHETORIC AND BEYOND

1. Introduction

In the late sixties (the same time that Muilenburg named the method he had been using for years) the field of classical rhetoric began to expand. Major impetus came from the work of the European philosophers Chaim Perelman and L. Olbrechts-Tyteca a decade earlier (1958). An English translation of their original French edition appeared in 1969 under the

---

1. Cf. the chiastic structure (*dispositio*) of the subject matter (*inventio*) in chapter 2, the center of the *inclusio*.
2. Let the reader be warned that the use of big words in the ensuing discussion (i.e., the proliferation of multisyllabic discourse in the disquisition), including many nominalizations, fits the confusion of tongues. In describing abstract concepts, the writer can only strive for clarity. Cf. Joseph M. Williams, *Style: Toward Clarity and Grace* (Chicago: University of Chicago Press, 1990), 17–45.

55

title *The New Rhetoric: A Treatise on Argumentation.*[3] This rhetoric actually revived the old rhetoric of Aristotelian thought; it focused on persuasion and its means. The authors explicated a philosophical base for the domain of argumentation. They held that through agreed upon principles argumentation seeks to establish a community of minds for debating issues and obtaining assent. Of the five parts of classical rhetoric, they privileged *inventio* and *dispositio*, subordinated *elocutio* to its function within argumentation, and omitted *memoria* and *actio* as inapplicable to contemporary culture. Of the three elements involved in every act of communication (speaker, speech, and audience), they privileged the relationship of speaker and audience and thus the social-historical context for rhetoric. Of the three types of speech, they appealed to each: the *epideictic*, the deliberative, and the judicial. Though they declared that rhetoric characterizes all human discourse, the bulk of their discussion classified and described techniques of argumentation.[4] Their conclusion stressed the possibilities for argumentation as the language of social-historical communities. Neither compelling nor arbitrary, classical rhetoric restated (the new rhetoric) can make available reasonable choices. It can enhance human freedom.

In the burgeoning field of rhetorical criticism, "the new rhetoric" hardly signified the last word. A collection of primary texts with commentary by Bernard Brock, Robert Scott, and James Chesebro suggested an endless development of perspectives.[5] Defining rhetoric "as the human

3. Ch. Perelman and L. Olbrechts-Tyteca, *The New Rhetoric: A Treatise on Argumentation,* trans. John Wilkinson and Purcell Weaver (South Bend, Ind.: University of Notre Dame Press, 1969). For a brief assessment, see Barilli, *Rhetoric,* 104–6. For a distillation, see Ch. Perelman, *The Realm of Rhetoric,* trans. William Kluback, with intro. by Carroll C. Arnold (South Bend, Ind.: University of Notre Dame Press, 1982), 2. Though Perelman is often cited with the first name Chaim, rather than the abbreviated "Ch.," Olbrechts-Tyteca remains hidden through the capital letter "L.," rather than revealed through the first name Luci. If few readers know of her female identity, Perelman himself fails even to mention her in his foreword to the American edition of their book (v–vi). Instead, he presents the work as "my ideas." On the heavy patriarchal bias of scholarship in classical rhetoric, along with present efforts to recover a lost past and carve a different future, see Corbett, *Classical Rhetoric for the Modern Student,* 576–78.

4. Perelman and Olbrechts-Tyteca, *New Rhetoric,* 185–508.

5. Bernard L. Brock, Robert L. Scott, James W. Chesebro, eds., *Methods of Rhetorical Criticism: A Twentieth-Century Perspective,* 3rd ed. rev. (Detroit: Wayne State University Press, 1989). Whatever its inadequacies, the collection offers a manageable introduction to a complex subject.

effort to induce cooperation through the use of symbols,"[6] these authors intended by imprecision to embrace process and product. Yet the purposes of rhetoric expanded even beyond their definition. Alongside the aim to induce cooperation (the persuasive) came the motivation to learn about things (the pedagogical) and to produce and test insights (the theoretical). In achieving these diverse purposes, rhetorical criticism involved the three tasks of description, interpretation, and evaluation.[7]

Appropriating the work of Thomas Kuhn,[8] the authors observed that the field of rhetorical criticism has grown in the twentieth century not by a gradual accumulation of insights, one building upon another, but by different proposals and programs, each shifting the ground of the discipline. Over time, the old paradigm, the traditional model of reality, broke down from the weight of its own weaknesses, and new paradigms competed for allegiance. Accordingly, the authors treated first the traditional perspective and then four perspectives that countered it. They described each by its orientation, assumptions, and consensus. This collection of texts with commentary demonstrated the explosion and confusion of its subject matter.

2. Five Perspectives

a. The Traditional Perspective

The traditional perspective, as reshaped in the first half of the century, differentiated literature and rhetoric.[9] The former concerned itself with the permanent value of discourse; the latter with the effect imparted to hearers. Given this difference, the orientation concentrated upon the expertise of the speaker. The assumptions involved first the positing of a stable situation throughout history to which established categories of discourse apply and then the understanding of rhetoric as mimetic in reflecting and describing an assumed reality. The consensus held that Aristotle formulated the basic program, especially with his definition of rhetoric as "the faculty of discovering the possible means of persuasion in

---

6. Ibid., 14.
7. Ibid., 15–17.
8. Thomas S. Kuhn, *The Structure of Scientific Revolutions,* 2nd ed. (Chicago: University of Chicago Press, 1970).
9. Brock, Scott, Chesebro, eds., *Methods of Rhetorical Criticism,* 24–31. Cf. the distinction Wuellner made between literary and rhetorical structure; see note 68 in chapter 2.

reference to any subject whatever."[10] The traditional perspective appeared in two strands. The neo-Aristotelian adhered to the full classical program; the historical narrowed the focus to the speaker, the speech, and the times. Regarding the tasks of rhetorical criticism, both strands tended to stress the descriptive over the interpretive and the evaluative. In the 1960s came major challenges to this perspective.[11] Its comprehensiveness made full use virtually impossible, and its orientation toward the speaker failed to account for social, political, and economic forces that also shape rhetorical discourse. Meantime, the role of readers in the act of communication acquired greater prominence; indeed, interest expanded to the complex interrelation of speaker, speech, audience, situation, and society. Though the traditional paradigm has survived, no longer is it in ascendancy. Nor is any other single perspective.

b. The Experiential Perspective

The experiential perspective moves away from a systematic program and a speaker orientation to the critic who makes judgments, experiences insights, and presents arguments.[12] Two strands appear. The eclectic accents the critic's ability to select the best standards, principles, and ideas from many sources, sort them without the restraints of an imposed system, and show the diversity at work in the rhetorical act. The epistemic accents knowledge as intersubjective rather than objective. Neither fixed nor final, it is shaped moment by moment as language develops a worldview. No one starting point marks the orientation of the perspective; it depends upon choices the critic makes. The assumptions posit that society is in process, that an infinite mixture of ideas, methods, and attitudes shape public discourse, and that any system of analysis is basically arbitrary. The consensus holds that discourse needs continual fresh study.

c. The Dramaturgical Perspective

Behind the label "dramaturgical" lies a history. It begins with the rubric "the new rhetoric," the title (in French and English) of the volume by Perelman and Olbrechts-Tyteca. In time, the plural "new rhetorics" replaced the singular to indicate diversity. This change Brock and Scott

---

10. Aristotle, *Rhetoric*, LCL, I.ii.2.
11. See esp. Edwin Black, *Rhetorical Criticism: A Study in Method* (New York: Macmillan, 1965; repr. with a new foreword, Madison: University of Wisconsin Press, 1978).
12. Brock, Scott, and Chesebro, *Methods of Rhetorical Criticism*, 86–95.

incorporated in the first two editions of their collection.[13] Now, in the third edition, the "new rhetorics" has yielded to two distinct perspectives, the dramaturgical and the sociological.[14]

The dramaturgical focuses on symbol as the core of rhetoric. It incorporates three approaches. The dramatistic approach shifts rhetorical emphasis from persuasion to motive, thereby accenting the psychological component.[15] The approach of fantasy theme explores the speaker-audience drama to bring about "rhetorical vision."[16] The narrative approach establishes a dialectical synthesis between two rhetorical emphases, the persuasive and the aesthetic.[17] No single theory governs the dramaturgical perspective. In general, the orientation seeks stable relationships for understanding social intercourse. The assumptions posit that society is in process but that stable relationships rule human interactions, that a flexible framework can be fashioned to study public discourses, and that a specific symbol guides human understanding of reality. The consensus holds that rhetorical criticism requires a unified framework for productive study.

d. The Sociological Perspective

As the second perspective that has replaced the "new rhetorics," the sociological centers upon the interrelationship between society and communication.[18] Four major approaches emerge. The sociolinguistic studies language in relationship to society; the generic explores how conventional forms of communication function in society; the social examines the discourse of movements to account for their choices and the effects; the feminist investigates the rhetoric of gender as a "stable variable" in accounting for social systems, classes, processes, and decisions. The orientation of the perspective stresses continuous and mutual interaction between society and communication. Its assumptions posit that societies

13. Chesebro joined Brock and Scott only in the editing of the third edition.

14. Brock, Scott, and Chesebro, *Methods of Rhetorical Criticism*, 172–82.

15. Cf., e.g., Kenneth Burke, *A Grammar of Motives* (Englewood Cliffs, N.J.: Prentice-Hall, Inc., 1945); *A Rhetoric of Motives* (Englewood Cliffs, N.J.: Prentice-Hall, Inc., 1950).

16. Cf., e.g., Ernest G. Bormann, "Fantasy and Rhetorical Vision: The Rhetorical Criticism of Social Reality," *Quarterly Journal of Speech* 58 (1972): 396–407.

17. Cf., e.g., Walter R. Fisher, *Human Communication as Narration: Toward a Philosophy of Reason, Value, and Action* (Columbia, S.C.: University of South Carolina Press, 1987).

18. Brock, Scott, and Chesebro, *Methods of Rhetorical Criticism*, 274–302.

tend to promote stability and downplay change, that societal values and methods set the boundaries for communication, that societal symbols determine rhetorical possibilities for individuals, and that society governs the relationship of word-thought-thing. While allowing for multiple theories, the consensus holds that the foundation of rhetorical criticism comes through an examination of society.

e. The Postmodern Perspective

Coming into prominence during the early 1980s, the postmodern perspective asserts that a major shift has happened globally about the nature of society.[19] The shift emerges through at least five categories of contrast. First, the modern critic views information as extrinsic to the individual who then relates to it. The postmodern critic sees the individual processing selectively and so making information. Second, the modern critic separates form, the artistic and symbolic product of creativity, from criticism, the response to form. The postmodern critic collapses the distinction, seeing both form and criticism as modes of persuasion or social power. Third, the modern critic posits a dichotomy of objectivity and subjectivity. The postmodern critic claims that all views are ideological; there is no objectivity. The biases of the individual in a given time and place shape even description. Fourth, the modern critic sees society as ordered with universals and controlled by experts. The postmodern critic sees society as full of contradictions reflecting the populace. Fifth, the modern critic endeavors to formulate theories for explaining society. The postmodern critic underscores the uniqueness or particularity of every situation and so eschews theory.[20]

This major shift about the nature of society requires a different rhetoric. Accordingly, the postmodern critic posits a crucial distinction between the concepts of "text" and "work." The latter is only a physical object; the former extends to any response or experience derived from the work. Reactions to works constitute texts. As a mode of textual analysis, rhetorical criticism brings the original work into new settings, thereby changing or even displacing it. In turn, the criticism becomes itself an original work, subject to textual analysis. Criticism is then an ideological construct. It derives from the biases and needs of actual readers to yield multiple and

---

19. Ibid., 428–40.
20. Though Brock, Scott, and Chesebro accurately report postmodernist claims to "eschew" theory, these claims actually promote theory.

contradictory meanings that are inherent and inevitable. Plurality of meanings and the distinction between work and text define postmodern rhetorical criticism.

Four underlying strategies mark the endeavor: to identify the difference between the author's original work and the critic's text; to articulate the ideological base or the worldview of these differences; to explore their societal implications; to evaluate the political or power relationships emerging in the work of the author and in the text of the critic. Two methodologies, the constructionist and the deconstructionist, accompany the strategies. The constructionist discloses the inevitable contradictory responses that different audiences generate toward a single work. The deconstructionist discloses how the power symbols within a work undermine themselves.

The orientation of the postmodern perspective focuses on the critic exploring the power and contradiction of texts. The assumptions posit that the modern industrial world uses symbolic constructs (texts) as forms of social control, that the critic must identify these constructs, that the critic functions as social activist, and that the connection of word-thought-thing is arbitrarily invented to support power relationships of domination and subordination. The consensus rejects universal meanings to hold that specific contexts such as background, value, time, place, gender, race, and class determine how human beings produce and use symbols. In this sense, the postmodern perspective claims to be antitheoretical.[21]

o   o   o   o   o   o   o

Summary. a. *For classical rhetoric and beyond.* Brock, Scott, and Chesebro describe contemporary rhetorical criticism as nonparadigmatic.[22] Many ideas compete and combine, overlap and separate, as they reflect the ambiguous and arbitrary nature of language. Pluralism reigns. Yet these authors suggest that in time distinctions among many of the perspectives may cohere to produce an expanded interdisciplinary, even transcendent, definition of rhetoric.

b. *For biblical rhetorical criticism.* Not surprisingly, the pluralism of contemporary rhetorical criticism resides in biblical scholarship. Samples

---

21. Again, the word "antitheoretical" misleads. To reject universal meanings for specific contexts and for unstable or arbitrary interpretations constitutes theory. For a critique, see Christopher Norris, *What's Wrong With Postmodernism* (Baltimore: The Johns Hopkins University Press, 1990).

22. Brock, Scott, and Chesebro, *Methods of Rhetorical Criticism*, 502–14.

presented in chapter 2 provide illustration. Gitay appropriates the traditional perspective.[23] Lundbom models the sociological. Craven reflects the experiential and the dramaturgical. Patrick and Scult display the experiential. Clines represents the postmodern. Such pluralism helps to situate the contribution of Muilenburg historically and sociologically. During the 1960s, when rhetorical criticism began to expand, he offered a reformulation. In ensuing years, the proliferation of perspectives has allowed his contribution to develop in different ways. In other words, his "work" has elicited many "texts," thereby relativizing critiques of his program. A pluralistic stance eliminates the supposition that biblical rhetorical criticism must fit a single model.[24] It undercuts the negative judgment that the pursuit seems "undistinguishable from literary criticism,"[25] and it tempers the criticism that rhetorical analysis fails to recognize speech as political power.[26] This postmodern judgment would restrict rhetoric to a single phenomenon or, conversely, attribute to that phenomenon a broad meaning that restricts rhetoric. Either way, a large claim becomes the narrow view it decries. But in a pluralistic setting, models change, borders between disciplines open, and there are more possibilities than power dreams of. A plethora of rhetorical perspectives allows the Muilenburg mode a place to be without mandating that it stay in its place.

B. LITERARY CRITICAL THEORY

Like classical rhetorical criticism, literary criticism has exploded since the 1960s. Though the model proposed earlier by Abrams endures, mimetic, pragmatic, expressive, and objective theories have undergone significant alterations. This overview outlines some of them.

1. Introduction: Frye on the Boundary

The publication in 1957 of Frye's *Anatomy of Criticism* marked a decisive turn from the objective theories that dominated the first half of the

---

23. For the traditional perspective in New Testament studies, including the "new rhetoric," see, e.g., George A. Kennedy, *New Testament Interpretation through Rhetorical Criticism* (Chapel Hill: The University of North Carolina Press, 1984); Mack, *Rhetoric and the New Testament.* Cf. Antoinette Clark Wire, *The Corinthian Women Prophets: A Reconstruction through Paul's Rhetoric* (Minneapolis: Fortress Press, 1990), esp. 1–38; 197–201.
24. Contra Wuellner, "Where Is Rhetorical Criticism Taking Us?" 451.
25. Ibid., 452.
26. Cf. Brueggemann, "At the Mercy of Babylon," 17–22.

twentieth century.[27] Frye deplored the isolationist tendencies of New Criticism, the separation of a single piece of literature from any conceptual whole. He denounced the rubric of "art for art's sake," declaring close readings futile without a comprehensive system for analysis. He also rejected expressive theories that exalt individual authors and so moved toward the pragmatic or affective orientation. Literature is an "order of words" in a coherent literary context. The critic must take account of a framework variously called structural principles, conventional modes, archetypal taxonomies, and underlying laws.

One of the four essays in which Frye laid out a scheme for the systematic study of literature is entitled "Rhetorical Criticism: Theory of Genres." He noted that rhetoric has two traditional meanings, ornamental speech and persuasive speech. The former is inseparable from literature; the latter applicable to it. Embracing both meanings, he described literature as "the rhetorical organization of grammar and logic."[28] Genres constitute the rhetoric of presentation: whether words are acted, spoken, or written.[29] To the classical categories of drama, epic, and lyric, he added "the genre of the printed page," arbitrarily dubbed "fiction." The purpose of genres is not just to classify but, more importantly, to clarify large numbers of literary relationships.

For biblical studies, Frye's work would seem to resonate with the literary side of form criticism. He espoused conventions, archetypes, and literary history; he minimized the power of individual texts. Yet recognition that rhetoric as artful speech is inseparable from literature also fitted the Muilenburg mode. For literary critical studies, Frye's contribution had a Janus-like appearance. It looked back to New Criticism and forward to new developments.

2. Four Developments

Four developments exemplify the accelerating explosion of theories: poetics, structuralism, reader-response criticism, and deconstruction.

---

27. Frye, *Anatomy of Criticism*. For critical assessment, see, *inter alia,* Frank Lentricchia, *After the New Criticism* (Chicago: University of Chicago Press, 1980), 3–26; Vincent B. Leitch, *American Literary Criticism from the Thirties to the Eighties* (New York: Columbia University Press, 1988), 136–44.

28. Frye, *Anatomy of Criticism*, 245.

29. Ibid., 246–51.

a. Poetics

Frye defined poetics with respect to literary types and their functions: the construction of plot, the constituent elements of the whole, and related matters. Drawing upon Aristotle,[30] he designated poetics the science of poetry, thereby distinguishing it from poetry itself and from the experience of poetry. Since his work, however, the study of poetics has moved from archetypal categories to modern linguistics. Rather than devising a systematic theory to govern individual works, it has sought to articulate the structures, rules, and conventions of discourse. The goal has been a grammar of literature.

Representative of this heterogeneous endeavor, Tzvetan Todorov first differentiated poetics from interpretation, that is, from interest in the meaning of the individual text.[31] As the study of grammar is separated from the meaning of sentences, so the grammar of literature (poetics) is separated from the meaning of literature. Nonetheless, a complementary relationship exists between interpretation and poetics. Individual works are instances (but only instances) of the general structure of literature. They permit the abstract properties to emerge. Todorov next related linguistics and poetics. The former examines components of sentences; the latter examines sentences as compounds of literary units.[32] The units combine to produce characters, plots, and thematic structures. Study of these features establishes norms and effects. The resulting topology produces genres, which are neither prescriptive norms nor descriptive catalogues. Instead they designate sets of convention that account for the meanings produced. These meanings always move to the general, to a grammar of literature.[33] The aim of poetics, then, is "to propose a theory of the structure and functioning of literary discourse."[34]

30. Ibid., 14–15. Frye uses the Bywater translation of Aristotle. The Golden translation reads: "Let us discuss the art of poetry, itself, and its species, describing the character of each of them, and how it is necessary to construct plots if the poetic composition is to be successful and, furthermore, the number and kinds of parts to be found in the poetic work, and as many other matters as are relevant. Let us follow the order of nature, beginning with first principles" (*Aristotle's Poetics*, I.1; Golden, 3).

31. See Tzvetan Todorov, *Introduction to Poetics*, trans. Richard Howard, vol. 1 of *Theory and History of Literature* (Minneapolis: University of Minnesota Press, 1981), esp. 3–12.

32. See Tzevetan Todorov, *The Poetics of Prose*, trans. Richard Howard (Ithaca, N.Y.: Cornell University Press, 1977). In the foreword Jonathan Culler provides a helpful summary; ibid., 7–13.

33. Ibid., 236.

34. Todorov, *Introduction to Poetics*, 7.

As with Frye's project, poetics exhibits greater affinity to biblical form criticism than to rhetorical criticism. Interest in producing a science of literature based on the study of conventions and norms suits Gunkel's goal of writing a history of Hebrew genres rather than Muilenburg's emphasis on the specificities of texts. Further, the separation of grammar from meaning runs counter to the insistence upon the inseparability of form, content, and meaning. Though such differences may shrink in the activity that Todorov calls "reading," dissimilarities between poetics and rhetorical criticism continue.[35]

b. Structuralism

Derived from the linguistic work of the nineteenth century Swiss scholar Ferdinand de Saussure,[36] structuralism is a method for organizing all human social phenomena—all systems of communication with set rules.[37] It studies complex structures, the network of interrelationships that constitute the whole over the parts. These structures are said to lie not on the surface but behind or below observed reality. Deep structures, as contrasted with surface structures, generate and limit particular activities. They relate not to historical processes but to a network of internal relationships known as binary oppositions: pairs of mutually exclusive and exhaustive categories such as life/death and male/female. Study of these relationships is synchronic, not diachronic. Structuralism rejects the

---

35. For Todorov's response to the charge that poetics ignores the specificities of texts and for his thesis on "reading," see *The Poetics of Prose*, 234–46. On the use of poetics in biblical studies, see, e.g., Adele Berlin, *Poetics and Interpretation of Biblical Narrative* (Sheffield: Almond Press, 1983). See also Herbert Chanan Brichto, *Toward a Grammar of Biblical Poetics: Tales of the Prophets* (New York: Oxford University Press, 1992). Cf. the exegetical essay, "'And Much Cattle': YHWH's Last Words to a Reluctant Prophet," ibid., 67–87. For a book-length study, see Kenneth M. Craig, Jr., *A Poetics of Jonah: Art in the Service of Ideology* (Columbia, S.C.: University of South Carolina Press, 1993). These poetic analyses arrived too late for the discussion of Jonah in Part Two.

36. See Ferdinand de Saussure, *Course in General Linguistics*, ed. and annotator Roy Harris (London: Duckworth, 1983). The original French work was published in 1916 under the title *Cours de linguistique générale*. For an introduction, see Jonathan Culler, *Ferdinand de Saussure*, Penguin Modern Masters, ed. Frank Kermode (New York: Penguin, 1977).

37. For a valuable study, including representative texts, see Michael Lane, ed., *Introduction to Structuralism* (New York: Basic Books, 1970); cf. Terence Hawkes, *Structuralism and Semiotics* (Berkeley: University of California Press, 1977).

concept of cause and effect. Instead, it perceives laws of transformation, the changing of one structure into another.[38]

As a literary endeavor,[39] structuralism appears (on the surface) to continue emphases of Frye and New Criticism. It seeks the conventions and contexts that make literature possible. It gives intrinsic readings, eschews historical interpretation, and rejects authorial intention. Nevertheless, interest lies not in the interpretation of genres but in the underlying or innate principles that govern all language; not in aesthetic objects (individual texts) but in systems of communication. Structuralism decodes surface structures, whether the archetypes of Frye or the close readings of New Criticism, to expose abstract messages in deep structures.[40]

In the 1970s structuralism entered biblical scholarship.[41] As a method for reading texts, it offered surface similarities to rhetorical criticism. Both approaches use the word "structure," present charts and diagrams in analyzing texts, accent synchronic interpretation, and pursue intrinsic readings. But the similarities deceive. From a structuralist perspective, rhetorical criticism works with surface, not deep, structures. It concentrates on particularities in texts rather than on relationships that form the system of literary conventions. It disavows the separability of form (structure), content, and meaning. The two methods diverge in basic ways.

c. Reader-response Criticism

Another development since Frye's *Anatomy* is reader-response criticism.[42] It departs from objective theories to accent readers (audience) and reading over the text. In Abrams's model it belongs to the pragmatic or affective orientation. Yet it would destabilize the model by dethroning the literary work, which Abrams placed in the center of his triangle, and

---

38. Lane, *Introduction to Structuralism*, 11–39.

39. See Jonathan Culler, *Structuralist Poetics* (Ithaca, N.Y.: Cornell University Press, 1975). For a critique of Culler, see Lentricchia, *After the New Criticism*, 103–12. Cf. also Robert Scholes, *Structuralism in Literature: An Introduction* (New Haven: Yale University Press, 1974).

40. For further analysis, see Leitch, *American Literary Criticism*, 238–66.

41. For bibliography, see the extended note at the end of the chapter.

42. The terminology "reader-response criticism" prevails in the United States. For comparison with the German school of Reception Theory, see Robert C. Holub, *Reception Theory: A Critical Introduction* (New York: Methuen, 1984).

enthroning the reader, whom he placed in the right-hand corner.[43] Further, the reader signifies a catalog of candidates heretofore not perceived: implied reader, original reader, ideal reader, informed reader, interested reader, and actual reader.[44]

Susan Suleiman identified six approaches within reader-response criticism: rhetorical, semiotic and structuralist, phenomenological, subjective and psychoanalytical, sociological and historical, and hermeneutic.[45] Even then she found it difficult to anchor the floating work of the critic Stanley Fish. He began his literary voyage by countering New Criticism.[46] "Meaning" is not the end result of analyzing formal structures but rather develops as the reader experiences the text. So he dislodged the text in a spatial context to install the reader in temporal experience. The shift required positing a common level of reader experience that preceded various emotional or intellectual interpretations. Yet a common level hooked Fish into assuming once again the stability of the text for controlling the reader's experience. To overcome the contradiction he reconceived the reader as a member of an interpretive community that itself decides what the text is.[47] Members of the same community agree on how they read the text; members of different communities disagree. The text remains radically unstable. In short, community "makes" literature; interpretive strategies shape texts.[48] This way of thinking propelled Fish to understand criticism as persuasion, a political act "endlessly negotiated."[49] He wrote of the "rhetoricizing" nature of his task, the constant transformation of interpre-

43. Cf. the sketch of Abrams's model in chapter 1. For a concise introduction to reader-response criticism, which begins with this model, see Elizabeth Freund, *The Return of the Reader* (New York: Methuen, 1987). For an overview and evaluation, see Leitch, *American Literary Criticism*, 211–37. Cf. Jane P. Tomkins, ed., *Reader-Response Criticism: From Formalism to Post-Structuralism* (Baltimore: The Johns Hopkins University Press, 1980).

44. Cf. the comments on the ideal reader in Patrick and Scult, *Rhetoric and Biblical Interpretation*, 18–24, 134–39.

45. See Susan R. Suleiman, "Introduction: Varieties of Audience-Oriented Criticism," *The Reader in the Text: Essays on Audience and Interpretation*, eds. Susan R. Suleiman and Inge Crosman (Princeton: Princeton University Press, 1980), 3–45.

46. The following summary draws from Stanley Fish, *Is There a Text in this Class? The Authority of Interpretive Communities* (Cambridge, Mass.: Harvard University Press, 1980), 1–17. For a review, see Richard Wollheim, "The Professor Knows," *The New York Review of Books*, vol. 28 (17 December 1981): 64–66.

47. Cf. the discussion of the interpretive community in Patrick and Scult, *Rhetoric and Biblical Interpretation*, 22–24.

48. Fish, *Is There a Text in this Class?*, 11.

49. Ibid., 17.

tation. The process meant, however, that the reader no longer controlled the text. At the end of Fish's voyage, the reader did not respond so much as disappear into the belly of "rhetoricizing."[50]

Of Suleiman's six approaches, the rhetorical and the phenomenological hold particular interest for biblical rhetorical criticism. The rhetorical understands the text as shared communication sent by the author to the reader.[51] In turn, the reader decodes what the text encodes. Wayne Booth, for example, posited the ideas of the implied author and the ideal reader. The first designates the values and commitments inherent in every literary artifact; it relates as a "second self" to the real author.[52] The second designates the reader whom the implied author makes and the literature addresses.[53] For reading to work successfully, the actual reader must agree to become the implied reader, to subordinate his or her own ideas to textual values and commitments. The desired identification of implied author and ideal reader ought to happen through the rhetoric of the text. There the author tries through various strategies to communicate meaning and so achieve intended effects. Overall, the circularity of implied author and implied reader inherent in the rhetoric of the text becomes an interpretive construct that guarantees the consistency of specific readings. In the process author, text, and reader converge.

This rhetorical approach accords well with some aspects of biblical rhetorical criticism. (At least the reader so interprets.) Though Muilenburg worked with the concept of the real author, his focus lent itself to the concept of the implied author. As he sought the proper way to read, he subordinated his own ideas to the values inherent in the text. Hence he also anticipated the concept of the implied reader. The entire process happened through rhetoric, the communication of meaning. Yet unlike Booth's approach, the Muilenburg mode did not so much engage a panorama of texts as concentrate on the specificities of single texts. Its close readings were more in keeping with the procedures (but not the assumptions) of New Criticism.[54]

50. But the voyage did not end. Instead, it carried Fish from reader-response criticism to deconstruction; see below. For critiques of Fish, see Lentricchia, *After the New Criticism*, 146–48; Leitch, *American Literary Criticism*, 214–19.
51. Suleiman, "Introduction," *The Reader in the Text*, 7–11.
52. Wayne C. Booth, *The Rhetoric of Fiction* (Chicago: University of Chicago Press, 1961), esp. 67–86 and *passim*.
53. Ibid., 49, 50, 70, 136–40.
54. For a helpful discussion of reader-response criticism in reference to the Bible (though it regrettably omits rhetorical criticism), see Edgar V. McKnight, *Post-Modern Use*

Two practitioners represent the phenomenological approach. Roman Ingarden distinguished between the literary work as "an objectivity *in itself*" and its concretizations, "what is constituted during the reading."[55] The latter must not be confused with subjective experiencing but rather signifies the realizing of the work, albeit partially. The work as an organic whole does not reside in the mind of the reader, but the reader submits to the work, including its indeterminacies, for the purpose of appropriating it to yield a single harmonious interpretation. Though influenced by Ingarden, Wolfgang Iser allowed the reader greater play in determining meaning.[56] He described the reading process as "a dynamic *interaction* between text and reader."[57] The reader wanders through the text to grasp its manifold interconnecting perspectives. Different readers may realize it "in different, equally valid, ways."[58] No single interpretation exhausts the possibilities. Indeed, "gaps" within the text stimulate readers to fill them in various ways. "When the reader bridges the gaps, communication begins."[59] Iser imposed one stricture upon this asymmetrical process. In the act of reading, the reader must interpret the text so as to bring about internal consistency. Adherence to consistency-building throughout the "wandering" (reading) process discloses the gestalt of the text, enabling the reader to experience it as actual event.[60]

The stance of multiple readings wed to consistency-building bespeaks an unresolved ambiguity in Iser's approach.[61] Such ambiguity also

---

of the Bible: The Emergence of Reader-Oriented Criticism (Nashville: Abingdon Press, 1988); cf. Mark G. Brett, "The Future of Reader Criticisms?" *The Open Text: New Directions for Biblical Studies?*, ed. Francis Watson (London: SCM Press Ltd., 1993), 13–31.

55. Roman Ingarden, *The Literary Work of Art*, trans., with introduction, by George G. Grabowicz (Evanston: Northwestern University Press, 1973), 331–55. The original German publication appeared in 1931; two subsequent editions followed in 1960 and 1965, plus an amended Polish translation in 1960. More than forty years later came the English translation, thereby making this work accessible to a larger audience only in the post-1968 period.

56. For Iser's critique of Ingarden, see, e.g., *The Act of Reading: A Theory of Aesthetic Response* (Baltimore: The Johns Hopkins University Press, 1978), 170–79.

57. Ibid., 107–34. For further discussion see Wolfgang Iser, "The Reading Process: A Phenomenological Approach," *The Implied Reader* (Baltimore: The Johns Hopkins University Press, 1974), 274–94.

58. Iser, *The Act of Reading*, 178.

59. Ibid., 169.

60. Ibid., 118f; 122–34. Cf. the comments on consistency-building in Patrick and Scult, *Rhetoric and Biblical Interpretation*, 85f.

61. For critiques of Ingarden and Iser, cf. Eagleton, *Literary Theory*, 74–85; Suleiman, "Introduction," *The Reader in the Text*, 22–27.

describes varieties of biblical rhetorical criticism that operate at the boundary of text and reader. However that may be, in both the phenomenological approach and the biblical discipline, the reader submits to the text, wandering through its specificities to discern internal coherence. She realizes and appropriates the text as an organic whole.[62]

d. Deconstruction

Deconstruction is another development since Frye's *Anatomy*.[63] A complex and bewildering concept, it exemplifies the post-modern perspective to indicate variously a philosophical stance, political maneuver, intellectual game, or literary project. Jonathan Culler explains the last category as follows: "to deconstruct a discourse is to show how it undermines the philosophy it asserts, or the hierarchical oppositions on which it relies, by identifying in the text the rhetorical operations that produce the supposed ground of argument, the key concept or premise."[64] Primarily through the French philosopher Jacques Derrida deconstruction has become a critique of structuralism. Appearing at times under the banner of post-structuralism,[65] it rejects the idea that structures are inherent or objectively present in texts. It rejects the claim that structures reflect the deep levels of the mind, levels that determine the limits of meaning. And it rejects the primacy of speech over writing, holding instead that the latter constitutes the origin of language. Writing signifies more than graphic representation; it includes all forms of articulation and differentiation. It embodies the element of "free play," of indeterminacy within every communication. Writing subverts what it says; language remains inherently unstable.

---

62. Cf. Patrick and Scult, *Rhetoric and Biblical Interpretation,* esp. 19–21.

63. For an excellent introduction, see Christopher Norris, *Deconstruction: Theory and Practice* (New York: Routledge, rev. ed. 1991). Except where documented otherwise, the above summary is indebted to this book, to Lentricchia, *After the New Criticism,* 156–210, and to Leitch, *American Literary Criticism,* 270–306.

64. Jonathan Culler, *On Deconstruction: Theory and Criticism after Structuralism* (Ithaca, N.Y.: Cornell University Press, 1982), 86.

65. See, e.g., Jacques Derrida, *Writing and Difference,* trans. with intro. by Alan Bass (Chicago: University of Chicago Press, 1978); cf. John Sturrock, ed., *Structuralism and Since: From Levi-Strauss to Derrida* (Oxford: Oxford University Press, 1981); Harold Bloom et al., *Deconstruction and Criticism* (New York: Seabury, 1979). Cf. Madan Sarup, *An Introductory Guide to Post-Structuralism and Postmodernism,* 2d ed. (Athens: The University of Georgia Press, 1993).

As an activity of reading, deconstruction stays bound to the text it questions, never becoming an independent system. Two interrelated strategies mark its presence. First, a critic uses a system against itself. Reading within the system, the deconstructor reads against it and so reverses established hierarchies. Second, the critic moves outside the system, views it from a perspective of discontinuity and difference, and so displaces the system. In advocating this strategy of double reading, Derrida sought to disassemble not only the order of priorities within a text but also the system of conceptual opposition that produced the order.

Double reading decenters the text and defers meaning. Decentering claims that there is no place (i.e., no structure, no signifier) outside the text to determine its boundaries. Indeed, no fixed text exists, only the multiplication of texts through the act of reading. Deferring plays with the anomalous and unstable French word *différance*. It embodies the sense of both to differ and to defer. A basic dissimilarity characterizes all texts, even similar ones, because similarities proceed from differences. The underlying difference in fashioning and reading texts leads to the continual deferring of their meaning. Free play prevents a single, homogeneous reading. To fix meaning falsifies the nature of a text as open and indeterminate.

Though the complexities of deconstruction prevent easy summary, juxtaposition to classical literary theories (mimetic, expressive, affective, and objective) may underscore basic features. The relationship to mimesis remains ambivalent. Some critics ignore any connection. Others explore a possibility in the concept of referentiality, namely that a text refers to something outside itself.[66] They maintain that this concept embraces hierarchical oppositions between the universe and artistic representation, between the original and the imitative. These oppositions deconstruction seeks to reverse and displace.[67] Whether mimesis be condemned, neutralized, or ranked superior to the original, it can become a textual strategy. By contrast, expressive theories as traditionally conceived offer little to deconstruction, though the meaning and role of the "author" remains a major issue for debate.[68] Efforts to construe the text apart from context have led from the assertion that the author is dead to the redefinition of

---

66. Cf. Culler, *On Deconstruction*, 185–87; Leitch, *American Literary Criticism*, 284f.

67. Note in the sentence the use of the device anastrophe (literally, "turning back"): inversion of the usual word order. Cf. Appendix B.

68. See Donald E. Pease, "Author," *Critical Terms for Literary Study*, 105–17.

the concept author as a fundamental cultural function of discontinuity to the displacement of the author by the critic (the authorless subject) and on to continuing controversy.

Affective theories past and present interact positively and negatively with deconstruction. One formulation has the reader as subject acting upon the text as object.[69] A variation has the reader making the text, even deferring its meaning. Another cites the hermeneutic penchant in reader-response criticism for interrogating the text, undermining objectivity, and stressing free play.[70] But a contrasting formulation claims that reader-response criticism and deconstruction diverge significantly.[71] The former explores the literary reader from many vantage points; the latter investigates not the reader but the text. The former seeks to rationalize textual discontinuities; the latter embraces them. Contradictory observations attest to an unstable relationship (and to unstable scholarship). In reference to objective theories a similar situation prevails. Like them, deconstruction pursues close readings. It is text-centered and so privileges literary language.[72] Nevertheless, deconstruction repudiates objective readings.[73] Against the autonomy of the text, it posits radical indeterminacy. Instability reigns.

True to its nature, deconstruction relates to biblical rhetorical criticism in unstable ways. The view that no fixed structures exist, that authorial intentionality does not prevail, and that meaning must be continually deferred decenters the Muilenburg stance. Yet rhetorical analysis itself characterizes deconstructionist activity. In dismantling texts, it investigates the persuasive power of language (as well as the lack thereof), delineates tropes and figures, and pursues close reading with focus on the particularities (rather than the similarities) of texts. Though with marked differences, rhetorical criticism (in the Muilenburg mode) and deconstruction eschew comprehensive systems for controlling texts.[74]

69. Lentricchia, *After the New Criticism*, 185.

70. Suleiman, "Introduction," *The Reader in the Text*, 38–45.

71. Leitch, *American Literary Criticism*, 288f.

72. See Joseph N. Riddel, "Response: A Miller's Tale," *Diacritics* 5 (Fall 1975): 56–65; cf. the discussion of Riddel in Leitch, *American Literary Criticism*, 279f.

73. See Norris, *Deconstruction*, esp. 99–105; Leitch, *American Literary Criticism*, 273–76.

74. This observation excludes Gitay's appropriation of Aristotelian theory and the endeavors of Patrick and Scult. On the larger issues, see Michael La Fargue, "Are Texts Determinate? Derrida, Barth, and the Role of the Biblical Scholar," *HTR* 81 (1988): 341–57.

Summary. Since Frye began to decenter New Criticism, literary critical theories and strategies have proliferated. The four sketched here—poetics, structuralism, reader-response criticism, and deconstruction—hardly cover the heterogeneity of the enterprise.[75] As in the reformulation of classical rhetorical theories, so in literary critical theories pluralism flourishes. The confusion of tongues, scattered abroad in the land, expands the background of biblical rhetorical criticism to enhance possibilities and increase difficulties.

C. LITERARY STUDY OF THE BIBLE

As literary critical theories have proliferated since the 1960s, so has their application to literary study of the Bible. Enormous outpourings in journals and books testify to innumerable methods and ever-changing points of view. This development constitutes a paradigm shift.[76] Biblical studies have moved from an historical to a literary orientation. Yet the long history of biblical studies shows that the historical interest was itself a recent phenomenon.[77] The shift to the literary signifies then not a new thing in the land but a return, *mutatis mutandis,* to an activity that extends, in the words of Muilenburg, "from the time of Jerome and before and continuing on with the rabbis and until modern times."[78]

The return of literary interest has involved both biblical and secular critics. Given their academic training, each group brings to the critical

---

For an excellent application of deconstruction to the Bible, see Edward L. Greenstein, "Deconstruction and Biblical Narrative," *Prooftexts* 9 (1989): 43–71.

75. A proliferation of reference works attests to the explosion even as it seeks to order it. For bibliography, see the extended note at the end of the chapter.

76. See Peter W. Macky, "The Coming Revolution: The New Literary Approach to the New Testament," in *A Guide to Contemporary Hermeneutics,* ed. Donald K. McKim (Grand Rapids, Mich.: William B. Eerdmans, 1986), 263–79. On paradigm shifts, see above, section A.

77. The historical critical method prevailed from the eighteenth through the middle of the twentieth century; see Edgar Krentz, *The Historical–Critical Method,* esp. 6–32, 73–88. Cf. the comments in chapter 1, section C. For an overview that relates the historical disciplines to newer literary trends, see John Barton, *Reading the Old Testament: Method in Biblical Study* (Philadelphia: Westminster Press, 1984). For one successful effort to join historical and literary paradigms, see Jon D. Levenson, "I Samuel 25 as Literature and as History," *CBQ* 40 (1978): 11–28. More recently, cf. the New Historicism as a development within literary criticism (see extended note 75 below).

78. Muilenburg, "Form Criticism and Beyond," 8.

task different skills, knowledge, and stances. Though some scholars work competently across the divide, the difference can make for problems.[79] Another distinction cuts across this divide: the perspectives of believers and non-believers.[80] Biblical and secular critics alike share the distinction; its effects are unpredictable. In general, the relatively stable tradition to which Muilenburg alluded has dissolved. An overview scans the situation from the 1960s into the 90s.[81]

1. The Sixties

Two biblical scholars writing in the 1960s deplored the paucity of literary studies even as their own works signaled a revival of interest.[82] Luis Alonso-Schökel, a Spanish Jesuit, examined the stylistic phenomenology of Hebrew poetry.[83] In later essays he compared his approach with New Criticism,[84] arguing for the integration of aesthetic and nonaesthetic readings.[85] Edwin Good, an American professor, investigated irony as a literary device that shapes theology and faith.[86] He traced intended incongruities through the Saul narrative and the books of Genesis, Isaiah, Jonah, Qoheleth, and Job. He did not align his analysis with any particular school

---

79. See, e.g., the exchange between two biblical scholars: James Kugel, "On the Bible and Literary Criticism," *Prooftexts* 1 (September 1981): 217–36; Adele Berlin and James Kugel, "On the Bible as Literature," *Prooftexts* 2 (September 1982): 323–32; see also Leland Ryken and Tremper Longman, "Introduction," *A Complete Literary Guide to the Bible,* eds. Ryken and Longman (Grand Rapids, Mich.: Zondervan Publishing House, 1993), 20–29.

80. Cf. Patrick and Scult, *Rhetoric and Biblical Interpretation,* 22–24.

81. Cf., e.g., Sandor Goodhart, "Biblical Theory and Criticism: Modern Criticism," *The Johns Hopkins Guide to Literary Theory & Criticism,* 84–90.

82. Just before the beginning of the decade appeared the illuminating study by Zvi Adar, *The Biblical Narrative,* trans. Misha Louvish (Jerusalem: Goldberg's Press, 1959). It analyzed literary characteristics in five stages: the short tale, the cycle of stories, the long story, the book, and the biblical narrative as a whole.

83. Luis Alonso-Schökel, *Estudio de poetica hebrea* (Barcelona: Juan Flors, 1963); see the revised English edition, *A Manual of Hebrew Poetics,* Subsidia Biblica, 11 (Rome: Pontifical Biblical Institute, 1988).

84. Luis Alonso-Schökel, "Narrative Structures in the Book of Judith," The Center for Hermeneutical Studies in Hellenistic and Modern Culture (Berkeley, 1975), 1–20, 45–47.

85. L. Alonso-Schökel, "Hermeneutical Problems of a Literary Study of the Bible," *Supplement to VT,* Congress Volume 28 (Leiden: E. J. Brill, 1975), 1–15.

86. Edwin M. Good, *Irony in the Old Testament* (Philadelphia: Westminster, 1965).

of literary theory.[87] Both these scholars acknowledged the inspiration of Muilenburg.

2. The Seventies

In the 1970s J. P. Fokkelman, a Dutch biblical scholar, published a book on narrative in Genesis.[88] Setting his analysis over against diachronic approaches in literary history and biblical scholarship, he described the text as a pole between the author and the reader. The author (often a code for a protracted process) creates the text; the reader recreates it through interpretation. Knowledge of the first act depends upon the second. The reader analyzes the text as an end unto itself. This artistic enterprise includes the drawing of theological conclusions. Only then does the reader explore the text as a transparency, a means to other ends. The subtitle of Fokkelman's book, "Specimens of Stylistic and Structural Analysis," evoked the classical categories *elocutio* and *dispositio*. His synchronic method of close reading approximated New Criticism, and his overall approach resembled biblical rhetorical criticism.[89]

Another study in the craft of storytelling came from the Israeli scholar Jacob Licht.[90] He maintained that in just about every instance the biblical narrator pursued two ends: the historical (the conveying of information) and the aesthetic (the shaping of art). The latter quality should be studied in its own right and not as a marginal pursuit. Though the claim might seem obvious, it "has the nasty habit of disappearing from learned discussions."[91] Licht broke the habit by examining aesthetic features as they emerge in chosen stories. The features included scenes and basic structures, repetition, story time, and complex narrative units. His exposition

87. A second edition appeared in 1981 (Sheffield: University of Sheffield Press). Good held fast to an eclectic approach that includes rhetorical criticism but noted that, if he were to revise his work, he would sever the link between literary criticism and theology (though he did not object if others promoted it).

88. J. P. Fokkelman, *Narrative Art in Genesis: Specimens of Stylistic and Structural Analysis* (Assen, The Netherlands: Van Gorcum, 1975).

89. Cf. more recently J. P. Fokkelman, *Narrative Art and Poetry in the Books of Samuel:* vol. 1, *King David* (Assen, The Netherlands: Van Gorcum, 1981); vol. 2, *The Crossing Fates* (1986); vol. 3, *Throne and City* (1990); vol. 4, *Vow and Desire* (1993). For a review of vol. 1, see James S. Ackerman, "Book Review," *JSOT* 25 (1983) 119–24. For an introduction to other literary studies from the seventies, see Edward L. Greenstein, "Biblical Narratology," *Prooftexts* 1 (May 1981): 201–8.

90. See Jacob Licht, *Storytelling in the Bible* (Jerusalem: The Magnes Press, 1978).

91. Ibid., 23.

engaged secular and biblical literary studies from the ancient world to the present. Affinities to rhetorical criticism are many.

3. The Eighties

The 1980s witnessed a mushrooming of literary analyses. At the beginning of the decade, the American literary critic Robert Alter wrote *The Art of Biblical Narrative*.[92] Labeling biblical scholarship "antiquarian" and "excavative," he virtually dismissed the rich history of literary biblical study even though his own views echoed that history. He proposed that the Bible in its final form constitutes an artistic document with a full texture of interconnected unity. Close reading unfolds intended meanings. It exposes conventions, techniques, characterizations, and types of discourse that yield coherence. Though Alter minimized form criticism, his study of "type-scenes" resembled the discipline.[93] Though he ignored rhetorical criticism, his analysis reflected the discipline.[94]

The Israeli scholar Meir Sternberg published a comprehensive system for understanding biblical narrative.[95] Difficult to read, the book offered a poetics marked with dogmatic tendencies and untouched by post-structuralism. Like Alter, Sternberg passed harsh judgment on biblical scholarship, contrasting his discourse-oriented analysis with its source-oriented inquiry. For him three functional principles regulate biblical discourse.[96] The ideological principle affirms monotheism, ethics, and, most important, divine omniscience over against human limitations. The historiographic principle describes the truth claim (not the truth value) of the text. The aesthetic principle promotes the literary character of the text, its intentional and pervasive use of artistic features.

92. Robert Alter, *The Art of Biblical Narrative* (New York: Basic Books, 1981). Cf. the review by Jon Levenson; it noted deficiencies in Alter's knowledge (Book Reviews, *Biblical Archaeologist* 46, Spring 1983, 124–25). For a companion work, see Alter, *The Art of Biblical Poetry* (New York: Basic Books, 1985).

93. Cf. Robert Alter, "How Convention Helps Us Read: The Case of the Bible's Annunciation Type-Scene," *Prooftexts* 3 (May 1983): 115–30, esp. 118–19.

94. On this point see, e.g., the essays by R. N. Whybray, David Jobling, and Norman C. Habel, with a response by Alter, in *JSOT* 27 (1983): 75–117.

95. Meir Sternberg, *The Poetics of Biblical Narrative* (Bloomington, Ind.: Indiana University Press, 1985). Given the complexities of Sternberg's writing, the beginning student may well turn first to another study: Shimon Bar-Efrat, *Narrative Art in the Bible* (Sheffield: Almond Press, 1989). Cf. Michael Fishbane, "Recent Work on Biblical Narrative," *Prooftexts* 1 (January 1981): 99–104.

96. Sternberg, *Poetics*, 41–57.

In developing the aesthetic principle, Sternberg isolated two major narrative strategies.[97] First, the omniscient narrator has infused the text with gaps, omissions, and discontinuities.[98] They testify to the cognitive divide between divine and human. The reader must work responsibly to fill the gaps, and in this process the reader grows ethically. Second, the omniscient narrator has included a seemingly contradictory and yet actually complementary structure: the use of repetition, that is strategies of informational redundancy. They occur on various levels, from words to plots to themes, and in many types, from verbatim repetition to repetition with variation. Not unlike ellipsis, redundancy has its own gaps. At the same time, it closes gaps not of its making. While each of the two strategies signals a pole of incoherence, together they form a network through which the reader may find a "difficult coherence."

Rhetoric occupied a significant place in Sternberg's poetics.[99] Though recognizing communication as the broad meaning of the concept, he gave attention to the narrow meaning of persuasive communication. The Bible persuades "by organizing the past into a rhetoric of faith."[100] He identified fifteen rhetorical devices by which the text shapes the response of readers.[101] Affinities between his poetics and rhetorical criticism come not at the level of ideology but of exegesis. The skill Sternberg exhibited in reading the particularities of texts provides a wealth of insights into the interrelationship of form, content, and meaning.[102]

Building on the *Anatomy of Criticism*, Frye wrote about the artistry of the Bible.[103] He laid out an overarching narrative structure that includes both Testaments under the categories of language, myth, metaphor, and typology. He did not give detailed commentary on specific texts. By contrast, the British critic Gabriel Josipovici combined exegesis of selected texts with the scheme of the whole.[104] He sought the unity of

---

97. Ibid., 186–229; 365–440.

98. Cf. the concept of gaps in the work of Iser; see above, note 59.

99. Sternberg, *Poetics*, 441–515.

100. Ibid., 104.

101. Ibid., 475–81.

102. For critical reviews of Sternberg, see the extended note at the end of the chapter.

103. Northrop Frye, *The Great Code* (New York: Harcourt Brace Jovanovich, 1982). For a review, see Naomi Bliven, "The Good Book," *The New Yorker* (31 May 1982): 104–6. Cf. Susan Einbinder, "Alter vs. Frye: Which Bible?" *Prooftexts* 4 (1984): 301–8.

104. Gabriel Josipovici, *The Book of God: A Response to the Bible* (New Haven: Yale University Press, 1988). For a review, see Michael Fishbane, *JBL* 110/2 (1991): 323–25.

the Bible while attending to its "peculiarly fragmentary and elliptical mode of narration."[105] Moreover, he used biblical languages and engaged biblical scholarship. Though both these scholars showed sensitivity, even commitment, to theological meaning, they did not offer links to rhetorical criticism.

A compendium of literary analyses appeared near the end of the decade.[106] Edited by Alter and Frank Kermode, a British literary critic, it included twenty-four males and one female from the United States, Europe, and Israel. They wrote general articles as well as essays on each book in the Jewish and Protestant canons. Some wrote as biblical scholars, some as literary critics, and a few as both. Many wrote as believers; some did not. Despite its claim to be "the" definitive guide, this volume considered only selected trends. It excluded rhetorical criticism.[107]

4. The Nineties

In the early 1990s secular literary critics produced quite different books about the Bible. Harold Bloom's effort perhaps merits note because it dealt not with the final form of the text, as is usual in literary studies, but with a hypothetical source dependent upon historical research.[108] Frye, in a sequel to his earlier work, continued to promote archetypal criticism.[109] He treated the poet's authority as bound to the authority of poetic lan-

105. Josipovici, *The Book of God*, 23.

106. Robert Alter and Frank Kermode, eds., *The Literary Guide to the Bible* (Cambridge, Mass.: Belknap, 1987).

107. For reviews, see, e.g., James L. Crenshaw, "What Does One Need to Know to Understand the Bible?" *Books and Religion* 16 (Fall 1989): 6, 9, 10, 24; Mieke Bal, "Literature and Its Insistent Other," *JAAR* 57/2 (1989): 373–83; Edgar V. McKnight, "New Criticism and Old," *JAAR* 57/2 (1989): 385–91; David Jobling, "A Discourse About the Meanings of the Whole," *Int* 46 (1992): 181–82.

108. Harold Bloom, *The Book of J* (New York: Grove Weidenfeld, 1990). Reviews have been overwhelmingly unfavorable. For an extended discussion, see the articles in *Iowa Review* 21 (1991) by Richard Eliot Friedman, Jay Holstein, Carol Meyers, and Phyllis Trible.

109. Northrop Frye, *Words with Power: Being a Second Study of "The Bible as Literature"* (San Diego: Harcourt Brace Jovanovich, 1990). For critical reviews, see Robert M. Adams, "God and the Critics," *The New York Times Book Review* (31 March 1991): 14f; Denis Donohue, "Mister Myth," *New York Review of Books* 39 (9 April 1992): 25–28.

guage, and he explored four biblical variations of the *axis mundi:* mountain, garden, cave, and furnace. Myth and metaphor shaped the reading. Disagreeing with Bloom and Frye, Alter produced a book that tried "to move from the specific texts to an apprehension of that world of writing, how it turns, how and why it is literary."[110]

In addition to these contributions came another compendium that took its departure from perceived failures in the volume edited by Alter and Kermode.[111] The work included twenty-seven males and three females, all from the United States. Beginning with the editors Leland Ryken, a professor of English, and Tremper Longman, a professor of Bible, the writers were equally divided between literary and biblical scholars. Most represented conservative Christian contexts.[112] Yet another development of the decade has been the journal *Biblical Interpretation.*[113] It promises to highlight multiple literary approaches alongside other trends.

◊   ◊   ◊   ◊   ◊   ◊   ◊

Summary. Frye observed that literary critics interested in the Bible and biblical critics interested in literary criticism are today numerous in the land.[114] This overview only suggests the breadth and depth of the enterprise. Time fails the chronicler to write of literary critics Bal, Damrosch, Fuchs,[115] and a host of biblical critics: Ackerman, Berlin, Conrad,

110. Robert Alter, *The World of Biblical Literature* (New York: Basic Books, 1992), xii. For his scathing review of Bloom's *The Book of J,* see ibid., 153–69. For critical reviews of Alter's work, see Stephen A. Geller, "Some Pitfalls in the 'Literary Approach' to Biblical Narrative," *JQR* 74 (1984): 408–15; Edward Greenstein, "Grasping the Meaning of a Peculiar Literature," *Forward* (15 May 1992): 10.

111. Leland Ryken and Tremper Longman, eds., *A Complete Literary Guide to the Bible.* Not unlike the title of the volume edited by Alter and Kermode (see note 106 above), this title claims too much. The guide is far from "complete." It does not provide essays on every book of the Bible but instead offers "representative specimens."

112. One notable exception is the Jewish novelist Chaim Potok; another, the Christian novelist Frederick Buechner.

113. *Biblical Interpretation: A Journal of Contemporary Approaches,* eds. J. Cheryl Exum and Mark G. Brett, vol. 1– (Leiden: E. J. Brill, 1993–).

114. Frye, *Words With Power,* xvi.

115. See, e.g., Mieke Bal, *Death and Dissymmetry: The Politics of Coherence in the Book of Judges* (Chicago: University of Chicago Press, 1988); David Damrosch, *The Narrative Covenant: Transformations of Genre in the Growth of Biblical Literature* (San Francisco: Harper and Row, 1987); Esther Fuchs, "The Literary Characterization of Mothers and Sexual Politics in the Hebrew Bible," in *Feminist Perspectives on Biblical Scholarship,* ed. Adela Yarbro Collins (Chico, Calif.: Scholars Press, 1985), 117–36.

Crenshaw;[116] Exum, Fewell, Greenstein, Gunn;[117] Jobling, Kselman, O'Connor, Polzin.[118] Even the recital of these names leaves the North American discussion incomplete.[119] If a literary paradigm now pervades biblical studies in a way that Muilenburg in 1968 could hardly have anticipated, much less inspired, nevertheless it has not come about *de novo*.[120] To the contrary, it forms but a small part of a long and rich heritage that began before the Common Era.

116. See, e.g., James Ackerman, "Joseph, Judah, and Jacob," in *Literary Interpretations of Biblical Narratives*, vol. 2, ed. Kenneth R. R. Gros Louis (Nashville: Abingdon, 1982), 85–113; Ackerman, "Who Can Stand Before YHWH, This Holy God? A Reading of 1 Samuel 1–15," *Prooftexts* 11 (1991): 1–24; Adele Berlin, *The Dynamics of Biblical Parallelism* (Bloomington: Indiana University Press, 1985); Edgar W. Conrad, *Reading Isaiah* (Minneapolis: Fortress Press, 1991); James L. Crenshaw, *Samson* (Atlanta: John Knox Press, 1978).

117. See, e.g., J. Cheryl Exum, "Promise and Fulfillment: Narrative Art in Judges 13," *JBL* 99 (1980): 43–59; Exum, "Of Broken Pots, Fluttering Birds, and Visions in the Night: Extended Simile and Poetic Technique in Isaiah," *CBQ* 43 (1981): 331–52; Exum, "The Tragic Vision and Biblical Narrative: The Case of Jephthah," in *Signs and Wonders: Biblical Texts in Literary Focus*, ed. J. Cheryl Exum (Atlanta: SBL, 1989), 59–83; David M. Gunn and Danna Nolan Fewell, *Narrative in the Hebrew Bible* (New York: Oxford University Press, 1993); Edward L. Greenstein, "The Riddle of Samson," *Prooftexts* 1 (1981): 237–60; Greenstein, "Mixing Memory and Design: Reading Psalm 78," *Prooftexts* 10, Part 2 (1990): 197–209; David Gunn, *The Fate of King Saul*, JSOT Suppl. Ser. 14 (Sheffield: JSOT Press, 1980).

118. See, e.g., David Jobling, *The Sense of Biblical Narrative: Structural Analyses in the Hebrew Bible;* John S. Kselman, "Semantic-Sonant Chiasmus in Biblical Poetry," *Biblica* 58 (1977): 219–23; Kselman, "'Why Have You Abandoned Me?' A Rhetorical Study of Psalm 22," *Art and Meaning: Rhetoric in Biblical Literature*, ed. Clines, et al, 172–98; Kselman, "Psalm 3: A Structural and Literary Study," *CBQ* 49 (1987): 572–80; Kselman, "Psalm 146 in its Context," *CBQ* 50 (1988): 587–99; Kselman, "The Literary Study of the Bible," *America* (31 October 1987): 297–99; 310f; M. O'Connor, *Hebrew Verse Structure;* O'Connor, "Parallelism," *NPEPP*, 877–79; Robert Polzin, extended note 41 below.

119. The designation North American refers to literary critics who, though they may live elsewhere, have their point of reference in biblical scholarship within the United States or Canada. For a sampling outside the North American context, see the extended note at the end of the chapter.

120. For yet additional samples, see Paul R. House, ed., *Beyond Form Criticism: Essays in Old Testament Literary Criticism* (Winona Lake, Ind.: Eisenbrauns, 1992). For bibliographies, see Mark Allan Powell, compiler with the assistance of Cecile G. Gray and Melissa C. Curtis, *The Bible and Modern Literary Criticism: A Critical Assessment and Annotated Bibliography* (New York: Greenwood Press, 1992); Mark Minor, *Literary-Critical Approaches to the Bible: An Annotated Bibliography* (West Cornwall, Conn.: Locust Hill Press, 1992); Watson and Hauser, *Rhetorical Criticism of the Bible*.

D. FORM CRITICISM

1. Assessment of the Modern Discipline

Form criticism, the fourth component in the background of biblical rhetorical criticism, has undergone major changes since Muilenburg's time. Five years after the publication of his presidential address (1974), there appeared a collection of essays designed to examine past results and sketch present issues.[121] The editor John Hayes listed problems that stymied the discipline:[122] too close an association with only the oral stages of tradition; the erroneous assumption that the shortest and clearest forms reflect the oldest and purest stages; the questionable use of the discipline to date traditions and texts; excessive claims in the re-creation of settings for genres; and the confusion of genre elements with complete genres. Martin Buss traced the study of forms from classical theories through early and medieval biblical studies and into the eighteenth century.[123] Following an eclipse of a hundred years (1775–1885), renewed interest then led to modern form criticism with Gunkel as the chief proponent.

Buss set the framework for other scholars to assess research on prominent genres: narrative, law, prophecy, psalms, and wisdom. While reporting gains, these scholars continued to encounter difficulties: confused usages of the term "form"; separation of style and content; imprecise definitions of *Gattung* and *Sitz im Leben;* uncertain connection between genres and settings; and lack of uniform terminology. Such a formidable list, added to the problems cited by Hayes, threatened the demise of form criticism. In reviewing these essays Robert Wilson opined that even they showed the poverty of the discipline, an inability to disclose the meaning of the text for theological appropriation.[124] Posing the issue sharply, he wondered if, rather than the intended progress report, the collection was not an obituary.

---

121. John H. Hayes, ed., *Old Testament Form Criticism* (San Antonio, Tex.: Trinity University Press, 1974), xviii.
122. Hayes, "Preface," ibid., xviii. These problems paralleled many cited by Muilenburg; see chapter 2, section A.
123. Martin J. Buss, "The Study of Forms," ibid., 1–56; cf. Buss, "Form Criticism," *To Each Its Own Meaning,* 69–85.
124. Robert R. Wilson, "A Progress Report or an Obituary?" *Int* 30 (1976): 71–74.

2. A Revised Agenda

The judgment of impending death was exaggerated. Shortly before the publication of the Hayes volume, the journal *Interpretation* devoted an entire issue to new developments in form criticism. A programmatic essay by Rolf Knierim outlined revisions.[125] It engaged such broad fields as folklore research, structuralism, linguistics, and morphology. Deploring the monolithic character of traditional form criticism, it proposed flexible and multiple understandings of genres, settings, and their relationships. It argued that analysis of individual structure must precede delineation of the typical in order to substantiate the claim that typicality inherently determines the makeup of a text. And it concluded that, though the method may not apply to all texts, in a revised version it can continue to enrich exegetical investigation.

These and comparable observations have heralded a multivolume form critical commentary. Edited by Knierim and Gene M. Tucker, the series called FOTL (The Forms of the Old Testament Literature) began to appear in 1981.[126] Its editors sketched a fourfold agenda: study of structure, genre, setting, and intention. Structure involves the outlining of a text to distinguish typical from individual features. This procedure leads to identifying literary form (genre). The form must then be connected to sociocultural contexts (settings). Discerning functions of the genre within settings unfolds its intentions. Form critics investigate these interrelated elements first at the level of the final redaction and then, if appropriate, in prior stages. Analysis proceeds from the large to the small, from an entire book to its individual units.

In light of modern form criticism derived from Gunkel, four features of the revised agenda merit comment. First, the ambiguous word "form" yields to two distinct terms: structure and genre. The former designates the outline of a text; the latter specifies type of literature. Second, the investigation covers all stages of a text but most especially the final. It neither assumes nor concentrates on oral prehistory and short units. Third, the relationship between genre and setting expands and complicates. In addition to social institutions, setting may include linguistic milieu, literary connections, aesthetic features, psychological framework,

---

125. Rolf Knierim, "Old Testament Form Criticism Reconsidered," *Int* 27 (1973): 435–68.

126. The publishing company is William B. Eerdmans, Grand Rapids, Michigan. By 1994, eight volumes have appeared, covering fourteen of the thirty-nine books in the Protestant canon.

specific occasions, or even the general spirit of a place and time. All such variables, not just institutional phenomena, may shape genre. Furthermore, a particular setting does not determine or dictate a particular genre. The latter may enjoy multiple settings even as the former may embrace multiple genres. Fourth, the revised method seeks to establish standard nomenclature. In the past, form critics have assigned different, even contradictory, meanings to the same genre term;[127] conversely, they have used different terms to talk about the same literature.[128] Terminological confusion has reigned. The FOTL series proposes to rectify the problem.[129]

This revision of form criticism acknowledges the Muilenburg critique. It takes account of the particularities of texts even though it subordinates them to typicality. In other words, revised form criticism would subsume rhetorical criticism.[130] Yet the latter lives its own life.

❀ ❀ ❀ ❀ ❀ ❀ ❀

Summary of Part One. Arranged as an *inclusio* (ABA'), Part One has provided the context for understanding biblical rhetorical criticism. Chapter 1 has sketched the four components in the background as they led to the presidential address of Muilenburg: classical rhetoric, literary critical theory, literary study of the Bible, and form criticism. Chapter 2 has introduced the foreground, biblical rhetorical criticism, by presenting the Muilenburg program and by examining samples that illustrate rhetoric as the art of composition and as the art of persuasion. Chapter 3 has expanded the background by reporting developments within the four components since the time of Muilenburg. Corresponding in structure and subject matter (but not in length), chapters 1 and 3 surround chapter 2, thus making it the center of attention.

Throughout Part One rules of rhetoric have operated. First has come the collecting of material (*inventio*) pertinent to the subject. Arranging

---

127. For example, "myth" has been variously defined as stories of polytheism, of origins, and of the supernatural. Cf. Brevard S. Childs, *Myth and Reality in the Old Testament* (Naperville, Ill.: Alec R. Allenson, Inc., 1960), 13–16; J. W. Rogerson, *Myth in Old Testament Interpretation* (Berlin: Walter de Gruyter, 1974).

128. For example, the words "legend" and "saga" have been used for the same narratives in Genesis; cf. W. F. Albright, Introduction to *The Legends of Genesis*, by Hermann Gunkel, trans. W. H. Carruth (New York: Schocken Books, 1964), xi–xii; John Van Seters, *Abraham in History and Tradition* (New Haven: Yale University Press, 1975), 131–48.

129. If the FOTL series is the most comprehensive evidence for the continuing life of form criticism, many other signs persist. See the extended note at the end of the chapter.

130. This effort may account for Knierim's assertion that Muilenburg does not show where rhetorical criticism goes "beyond" form criticism (Knierim, "Old Testament Form Criticism Reconsidered," 458). See chapter 2, section A'.

this material as an *inclusio* with a chiasm in the middle has set the structure (*dispositio*). The writing itself has used a variety of stylistic devices (*elocutio*) that range from the succinct and the plain to the full and the elaborate. Three goals have influenced the presentation. The intellectual goal to teach has remained primary, but the emotional goal to touch the feelings and the aesthetic goal to please have also come into play. In other words, Part One has sought to be the rhetoric it reports. The composition of the context has become an effort to persuade.

EXTENDED NOTES

Note 41 on page 66

An entire issue of *Interpretation* pursued the subject of structuralism and the Bible: *Int* 28 (April 1974). See also various issues of *Semeia*: e.g., *Genesis 2 and 3: Kaleidoscopic Structural Readings*, ed. Daniel Patte, *Semeia* 18 (1980). See R. Barthes, et al., *Structural Analysis and Biblical Exegesis*, trans. Alfred M. Johnson (Pittsburgh, Penn.: The Pickwick Press, 1974); Robert M. Polzin, *Biblical Structuralism: Method and Subjectivity in the Study of Ancient Texts* (Philadelphia: Fortress Press, 1977); Polzin, *Moses and the Deuteronomist* (New York: Seabury Press, 1980); Polzin, *Samuel and the Deuteronomist* (San Francisco: Harper & Row, 1989); Polzin, *David and the Deuteronomist* (Bloomington, Ind.: Indiana University Press, 1993). See David Jobling, *The Sense of Biblical Narrative: Structural Analyses in the Hebrew Bible*, vol. 1, 2nd ed., and vol. 2 (Sheffield: University of Sheffield Press, 1986). Cf. Pamela J. Milne, *Vladimir Propp and the Study of Structure in Hebrew Biblical Narrative* (Sheffield: Almond Press, 1988). For a structuralist reading of Jonah, see "An Approach to the Book of Jonah: Suggestions and Questions," under the anonymous authorship of "a group from Rennes, France," *Semeia* 15 (1979): 85–96. For New Testament studies, see Daniel Patte, *Structural Exegesis for New Testament Critics* (Minneapolis: Fortress Press, 1990), including an Annotated Select Bibliography. Cf. Edmund Leach and D. Alan Aycock, *Structuralist Interpretations of Biblical Myth* (Cambridge, Eng.: Cambridge University Press, 1983).

Note 75 on page 73

Reference works on literary critical theories and strategies include T. V. F. Brogan, ed., *The New Princeton Handbook of Poetic Terms* (Princeton, N.J.: Princeton University Press, 1994); Lentricchia and McLaughlin, eds., *Critical Terms for Literary Study;* Stephen Greenblatt and Giles Gunn, eds., *Redrawing the Boundaries* (New York: The Modern Language Association of America, 1992); Philip Rice and Patricia Waugh, eds., *Modern Literary Theory* (London: Edward Arnold, 2nd ed., 1992); Makaryk, ed., *Encyclopedia of Contemporary Literary Theory;* Groden and Kreiswirth, eds., *The Johns Hopkins Guide to Literary Theory & Criticism*. In this discussion New Historicism might also have been included; see, e.g., Stephen Greenblatt, "Towards a Poetics of Culture," in *The New Historicism*, ed. H. Aram Veeser (New York: Routledge, 1989), 1–14; Louis Montrose, "New Historicisms," *Redrawing the Boundaries*, 392–418; Hunter Cadzow, "New Historicism," *The Johns Hopkins Guide to Literary Theory & Criticism*, 534–39.

Note 102 on page 77

Critical reviews of Sternberg include Adele Berlin, *Prooftexts* 6 (1986): 273–84; Naomi Segal, *VT* 38 (1988): 243–49; Jeremiah Unterman, *Hebrew Studies* 29 (1988): 194–205; Edward L. Greenstein, *Conservative Judaism* 42(4) (Summer 1990): 66–68; David M. Gunn, "Reading Right: Reliable and Omniscient Narrator, Omniscient God, and Foolproof Composition in the Hebrew Bible," in *The Bible in Three Dimensions*, JSOT Suppl. Ser. 87, ed. David J. A. Clines et al (Sheffield: Sheffield Academic Press, 1990), 53–64; also Danna Nolan Fewell and David M. Gunn, "Tipping the Balance: Sternberg's Reader and the Rape of Dinah," *JBL* 110 (1991): 193–211. Cf. Sternberg's reply to the last article: "Biblical Poetics and Sexual Politics: From Reading to Counter-Reading," *JBL* 111 (1992): 463–88. Cf. the critique of Sternberg and Alter by Burke O. Long, who observed that these scholars, by failing to engage the pluralism of modern literary study, would seek to limit legitimate study and deny their own ideologies under the guise of objectivism ("The 'New' Biblical Poetics of Alter and Sternberg," *JSOT* 51 [1991]: 71–84).

Note 119 on page 80

Literary critical studies of the Bible outside the North American context include the following: In Israel, Sternberg, Bar-Efrat, and Licht as presented above; also Meir Weiss, *The Bible from Within: The Method of Total Interpretation* (Jerusalem: Magnes Press, 1984); Athalya Brenner, together with the Dutch scholar Fokkelien van Dijk-Hemmes, *On Gendering Texts: Female and Male Voices in the Hebrew Bible* (Leiden: E. J. Brill, 1993). In Britain, Clines and Barton as presented in chapter 2 and Josipovici above. In Germany, Wolfgang Richter, *Exegese als Literaturwissenschaft* (Göttingen: Vandenhoeck & Ruprecht, 1971); Gottfried Vanoni, *Das Buch Jona: Literar- und formkritische Untersuchung* (St. Ottilien: EOS Verlag, 1978); Hagia Witzenrath, *Das Buch Jona: Eine literatur-wissenschaftliche Untersuchung* (St. Ottilien: EOS Verlag, 1978). In South Africa, Gerald O. West, *Biblical Hermeneutics of Liberation* (Pietermaritzburg: Cluster Publications, 1991), 104–41; G. T. M. Prinsloo, "Two Poems in a Sea of Prose: The Content and Context of Daniel 2. 20-23 and 6. 27-28," *JSOT* 59 (1993): 93–108. In Argentina, J. Severino Croatto, *Biblical Hermeneutics: Toward a Theory of Reading as the Production of Meaning*, trans. Robert R. Barr (Maryknoll: Orbis Books, 1987), 13–35; in Costa Rica, cf. Elsa Tamez, *Bible of the Oppressed*, trans Matthew J. O'Connell (Maryknoll: Orbis Books, 1982). In Japan, see Kiyoshi K. Sacon, "Isaiah 40:1–11: A Rhetorical-Critical Study," *Rhetorical Criticism*, 99–116; in Korea, cf. Ee Kon Kim, "'Outcry': Its Context in Biblical Theology," *Int* 42 (1988): 229–39; in Hong-Kong, see Khiok-khng Yeo, "A Rhetorical Study of Acts 17.22–31: What Has Jerusalem to Do with Athens and Beijing?" *Jian Dao* 1 (1994): 75–107.

Note 129 on page 83

In addition to the FOTL series, form-critical studies continue in numerous ways: (1) exploration of oral prose and narrative structure: e.g., Robert C. Culley, *Studies in the Struc-*

ture of Hebrew Narrative (Philadelphia: Fortress Press, 1976); (2) genre study with the goal of interpretation: e.g., George W. Coats, ed., *Saga, Legend, Tale, Novella, Fable: Narrative Forms in Old Testament Literature,* JSOT Supplement Series 35 (Sheffield: JSOT Press, 1985); (3) reassessment and use of folkloristic research: e.g., J. W. Rogerson, *Anthropology and the Old Testament* (Oxford: Oxford University Press, 1978; reprint Sheffield, 1984); Susan Niditch, *Underdogs and Tricksters: A Prelude to Biblical Folklore* (San Francisco: Harper and Row, 1987); Niditch, *Folklore and the Hebrew Bible* (Minneapolis: Fortress Press, 1993); Patricia G. Kirkpatrick, *The Old Testament and Folklore Study,* JSOT Supplement Series 62 (Sheffield: JSOT Press, 1988); (4) the first English translation ever of Gunkel's classic 1921 study: Hermann Gunkel, *The Folktale in the Old Testament.* Cf. chapter 1, note 74.

PART TWO
METHOD and the
BOOK of JONAH

4
Guidelines for Beginning

Drawing upon the context described in Part One, Part Two gives a full demonstration of biblical rhetorical criticism. It explores the book of Jonah. The arrangement (*dispositio*) of the material gathered (*inventio*) fashions another *inclusio*. Guidelines for beginning and continuing (chapters 4 and 10) surround the study of the text (chapters 5 through 9). The purpose is to teach method by showing the discipline at work on the book and the book at work on the discipline. Intellectual, emotional, and aesthetic goals persist, with the intellectual as primary. To commence the demonstration, this chapter analyzes the Muilenburg rubric and offers practical instruction.

A. GUIDING RUBRIC

Muilenburg proposed that "proper articulation of form yields proper articulation of meaning."[1] Another formulation makes explicit what he assumed, namely, that form and content are inseparable. Hence, proper articulation of form-content yields proper articulation of meaning. The sentence states purpose, gives direction, and keeps analysis on track. It also poses problems. Exegesis illuminates the possibilities.

1. Articulation of Form-Content

The hyphenated construction "form-content" signals the organic unity of a composition while distinguishing the ingredients. The word "form"

---

1. See chapter 2; cf. Muilenburg, "Form Criticism and Beyond," 7, where the word "form" yields to "linguistic patterns" and "precise formulations."

is ambiguous. In traditional form criticism it designates both genre and structure, but in rhetorical criticism only the latter designation obtains. Form means structure (or design).[2] Further, the meaning of structure differs from the form critical use. In the FOTL series, structure constitutes the topical outline of a passage. It designates not the text itself but a schematic synopsis that paraphrases and abridges the text. A word or phrase summarizes each section.[3] By contrast, in rhetorical criticism structure presents the *ipsissima verba* of the text. It shows the patterns of relationships residing in the very words, phrases, sentences, and larger units.[4]

Although structure and content may be distinguished for analytical purposes, they remain an inseparable whole. A literary artifact is not a container from which ideas or substance can be removed. Conversely, it is not a subject matter from which stylistic and structural wrappings can be removed. No form appears without content and no content without form. How a text speaks and what it says are mixed and mingled indissolubly to give meaning.[5] The concept of organic unity (form-content) underlies all rhetorical critical readings.[6]

Organic unity relates to the particularity of a text, which includes the conventional language it employs. This assertion requires careful explanation with reference again to form criticism, a discipline that stresses the conventional, the typical, the traditional, and the customary. By examining texts set within genres, form criticism discerns shared characteristics. Though it considers individual differences, it highlights similar elements.[7]

2. On the term "design" as related to "structure," see chapter 5.

3. See the sections marked "Structure" in each volume of the FOTL series. Note further that both form criticism and rhetorical criticism use the word "structure" quite differently from its use in structuralism; see chapter 3.

4. On the history of the word "structure," see John Carlos Rowe, "Structure," *Critical Terms for Literary Study*, 23–38.

5. This rhetorical formulation differs from the claim that "the medium is the message" (Marshall McLuhan, *Understanding Media: The Extensions of Man* [New York; New American Library, 1964]). The collapsing of any distinction between form and content ironically separates them, with a subsequent ignoring of content (message).

6. On the concept of organic unity, cf. the views of Samuel Taylor Coleridge, *Biographia Literaria or Biographical Sketches of My Literary Life and Opinions* (London: Routledge & Kegan Paul, 1983); *Lectures On Shakespeare* (London: J. M. Dent & Sons, Ltd, 1937). Cf. also Socrates, chapter 1 above, note 6.

7. Knierim has argued that recognition of the individuality of texts must be included in form critical analysis; indeed, it must precede the study of the typical "if the claim that such a typicality inherently determines an individual text is to be substantiated." See "Old Testament Form Criticism Reconsidered," *Int* 27 (1973): 461.

To write redundantly: form criticism interprets convention as conventional, tradition as traditional, type as typical. Like form criticism, rhetorical criticism recognizes both typical and individual features but shifts emphasis. It interprets convention not so much as conventional but more as particular to the text in which it appears. Thus the distinction between form criticism and rhetorical criticism does not correspond to a separation between the typical and the individual, with one category assigned to each discipline. Instead, the two categories belong together in each discipline, though they are valued differently. Rhetorical criticism interprets the particularity of the conventional as well as the particularity of the particular.[8] Organic unity comprises both elements.

Within organic unity the limits of a text vary. They may signify the entire Bible or a major division or a single book or chapters within a book or a single narrative or an episode or a poem or a proverb. However large or small the division, the criterion of form-content determines the boundaries. As the limits, so the approaches to a text vary. Critics may trace overall design and plot movement, follow the unfolding of a single stylistic device or motif, analyze selected portions, or pursue close reading of the parts and the whole. The last approach describes full rhetorical analysis; the others present facets. As the approaches, so the perspectives on a text vary. Not all critics see the same way; a multifaceted text invites numerous readings. Different definitions, approaches, and perspectives affect the concept of organic unity.

A related issue concerns composition: what form of a text does rhetorical criticism study? Here the word "form" means the putative history from earliest versions to the present (or final) shape. The usual answer to the question holds that rhetorical criticism studies the final form.[9] Unlike source criticism, it does not examine antecedent literary strands. Unlike tradition-history, it does not examine development and transmission. Rather than considering hypothetical sources or reconstructed processes, it interprets a text as it now appears. Rhetorical criticism practices synchronic, not diachronic, analysis.

---

8. In practice the relationship between form criticism and rhetorical criticism has fluctuated, with different scholars asserting different points of view. E.g., Melugin argued for "a balance of two one-sided approaches" ("The Typical Versus the Unique among the Hebrew Prophets," 331–41). By contrast, Craven considered rhetorical analysis a complete approach divorced from form criticism (*Artistry and Faith in the Book of Judith*). See chapter 2.

9. See Kessler, "A Methodological Setting for Rhetorical Criticism," esp. 9–14.

This answer to the question tells the truth but not the whole truth. It accepts too easily a separation between the diachronic and the synchronic. Full rhetorical reading includes conversation with textual criticism and with historical disciplines like source criticism, tradition history, and redaction criticism. The reading evaluates the findings of these disciplines in light of its own research and its own synchronic goal. Sometimes the rhetorical critic deems the findings suspect or gratuitous.[10] Other times the critic concludes that a particular text manifests a history. In those cases the critic ponders how that past affects the final form. The possibilities are several: literary harmony may prevail despite a turbulent past;[11] the final form may contain but not absorb disruption;[12] the final form may yield a hodgepodge that undercuts organic unity.[13] Decisions come text by text to meet the requirements of particularity. In general, rhetorical analysis begins and ends with the final form of a text, though it is not limited to that form.[14] Synchronic analysis allows for diachronic reflection.

Articulation of form-content raises questions about environment, the relationship of a text to a larger world. The adjectives "extrinsic" and "intrinsic" define two contrasting though not incompatible responses. The former concentrates on the environment; the latter, on the text. Rhetorical criticism belongs to the latter. Basically an intrinsic approach, it focuses on a text rather than on such factors as historical background, archaeological data, authorial intention, sociological setting, or theological milieu. Yet no text is an island unto itself. Thus the phrase "intrinsic reading" should not be seized upon by friend or foe to mean isolation. Extrinsic factors inevitably play a role in intrinsic analysis, though the weight assigned them varies. All rhetorical critics call, for example, upon theories of literature, technical vocabulary, and modern concepts alien to scripture

---

10. See, e.g., Allen, "Ezekiel 24:3–14: A Rhetorical Perspective," where rhetorical study discloses a carefully structured composition despite counterproposals emerging from textual, redactional, and form-critical analyses.

11. Genesis 3, with its mixture of poetry and prose and with aetiological fragments incorporated in the larger narrative, illustrates this possibility; see Phyllis Trible, *God and the Rhetoric of Sexuality* (Philadelphia: Fortress Press, 1978), 115–39.

12. E.g., Gen. 2:10–14; see Trible, *God and the Rhetoric of Sexuality*, 82–88.

13. Though this situation remains a theoretical possibility, research to date does not sustain it. Composers, compilers, and redactors seemed to know what they were doing even if readers cannot always follow their logic.

14. Cf. Edward L. Greenstein, *Essays on Biblical Method and Translations* (Atlanta: Scholars Press, 1989), 29–51.

itself. Analysis imposes other worlds upon a text. In addition, some rhetorical critics forge explicit connections among a single text, other texts, and a larger environment.[15] They understand that a text inhabits worlds other than its own and that reader-response is a major ingredient of interpretation. Nonetheless, the phrase "intrinsic reading" best identifies the focus of rhetorical study. Articulation of form-content remains primary; environment, secondary.

2. Articulation of Meaning

If the description "intrinsic" echoes New Criticism, the purpose of rhetorical criticism quells that sound. Another component of the sentence under examination, namely the phrase "articulation of meaning," clarifies the difference. Rather than being sufficient unto itself, articulation of form-content yields articulation of meaning. But the word "meaning" slips and slides, lending itself to innumerable meanings: historical, sociological, political, biographical, psychological, and philosophical as well as literary. Meaning functions as a collective noun denoting variety rather than singularity. One way to explore meaning situates it in the three elements that for classical rhetoric constitute the total act of communication: author, text, and audience.[16]

a. Authorial Meaning

Muilenburg equated meaning with authorial intentionality. By "author" he intended neither the implied nor the ideal but the flesh-and-blood individual(s) behind the words.[17] To articulate form-content "will reveal to us the texture and fabric of the writer's thought, not only what it is that he thinks, but as he thinks it."[18] The classicist George Kennedy has taken a similar stance: "The ultimate goal of rhetorical analysis, briefly put, is the discovery of the author's intent and of how that is transmitted

---

15. E.g., Walter Brueggemann, "Psalms 9–10: A Counter to Conventional Social Reality," *The Bible and the Politics of Exegesis*, 3–15.

16. Not unlike ancient rhetoricians, biblical critics weigh these elements differently. The difference, however, does not make one superior to the others. It may pertain to a particular situation or express the preference of the critic.

17. Cf. the historical study by Pease, "Author," *Critical Terms for Literary Study*, 105–17.

18. Muilenburg, "Form Criticism and Beyond," 7, 9.

through a text to an audience."[19] These formulations echo the expressive orientation in literary theory.

Questions arise. Is literature a window through which one sees the author's mind? Is meaning restricted to authorial intention? May not literature speak differently from what its author intended? Are authors not infrequently caught short when they discover meanings in their compositions they did not intend? Are these meanings valid? What is the connection of the flesh-and-blood author to the implied or ideal author? In considering these and other questions, scholars have given different responses. One, popular among New Critics, posits the concept of "the intentional fallacy."[20] Originally formulated to deny that authorial intention can be used for *evaluating* a work of art, the concept has since been applied to *interpreting* a work.[21] The intention of an author does not determine the meaning of a text. To hold otherwise commits the intentional fallacy. An extreme form of this view divorces text and author; a milder version separates the two. Yet another response to the questions raised is popular among some biblical critics. They first read a text precisely for the purpose of ferreting out authorial intention not otherwise known. Then they use this putative intention to interpret and control interpretation. Overlooked in this circular process is the role of the reader. To what extent does the reader's intention, imposed upon a text, decide the author's intention?

These questions need not forge a divorce between author and text. (That is certainly not this author's intention.) Texts do reveal authors: their

19. Kennedy, *New Testament Interpretation through Rhetorical Criticism*, 12. On the history of the term "intention," see Annabel Patterson, "Intention," *Critical Terms for Literary Study*, 135–46.

20. See W. K. Wimsatt, Jr., and Monroe C. Beardsley, "The Intentional Fallacy," in *The Verbal Icon* (University of Kentucky Press, 1954), 3–18: "[T]he design or intention of the author is neither available nor desirable as a standard for judging the success of a work of literary art" (3). Cf. T. S. Eliot, "Tradition and the Individual Talent," *Selected Essays* (New York: Harcourt, Brace, & World, Inc., 1964), 3–11. For a critique of this view, see E. D. Hirsch, Jr., *Validity in Interpretation* (New Haven: Yale University Press, 1967), who distinguishes between the meaning and the significance of a text. The former never changes; it is what the author intends. The latter designates a relationship between that meaning and anything else. The relationship can change and often does, though one pole (textual meaning) remains constant.

21. On the move from evaluation to interpretation, cf. E. D. Hirsch, Jr., "Carnal Knowledge," *The New York Review of Books* 36 (14 June 1979): 18–20, a review of Frank Kermode, *The Genesis of Secrecy: On the Interpretation of Narrative* (Cambridge: Harvard University Press, 1979).

resources, knowledge, issues, perspectives, and skills. Yet authorial intention constitutes a part, not the whole, of meaning. Texts (including this one) may reveal more or less or other than their flesh-and-blood authors intend. Such an understanding diverges from the Muilenburg mode.

b. Textual Meaning

A second center for meaning is the text: its content, interlocking structures, and artistic configurations. This center parallels judicial rhetoric in which speech (or text) predominates. But the emphasis lies not on justice nor does the purpose necessarily involve persuasion. This center also parallels New Criticism and deconstruction in which close readings perdure. Unlike the former, however, rhetorical criticism views a text as more than aesthetic object. Being and meaning intertwine. Unlike the latter, rhetorical criticism seeks rather than defers meaning. Though it understands that meaning is never fixed, it recognizes limits to language as well as the power of language to specify and signify.

Within biblical scholarship the text-centered focus for meaning aligns itself with textual criticism in pursuing close readings but departs from that discipline in not seeking an "original" text (*Urtext*).[22] The text-centered focus also aligns itself with canonical criticism in privileging the final form but departs from that discipline in embracing artistry and not dwelling on the failures of historical critical methods.[23] The text-centered focus distinguishes itself from all disciplines that view the text as a window through which meanings come, whether historical reconstruction, sociological speculations, authorial intentions, or ethical and theological extractions. Though the text may well be a window, one rhetorical approach perceives it primarily as a picture.[24] Hence the discipline articulates meaning by describing and interpreting the picture.

22. On textual criticism, see Emmanuel Tov, "Textual Criticism (OT)," *ABD*, vol. 6, 393–412; Tov, *Textual Criticism of the Hebrew Bible* (Minneapolis: Fortress Press, 1992), esp. 164–80.

23. On canonical criticism and its critique of historical methods, see Childs, *Introduction to the Old Testament as Scripture*, 71–75 and *passim*. On Childs' critique of Muilenburg's aesthetic interests, see chapter 2, note 84. Cf. Barton, who parallels canonical criticism to objective theories of literature, claiming that "here for the first time in Old Testament criticism we have a concentration on *the text itself* . . . rather than on its relation to other things" (*Reading the Old Testament*, esp. 140–57; 198–207). His analysis omits rhetorical criticism.

24. On the contrast between the text as window and picture, see Macky, "The Coming Revolution," 263–79. Cf. also note 28 below.

Questions arise. Can texts be isolated from authors and readers? Can they be severed from the life that surrounds them? Is not literature, like language, the product of society? Is power inherent in texts qua texts? Can texts be personified? Is aesthetics the idolatry of art? Can poetic language be separated from practical language?[25] Though these and other questions set constraints upon efforts to situate meaning in the text, they need not displace the centrality of the object.

c. Reader's Meaning

One valid retort to the text-centered approach observes that a text is mute. It does not speak; the reader gives it voice. The reader articulates form-content in order to articulate meaning. The philosopher Paul Ricoeur provides a helpful analogy: "The text is like a musical score and the reader like the orchestra conductor who obeys the instructions of the notation."[26] Though the conductor is not free to change the notes, she may produce multiple interpretations of a single score. The notes for a Bach cantata, for instance, remain set on the page, and yet renditions vary widely. Conductors and orchestras bring various skills, knowledge, and sensitivities to the interpretive process. They hear the same notes differently at different times and in different settings. By analogy with Ricoeur's analogy, rhetorical critics obey the "notes" while bringing to the interpretive task various skills, knowledge, and sensitivities. Faithful in describing the structure, style, and substance of a mute text, they produce in the end multiple renditions. When rhetorical criticism highlights this element in the total act of communication, it exhibits similarities to classical persuasive rhetoric, contemporary experiential rhetoric, pragmatic theories of literature, and reader-response criticism.

Questions arise. Who is the reader?[27] The ancient audience who first heard a text? the ideal or implied audience? the contemporary flesh-and-blood reader? Do not different readers in the same setting and similar readers in different settings and all combinations thereof guarantee heterogeneous responses? Is meaning then unfixed, even if a text remains stable? Does unfixed meaning foster "unrestrained subjectivity and literary anarchy"; does a reader-centered approach risk turning the text

25. Cf. I. A. Richards, *Practical Criticism* (New York: Harcourt, Brace & World, Inc., 1929).

26. Paul Ricoeur, *Interpretation Theory: Discourse and the Surplus of Meaning* (Fort Worth, Tex.: Texas Christian University Press, 1976), 75. Recall Craven's use of musical analogies to explicate rhetorical criticism (*Artistry and Faith in the Book of Judith*, 45).

27. Cf. the discussion in chapter 3 on reader-response criticism.

into a "mirror for narcissistic self-reflection"?[28] Though such questions constrain reader-centered meanings, they need not invalidate the orientation. After all, readers endure.[29]

o   o   o   o   o   o   o

Summary. Articulation of meaning offers many possibilities for author, text, and reader. Some critics find this situation untenable. A single meaning ought to prevail, and yet it does not. Other critics find the more meanings the better. Potential chaos seems not to matter. The rhetorical criticism developed here works between the alternatives: more than a single meaning and fewer than unlimited meanings. In addition, it works at the boundary of text and reader, with emphasis on the former. Whereas Muilenburg stressed authorial intention as the goal of the process, that concern recedes (though it does not disappear) in favor of a text-centered focus. Text designates the received tradition. The flesh-and-blood reader holds responsibility for articulating the meaning, an activity that happens in the presence of other readers (friends, foes, and foils) and other texts. Choices made by the reader shape and receive meanings, but they do not harness the text. Other meanings lie in wait. To adjudicate possibilities remains difficult. Indeed, the guiding rubric recognizes the problem when it uses the adjective "proper."

3. Proper Articulation

The formulation "proper articulation" occurs twice in the Muilenburg rubric, first for form-content and then for meaning. The adjective sets limits to analysis. "Proper" opposes improper. Not all articulation is valid, and not all valid articulation is equally valid. But the word "proper" does

---

28. Cf. Stephen A. Geller who used the metaphors of window and mirror to argue for a "relational and dialectical approach" between historical and aesthetic analyses. The window moves toward the author and the world; the mirror toward the reader ("Through Windows and Mirrors into the Bible: History, Literature and Language in the Study of Text," *A Sense of Text: The Art of Language in the Study of Biblical Literature*, JQR Supplement [1982] 3–40, esp. 21–22). Cf. Murray Krieger, who regarded the metaphor of window as describing pre-New Criticism and the metaphor of enclosed sets of mirrors as describing New Criticism. He then proposed a third way: "to see the mirrors as window too" (*A Window to Criticism* [Princeton, N.J.: Princeton University Press, 1964], 3). Omitted from these discussions is the metaphor of picture (cf. Macky, "The Coming Revolution," and note 24 above). All three metaphors can be related to the elements in the total act of communication: author (text as window); text (text as picture); reader (text as mirror).

29. Cf. Frank Lentricchia, "In Place of an Afterword—Someone Reading," *Critical Terms for Literary Study*, 321–38.

not itself identify what the limits are, who decides, and on what basis. Its meaning remains open to various interpretations. A classical rhetorician might define "proper" by how faithfully articulation adheres to the traditional system. An experiential critic might decide by how well it expresses intersubjective observations. A reader-response critic might invoke the agreement of interpretive communities. A New Critic might decide by how well articulation discloses interconnected elements of a text. A postmodern critic might argue that "proper" indicates how well articulation exposes contradictions in order to decenter a text, defer meaning, and disclose power struggles (and thereby show the impropriety of "proper").[30] Within biblical studies, Muilenburg identified "proper" with authorial intention. Craven gave the adjective two different definitions, the objectively verifiable related to form-content and the individually validated related to meaning. By extension, Gitay might link "proper" to appropriation of the classical system; Patrick and Scult might equate it with Dworkin's principle of "the best text"; and Clines might deconstruct it.[31]

These interpretations illustrate the indeterminacy of the word "proper." Even though Muilenburg intended (!) by its use to secure meaning, a disparity of meanings shows that the concept does not control author, text, or reader. What the word promises it cannot guarantee. Moralistic overtones may also detract from its value. In this regard, "appropriate" may be a more acceptable adjective. Though no term can stand unchallenged, "proper" or "appropriate" nevertheless alerts the reader to articulate with care: to develop readings that account for all elements of form-content as they "yield" meaning.

4. The Verb "Yield"

"Proper articulation of form-content yields proper articulation of meaning." The word "yield" functions as both linking and transitive verb. As linking verb, it connects the subject (proper articulation of form-content) to the subject complement (proper articulation of meaning). So it behaves much as the verb "to be;" it describes one activity by another. But it is not the verb "to be." Use of that verb would collapse any distinction between the two properties and leave the erroneous impression that to do the former is to do the latter.[32] As a transitive verb, "yield" connotes

---

30. Cf. chapter 3.
31. Cf. chapter 2.
32. See note 5 above on McLuhan.

completion and result. In signifying to "bring forth" or "disclose," it indicates activity beyond the action of articulating form-content. In other words, it holds the responsibility for moving the subject (proper articulation of form-content) to act upon the object (proper articulation of meaning). Where the two functions of the verb coalesce, description and interpretation mingle.

❧   ❧   ❧   ❧   ❧   ❧   ❧

Summary. The Muilenburg rubric does not yield a rule that accounts for every eventuality, dictates every move, explains every procedure, or guarantees every result. It does not even approach a comprehensive system. Those who seek one misunderstand the rhetorical enterprise. Fokkelman has made the point nicely: "But how to make a start? Not a single method warrants our access to the work in advance; every text requires its own hermeneutics and the annoying thing is that the outlines cannot be drawn until after the event."[33] The Muilenburg rubric offers perspective and guidance. It allows for, indeed requires, intuition and play. The test of its usefulness comes not in theory but in practice.

B. PRACTICAL INSTRUCTION

A few guidelines (often in apodictic form) facilitate rhetorical practice. In studying them, do not canonize the order of the list, not even the first instruction. Instead, allow to unfold the order best for you and the text. Do not assume that rote procedures can produce a rich harvest. Experiment; play with the text; be graceful in articulation. Relate these guidelines to the general rubric and remember that they do not exhaust the subject.

1. Begin with the text. Read it again and again. You may consult numerous English translations and then move to the Hebrew; you may reverse this order; you may handle the original and translations concurrently. If you do not know Hebrew, despair not. Consult someone who does and use an interlinear Bible (with due caution). As you read, keep literary questions at the forefront of your consciousness (see number 5). Jot down ideas that come your way. Some you may never use, but they all help to get the process started.

2. Read various scholarly works on the text and take notes. Do not limit your reading to literary analyses. Rhetorical criticism needs the nourishment of other disciplines even as it nourishes them. Do not limit your

---

33. Fokkelman, *Narrative Art in Genesis,* 8. He offers but a single guideline: "[G]o into the text carefully, in an attitude of confidence. . . ."

reading to either recent or early material. Consult the old and the new as you seek literary clues. They may be direct or indirect, coming through declarations, negations, or silences. Exegetical commentaries assume special importance because they treat details, sometimes line by line if not word by word.

3. Surround the study of the text with background knowledge to give depth and perspective. Choose from the components sketched in Part One at least two different areas for investigation. Let form criticism be one. But do not let the background overwhelm you. Use it for enrichment general and specific. It may serve as point and counterpoint.

4. Acquaint yourself with rhetorical terms.[34] Chapters 1, 2, and 3 have introduced some of them; others will follow. Though commentaries often use these terms to explain stylistic elements, less often do they develop their meaning for the particularities of the text. That is your job as rhetorical critic.

5. Attend closely to the following features of a text.

a. Beginning and ending. Remember that Muilenburg cited as the first task of the rhetorical critic the delimiting of literary boundaries. Though some boundaries are given (e.g., a book, psalm, or proverb), others require establishing (e.g., a story or poem within a larger whole). To determine limits, use the criterion of form-content. Make certain the two elements cohere. On a difficult text several tries may be necessary before beginning and ending fall into place. Even then critics may disagree.[35]

b. Repetition of words, phrases, and sentences. As a basic phenomenon in biblical speech, repetition (verbatim or modified) provides the backbone for discerning structures and meanings. Though it is not infrequently[36] accessible in translation, beware of pitfalls. Sometimes translators select different English words for the same Hebrew vocabulary and thereby obscure repetition.[37] Other times they use the same English word

---

34. See Richard A. Lanham, *A Handlist of Rhetorical Terms*, 2nd ed. (Berkeley: University of California Press, 1991).

35. Cf., e.g., the different analyses of the literary units within Isaiah 40–66 by Muilenburg, Gitay, et al. (cf. chapter 2).

36. Note that the phrase "not infrequently" illustrates the rhetorical device "litotes": expressing an idea by denial of the contrary.

37. E.g., in the NRSV translation of Jonah the Hebrew verb *qr'* is variously rendered "cry" (1:2), "call" (1:6), and "proclaim" (3:2). The verb *mnh* is variously rendered "provided" (1:17; [2:1, Hebrew]), "appointed" (4:6), and "prepared" (4:8). Cf., e.g., the difficulties encountered in Ceresko's translation (chapter 2, note 39).

for different Hebrew vocabulary and thereby feign repetition.[38] Rhetorical analysis needs to maintain in translation the exact consistencies and inconsistencies of the Hebrew vocabulary. When on occasion you must deviate from this principle, then by all means inform the reader. Moreover, throughout your translation and interpretation, be careful not to confuse the phenomenon of repetition with the recurrence of themes or ideas (see number 10).

c. Types of discourse. Discern how narrated discourse and direct discourse interact. Do they disclose tension or harmony between narrator and characters?[39] Different types of discourse engage the reader from different perspectives with different information. Identifying the differences may also be useful in delimiting boundaries.

d. Design and structure. Much like a building, an individual text has an overall design and numerous sections (cf. *dispositio*).[40] The two interrelate. Describing the architecture is your task. Struggle with how the parts and the whole cohere. Sometimes you may think you have identified a section only to see it differently in the context of the whole design. Conversely, the whole may appear differently in the context of the parts. At all levels seek to discern the interrelationship of form-content. (See numbers 6, 8, and 10).

e. Plot development. Trace the movement of narratives from their beginnings to their ends. Observe how, when, where, and what changes happen: those that work for the movement, those that work against it, and those that seem to make no difference. (The last may have thematic value.) Poetic texts may or may not contain plots. In any event, strive for the sense of the whole and the parts.

f. Character portrayals. Observe interaction (or lack thereof) among characters. Pay attention to whether they are given names and speech: where their names and speech do and do not occur, how they address one

---

38. E.g., in the RSV translation of Jonah the Hebrew verbs *bô'* and *hlk* are both translated as "go": *bô'* in 1:3 and 3:4, and *hlk* in 1:2 and 3:2. On this problem, see the discussion in chapter 7.

39. E.g., at the end of chapter 1 in Ruth, Naomi speaks calamity and the narrator indicates hope (1:20-22); at the end of chapter 2, Naomi speaks hope and the narrator indicates calamity (2:22-23). By the end of chapter 3 the tension has been resolved. Naomi speaks hope; the narrator offers no countering tone (3:18). See Trible, *God and the Rhetoric of Sexuality,* 174–75, 181, 187.

40. On architecture as an analogue for literature, see Frank, *Literary Architecture.* Cf. this analogy with the analogy of music (note 26 above).

another, and how the narrator refers to them.[41] Analyze differences in gender, nationality, and class as they function in literary analysis.

g. Syntax. Note divergences from the usual order of Hebrew syntax. They may signal emphasis or contrast.[42] To the particularities of the text relate these divergences.[43]

h. Particles. Little words in Hebrew often have big functions. Particles such as *kî, hinnēh,* and *lākēn* can signal connection, movement, emphasis, and structure.[44] Particular meanings vary according to context. Observe where such words appear and how they function. Particles are no small matter.[45]

6. Show structure by using the very words of the text in the order they occur. Even at the risk of awkward constructions, preserve the Hebrew word order as much as possible in translation (see number 7). Remember

---

41. Three examples: (1) In Judg. 19:1-30, the woman betrayed, raped, tortured, murdered, and dismembered is given neither name nor speech, a telling commentary on her status in the story. (2) In Ruth, only Boaz among the male characters has both name and speech. He alone endures. The other males receive but one of these elements; they do not endure (1:1-5 and 4:1-8). On the other hand, all the female characters have name and speech; they signify life and hold narrative power. (3) In Genesis 16 and 21, the fact that the Hebrew matriarch Sarah never utters the name of her Egyptian slave Hagar nor speaks directly to her effects distance between the women and diminishes Hagar. See Phyllis Trible, *Texts of Terror* (Philadelphia: Fortress Press, 1984), 9–35, 65–91; Trible, *God and the Rhetoric of Sexuality,* 166–99.

42. E.g., in Jonah 1:4 the subject "Yhwh" precedes the verb "hurled," thereby emphasizing the divine action; in 1:5 the subject "Jonah" precedes the verb "went down," thereby contrasting his behavior with that of the sailors.

43. Note the use of anastrophe (inversion of normal word order) in the sentence cited. The purpose is twofold: to emphasize the concept particularity and to demonstrate what is being taught about Hebrew syntax.

44. On *kî,* see Muilenburg, "The Linguistic and Rhetorical Usages of the Particle כִּי in the Old Testament"; A. Schoors, "The Particle כִּי," *Remembering All the Way . . . ,* ed. Bertil Albrektson et al., Oudtestamentische Studiën XXI (Leiden: E. J. Brill, 1981), 240–76; Anneli Aejmelaeus, "Function and Interpretation of כִּי in Biblical Hebrew," *JBL* 105 (1986): 193–209; Barry Bandstra, "The Syntax of the Particle 'KY' in Biblical Hebrew and Ugaritic," unpubl. Ph.D. dissertation (New Haven: Yale University Press, 1982), attempts to refute the claim of an emphatic *kî* (ibid., 25–61; cf. 78). On *hinnēh,* see Berlin, *Poetics and Interpretation of Biblical Narrative,* 62f; Sternberg, *Poetics of Biblical Narrative.* On *lākēn,* see Johs. Pedersen, *Israel: Its Life and Culture,* I–II (London: Oxford University Press, 1926), 116–18; W. Eugene March, "*Lākēn:* Its Functions and Meanings," in *Rhetorical Criticism,* ed. Jackson and Kessler, 256–84; B. Jongeling, "*Lākēn* dans l'Ancien Testament," *Remembering All the Way . . . ,* 190–200.

45. Note two rhetorical devices in the sentence: pun (wordplay) and litotes (understatement or denial of the contrary).

to use the same English word for the equivalent Hebrew word; do not translate a single Hebrew word by a variety of English words (see number 5b). Formal or literal correspondence between the languages, rather than so-called dynamic equivalence, is required.[46] Remember also not to confuse structure with the outline of a text or with a summary of its themes, motifs, or ideas. Though these exercises have their place, they do not constitute rhetorical analysis. Only the *ipsissima verba* of the text can yield the structure.

7. Translate so as to retain not only the Hebrew syntax but also the original number of words. When a single Hebrew word requires more than one English word (a frequent occurrence), inform the reader by using hyphens to join the English words that convey the one Hebrew word. For example, the single word *wayyehî* may become in translation five connected words, "and-it-came-to-pass." The hyphenating procedure is necessary because only the Hebrew words exhibit and validate structure.

8. Devise a series of markers to indicate prominent features of the text, particularly repetition. The markers signal associations among words, phrases, clauses, or sentences. Within a unit, an unbroken line may indicate a first group of repetitions; a broken line, a second group; a set of dots, a third group, and so on. Though such markers are arbitrarily chosen, their use is purposeful and consistent.[47]

9. Once you have demonstrated structure in the *ipsissima verba*, with appropriate markers, then describe in clear prose what the structural diagram shows and interpret both diagram and description. The double task of description and interpretation you may intertwine or treat sequentially. Though difficult, this prosaic undertaking enables you to own the text and clarify it for the reader.[48]

10. Correlate your discoveries. How do structural units relate to plot development? Does a particular unit interrupt the narrative flow in order to slow down action, build suspense, or distract readers? How do narrated

---

46. On the contrasting principles of dynamic equivalence and formal correspondence, see Eugene A. Nida and Charles R. Taber, *The Theory and Practice of Translation* (Leiden: E. J. Brill, 1974), esp. 5–6, 22–31. The "dynamic" equivalent principle is of no use in rhetorical analysis because it separates form and content.

47. Cf. the underlining in the structural analyses by Lundbom and Craven (chapter 2), even though they did not use the model prescribed here.

48. Demonstrating, describing, and interpreting the structure of a text, word by word, does not presume its quality. Whether the structure is poor, good, indifferent, or exquisite, your job is to show what meaning the form-content yields.

introductions to direct discourse affect character portrayals?[49] What content does an *inclusio* enclose to give what meaning? Is repetition verbatim or altered? What difference does it make? Find the right questions for the text you are studying. A specific structure or device does not mean the same thing everywhere.[50] Nor do all its elements have equal value. Wrestle with the interrelationship of form-content and meaning.

❊   ❊   ❊   ❊   ❊   ❊   ❊

Rhetorical analysis unfolds by fits and starts, by hints and guesses. The Muilenburg rubric and these practical instructions are a beginning.[51] Working to see method and seeing method work happens best by studying the particularities of a text. That task becomes the next assignment. In the pursuit of it two modes of teaching contend. One takes the reader step by step through the process to explain the text and the subtext. Though this procedure may seem desirable, it becomes lengthy, tedious, and cumbersome. It also becomes impossible because the process often defies tracking. The other mode presents the finished product, leaving the reader to puzzle how it came forth. Aphorisms of Alonso-Schökel support this procedure.[52]

> With the sweat of your forehead you shall produce fruit.
> Share the fruit, not the sweat.
>
> Search and check and discard;
> and make no display of your toil.
>
> Follow your intuition,
> but never confess it.

The forthcoming study of Jonah nods to the first mode of teaching but adopts the second. Work and play, struggle and serendipity, yield the rhetorical fruit.

---

49. Is the speech of a male, for example, always preceded by his name (e.g., "and Abraham said") while the speech of a female never (e.g., "and she said")?

50. E.g., the *inclusio* in Gen. 3:1-4, with the words of the serpent surrounding the words of the woman, means that he has ensnared her. But *inclusios* in the Song of Songs bespeak the embrace of lovers; cf., e.g., Trible, *God and the Rhetoric of Sexuality*, 144–52.

51. Cf. Robert Scholes, *Elements of Fiction* (New York: Oxford University Press, 1968); Scholes, *Elements of Poetry* (New York: Oxford University Press, 1969). Though these studies pertain to English literature, they can be helpful for many issues considered here.

52. L. Alonso-Schökel, "Aphorisms on Biblical Scholarship," in *Narrative Structures in the Book of Judith*, Colloquy 11, ed. W. Wuellner (Berkeley: Center for Hermeneutical Studies, 1975), 70.

5
External Design of Jonah

A. INTRODUCTION

Several reasons motivate the selection of Jonah. The book fits the spatial need for a short text. It fits the pedagogical need for a complete text. The combination of prose and poetry enhances its usefulness. The abundance of artistic features works well for didactic purposes.[1] Indeed, so captivating is the narrative that the writer and the reader must take care to keep the assignment on course: to distinguish between the overlapping tasks of using Jonah to teach rhetorical criticism and using rhetorical criticism to teach Jonah. The former receives the emphasis.

1. The Context of Other Biblical Disciplines

A brief overview of what other biblical disciplines say about Jonah helps to situate rhetorical analysis.[2] Textual criticism finds no major problems in the book.[3] The Hebrew text and the versions (e.g., Greek and

---

1. Cf. the judgment of Licht that Jonah's "freedom from the awkwardness of fact" makes it "a perfect example of the narrator's art, on a higher, more complex level than usual in the Old Testament" (*Storytelling in the Bible*, 124).
2. For recent commentaries in English, see esp. Leslie C. Allen, *The Books of Joel, Obadiah, Jonah and Micah* (Grand Rapids, Mich.: William B. Eerdmans, 1976); Hans Walter Wolff, *Obadiah and Jonah*, trans. Margaret Kohl (Minneapolis: Augsburg Publishing House, 1986); Jack M. Sasson, *Jonah*, AB 24B (New York: Doubleday, 1990). Cf. the ample bibliography in Sasson, *Jonah*, 31–62. The work by James Limburg, *Jonah: A Commentary* (Louisville, Ky.: Westminster/John Knox Press, 1993), arrived too late for this conversation. But see his exposition of Jonah in *Hosea–Micah*, Interpretation (Atlanta: John Knox Press, 1988), 137–57.
3. For a complete text critical study, see Sasson, *Jonah*.

Latin) have been well preserved. By contrast, historical criticism struggles without resolution to determine author, date, setting, and purpose.[4] The major source critical problem centers on the psalm in chapter 2:3-10.[5] Is it original to the story or a later insertion? If an insertion, then redaction criticism explores how the resulting "second edition" shapes the theological framework.[6] Canonical criticism follows to study the theology of the whole.[7] But the study depends in part upon the identification of the narrative genre. Form criticism offers no certainty, only an array of proposals: allegory, fable, fairy tale, folktale, legend, *Märchen, māšāl, midrash,* novel, parable, prophetic tale, saga, satire, sermon, short story, and even tragedy.[8] Theologies of Jonah differ strikingly.[9] Some would reduce meaning to a single theme such as universalism versus nationalism, true versus false prophecy, divine justice versus divine mercy, the commanding presence and power of God, deliverance by God, or repentance human and divine. Other theologies grapple with the complexities of interrelated subjects. Among all such disciplines rhetorical criticism finds its place, though it does not always stay there.

4. For the consensus of older historical critics, see S. R. Driver, *An Introduction to the Literature of the Old Testament* (New York: Meridian Books, 1956), 321–25. The first edition was published in 1891; this printing comes from the edition of 1897. See also Otto Eissfeldt, *The Old Testament: An Introduction,* trans. Peter R. Ackroyd (New York: Harper and Row, 1965), 403–6; Ernst Sellin and Georg Fohrer, *Introduction to the Old Testament,* trans. David E. Green (Nashville: Abingdon Press, 1968), 440–43. On the present state of these issues, consult the commentaries listed in note 2 above. Cf. a restatement of the older consensus in John Day, "Problems in the Interpretation of the Book of Jonah," *In Quest of the Past: Studies on Israelite Religion, Literature and Prophetism,* ed. A. S. Van der Woude (Leiden: E. J. Brill, 1990), 32–47.

5. A minor source critical question concerns the location of 4:5. See the discussion later in this chapter.

6. The discipline of redaction criticism is associated more with New Testament than with Old Testament studies, where it is often subsumed under tradition history. See, e.g., Norman Perrin, *What Is Redaction Criticism?* (Philadelphia: Fortress Press, 1969); Walter E. Rast, *Tradition History and the Old Testament* (Philadelphia: Fortress Press, 1972), 1–32. Both disciplines study how redactors shape the theological frameworks of books. They investigate editorial stages leading to the final form.

7. See Childs, *Introduction to the Old Testament as Scripture,* 421–27.

8. Some of these proposals reflect disagreements about the book; others, disagreements about nomenclature for genres (cf. chapter 3, note 128). This summary excludes the FOTL series, which has yet to publish research on Jonah.

9. For interpretations throughout history, see Elias Bickerman, *Four Strange Books of the Bible* (New York: Schocken Books, 1967), 3–49; cf. the commentaries for other treatments; also John H. Walton, "The Object Lesson of Jonah 4:5–7 and the Purpose of the Book of Jonah," *BBR* 2 (1992): 47–57.

2. Literary Overview: Structure, Characters, and Plot

Even a first reading of Jonah in English can detect the basic structure, identify the characters, and trace the plot. In the NRSV chapter 1:1 opens, "Now the word of the LORD came to Jonah son of Amittai, saying." Chapter 3:1 repeats all but the appositive and then adds a telling phrase: "The word of the LORD came to Jonah a second time, saying." The repetition plus the addition "a second time" signifies that the narrative falls into two major parts (or scenes).[10] At the beginning the two major characters are named: the deity Yhwh and the man Jonah. They contend throughout as protagonist and antagonist. The other human characters are unnamed. They come in groups, each with a leader, and they divide between the scenes. In the first appear sailors and their captain; in the second, Ninevites and their king. Phenomena of nature also play major roles: in scene one, wind, storm, sea, dry land, and fish; in scene two, flocks and herds, plant, worm, sun and wind. The plot thrives on divine activity; human and natural responses mark the turning points. In scene one the words and actions of Yhwh elicit from diverse characters disobedience, fear, confession, sacrifice, and piety. At the close some issues have found resolution, but not the command (1:1) that initiated the plot. Instead a stalemate results. In scene two the plot continues by beginning a second time. The words and actions of Yhwh elicit from diverse characters capitulation, proclamation, repentance, anger, and disputation. At the close some issues have found resolution, but the final question leaves the plot open-ended. This literary overview, derived from a first reading of Jonah in English, prepares the reader to consider the external design of the book.[11]

B. EXTERNAL DESIGN

1. Introduction

Appropriating architectural and artistic language, the description "external design" signals the end of a long, tedious, and rewarding process.[12] It involved no particular order of research but rather the gathering of

10. On the choice of the term "scenes" for these divisions, see below.

11. Note one difference in verse numbering between the English and Hebrew texts. In the English, chapter 1 has 17 verses and chapter 2 has 10 verses. In the Hebrew, chapter 1 has 16 verses and chapter 2 has 11. In other words, 1:17 in the English equals 2:1 in the Hebrew. Throughout this study, the Hebrew numbering, not the English, is used. Unless otherwise specified, the translations of the Hebrew are my own.

12. Note the use of the term "external design" (along with "internal structure") in the work of Craven; see chapter 2, section B.

clues (*inventio*) from reading the text and secondary literature. Along with the gathering went conscious (and unconscious) reflection on the Muilenburg rubric. In time, the parts and the whole came together. Important clues were the recognition of two scenes, of numerous verbal repetitions, and of contrasting characters. These phenomena led to the question of whether other parallels might obtain between chapters 1–2 and chapters 3–4. Playing with possibilities brought an affirmative answer: the scenes exhibit symmetrical design. (As you peruse the following chart, check it with the text of Jonah.)

External Design: A Study in Symmetry

Scene One: Chapters 1–2

1. Word of Yhwh to Jonah (1:1)

2. Content of the word (1:2)

3. Response of Jonah (1:3)

4. Report on impending disaster (1:4)

5. Response to impending disaster (1:5)
 - by the sailors
 - by Jonah

6. Unnamed captain of the ship (1:6)
 - efforts to avert disaster by
 • action
 • words to Jonah
 • hope

7. Sailors and Jonah (1:7–15)
 - sailors' proposal (1:7ab)
 - sailors' action and its result (1:7cd)
 - sailors' questions (1:8)
 - Jonah's reply (1:9)
 - sailors' response (1:10)
 - sailors' question (1:11)
 - Jonah's reply (1:12)
 - sailors' action (1:13)
 - sailors' prayer (1:14)
 - sailors' action (1:15ab)
 - result: disaster averted (1:15c)

Scene Two: Chapters 3–4

1. Word of Yhwh to Jonah (3:1)

2. Content of the word (3:2)

3. Response of Jonah (3:3–4a)

4. Prophecy of impending disaster (3:4b)

5. Response to impending disaster (3:5)
 - by the Ninevites

6. Unnamed king of Nineveh (3:6–9)
 - efforts to avert disaster by
 • action
 • words to the Ninevites
 • hope

7. Ninevites and God (3:10)

 - Ninevites' action (3:10ab)

 - result: disaster averted (3:10cd)

8. Response of the sailors (1:16)	8. Response of Jonah (4:1)
9. Yhwh and Jonah (2:1-11)	9. Yhwh and Jonah (4:2-11)
- Yhwh's action and its result (2:1)	
- Jonah's prayer (2:2-10)	- Jonah's prayer (4:2-3)
	- Yhwh's question (4:4)
	- Jonah's action (4:5)
- Yhwh's response and its result	- Yhwh's response and its result
• by word (2:11a)	
• by nature: fish (2:11b)	• by nature: a plant (4:6abcd)
	- Jonah's response (4:6e)
	- Yhwh's response and its result
	• by nature: worm (4:7)
	sun and
	wind (4:8abc)
	- Jonah's response (4:8d)
	- Yhwh's question (4:9a)
	- Jonah's response (4:9b)
	- Yhwh's question (4:10-11)

A chart, whether presented at the beginning, middle, or end of a discussion, requires description and interpretation. Though this double task may occur in separate stages, most often it intertwines. In the design set forth here, the numberings 1 through 9 on the left-hand side of each scene are for convenience of reference. Each marks a section of narrative designated a "unit," the term to be used in the commentaries that follow.

2. Commentary on Symmetry

a. Repetition of words and phrases abound at the beginnings of Jonah 1 and 3 (units 1 and 2, extending into units 3). These verbal parallels establish the two scenes. Chapter 3:1 repeats 1:1 almost verbatim, with the word *šēnît* (a-second-time) alerting the reader to the connection and the division.[13] In addition, most of 3:2 repeats 1:2, and the first two words of 3:3 replay 1:3. The preponderance of parallels accents Yhwh's word. It forces Jonah to respond. That his response begins the same each time ("and-arose Jonah") shows narrative continuity; that it diverges thereafter allows the plot to develop. But in both scenes the development remains

---

13. Cf. a similar use of *šēnît* in Gen. 22:15 to introduce a unit parallel to the one beginning in 22:11. On repetition and variation, see, inter alia, Alter, *Art of Biblical Narrative*, 88–113; Sternberg, *Poetics of Biblical Narrative*, 365–440; Licht, *Storytelling in the Bible*, 51–95.

tied to the commanding power of the same Yahwistic words, "arise," "go," and "call." The many repetitions at the beginnings forge symmetry, set tone, and provide meaning.[14]

b. In contrast to the extensive repetitions between units 1, 2, and 3, units 4 offer a lesser type of juxtaposition: only the theme of impending disaster. Chapter 1:4 employs narrated discourse in a thirteen-word sentence in which Yhwh hurls a great wind, a tempest ensues, and the ship threatens to break up. Chapter 3:4b employs direct discourse in a seven-word sentence in which Jonah predicts the overturn of Nineveh. By itself the shared theme does not establish the structural relationship of these verses to each other or to the overall design. (Thematic analysis can be arbitrary and slippery.) But the theme acquires symmetrical validity vis-à-vis the corresponding position of these verses, the subject matter, and the surrounding content. To secure further the relationship between units 4 requires attention to units 5.

c. In unit 5 of scene one the sailors respond to the impending disaster sent by Yhwh. Three verbs in narrated discourse describe them: "they-feared," "they-cried," and "they-threw" (1:5abc). In unit 5 of scene two the Ninevites respond to the impending disaster announced by Jonah. Three verbs in narrated discourse describe them: "they-believed," "they-called," and "they-put-on" (3:5). Though the sets of verbs in these units use different vocabulary, they match in number, order, and kind. First come inward responses: "they-feared" and "they-believed." Second come articulated responses: "they-cried" and "they-called." Third come outward responses: "they-threw" and "they-put-on." In addition, the narrator paints a favorable portrait of each group as it appeals to the divinity *'elōhîm*. The sailors "cried, each-man to his-*'elōhîm*," and "the-Ninevites believed in-*'elōhîm*." (These portraits of foreigners allow an implied contrast to the character Jonah.) Parallel in number (collective) and in kind (foreigners), the sailors and the Ninevites respond similarly to impending disaster.[15] Units 5 have equivalent length, equivalent verb forms, equivalent characters, equivalent themes, and equivalent locations within the external design.

---

14. Commentators diverge on the importance they attach to the parallelism between 1:1-3a and 3:1-3a. E.g., Allen stresses it (*The Books of Joel, Obadiah, Jonah, and Micah*, 197); Sasson minimizes it (*Jonah*, 225–27). Cf. also Licht, note 21 below.

15. If you are reading closely, you notice that at the close of units 5 the symmetry falters. The response of Jonah to threatened disaster in scene one (1:5c) has no counterpart in scene two (cf. 3:5). See the discussion below.

d. Units 6 contrast the captain and the king. The captain appears close up. He is the subject of one verb of action and one of speech: "And-drew-near to-him the-captain-of the-ship and-he-said." The king appears first at a distance. He is the object within a preposition phrase: "And-reached the-word to-the-king-of Nineveh." Then he becomes the subject of four verbs of action: "and-he-arose," "and-he-removed," "and-he-covered," "and-he-sat." Two verbs of speech follow: "and-he-cried and-said." The narrated portraits of the leaders correspond in location and in manner of presentation (action and speech). They diverge in length and information, with the extended portrait of the king highlighting his more prominent role. The direct discourse that follows in each case provides further comparison and contrast. Addressing Jonah (1:6c), the captain utters short sentences. Addressing the Ninevites (3:7b-9), the king issues a lengthy decree. Though the two speeches differ in length, object of address, and type of discourse, their conclusions correspond in theme, vocabulary, and syntax. They open with parallel rhetorical expressions that anticipate but do not guarantee salvation. "Perhaps" (*'ûlay*), says (*'mr*) the captain; "who knows" (*mî yôdēaʿ*), says (*'mr*) the king.[16] Next come identical subjects with different verbs. "Perhaps will-think the-god (*hā-'elōhîm*) to-us," says the captain. "Who knows, will-return and-repent the-god (*hā-'elōhîm*)," says the king. Identical words conclude the speeches: "and-not we-will-perish (*welō' nō'bēd*)," says the captain; "and-not we-will-perish (*welō' nō'bēd*)," says the king. Both foreign leaders proclaim a theology of hope. Their juxtaposition in the design of the book shows asymmetries residing within symmetry.

e. Two other instances of the verb "perish" (*'bd*) further the symmetry and the sense. In unit 7 of scene one the sailors beseech Yhwh, "Not, please, let-us-*perish* for-the-*nepeš*-of-the-man the-this" (1:14).[17] In unit 9 of scene two Yhwh speaks to Jonah about the plant "which-a-child-of-the-night became and-a-child-of the-night *perished*" (4:10). These near correspondences in placement join the exact correspondences in units 6 to provide artistic balance and thematic emphasis. Moreover, all the instances of "perish" belong to direct discourse. The captain, sailors, king, and

---

16. Cf. James L. Crenshaw, "The Expression *MI YODEAʿ* in the Hebrew Bible," *VT* 36 (1986): 274–88, who discusses the *rhetorical* value of this question in its ten occurrences.

17. The word *nepeš* is difficult to translate. The restricted meaning is "throat" or "neck" (Jonah 2:6). The extensive meanings include "life," "self," "person," and "soul." See Hans Walter Wolff, *Anthropology of the Old Testament*, trans. Margaret Kohl (Philadelphia: Fortress Press, 1974), 10–25.

Yhwh—but never Jonah—use it. (Jonah employs instead the word "die," which the other characters never use.) Three times the verb "perish" (*'bd*) occurs with the adverb "not" (*lō'*) to express hope or make a plea; the fourth time it occurs in the affirmative to report the demise of the plant. Its strategic use in design and dialogue pinpoints a pervasive motif.

f. In units 7 the sailors and the Ninevites reappear (cf. c above). Parallelism of position does not entail, however, parallelism of length, form and content. A long section mixing narrated and direct discourse features the sailors and Jonah (1:7-15); a brief section of only narrated discourse presents the Ninevites and God (3:10). The striking imbalance recalls the reverse contrast in units 6 (a brief portrait of the captain and a longer portrait of the king) and presages another imbalance of length in units 9 (see subsection h below). However many differences mark units 7, they end on the shared theme of disaster averted. "And-ceased the-sea from-its-raging" (1:15c); "and-repented the-God concerning the-evil which he-said to-do to-them and-not he-did" (3:10cd). Much like the thematic association between units 4 (see subsection b above), this one gains stability from all the verbal parallels that surround it. In addition, the imbalances between units 7 contribute to the balance of the whole. But that observation awaits the telling.

g. Human responses to averted disaster occupy units 8. Though matched in grammar, vocabulary, and subject matter, they depart from the usual pairing of characters (cf. units 5, 6, 7). In scene one the sailors respond; in scene two Jonah (not the Ninevites) responds. Literary symmetry diverges from logical symmetry. But in both units verbs with cognate objects modfied by the adjective "great" describe states of being. "And-feared the-sailors a-fear great" (1:16); "and-was-evil to Jonah an-evil great" (4:1). The great fear of the sailors leads to cultic activities reported by verbs with cognate objects: "they-sacrificed a-sacrifice" and "they-vowed vows." Narrated discourse completes their appearances. By contrast, the great evil to Jonah leads to inner turmoil reported by a single verb and a prepositional phrase: "and-it-burned to-him." Narrated discourse signifies that for him matters are incomplete.

h. The two scenes conclude, as they open (units 1 and 2), with Yhwh and Jonah (units 9). Yet the endings far outstrip the beginnings in length and complexity. Compared to each other, however, the first ending is shorter, a difference that increases dramatically if the psalm be deemed a later insertion. The second ending, by virtue of its location and function, receives double stress and so is more expansive.[18] The endings share verbs exclusive to the units. The verb "appoint" (*mnh*) occurs once in scene one (2:1) and three times in scene two (4:6, 7, 8). Each time the deity is subject and elements of nature are objects. Yhwh appoints a fish; Yhwh God or (the) God appoints a plant, worm, and wind. The verb "pray" (*pll*) occurs in corresponding positions (2:1 and 4:2) with "Jonah" (or "he") as subject and the phrase "to Yhwh his-God" or "to Yhwh" as object. But similarities herald differences (as deconstructionists would surely assert). The ending of scene one gives a psalm as the content of Jonah's prayer (2:2-9); the ending of scene two gives a prose speech that contains an ancient credo (4:2b-3). The difference in genres matches the difference in tone and content. Contrasting portraits of Jonah emerge. Modeling piety, he concludes with thanksgiving to Yhwh for deliverance. Proclaiming self-justification, he concludes with a petition to Yhwh for death.[19] On the two occasions Yhwh responds differently. The first time the deity makes no verbal reply to Jonah's prayer; narrated discourse sets distance between Yhwh and Jonah (2:11). The second time Yhwh replies directly, "Is-it-good it-burns to-you?" (4:4). When Jonah continues to express his death wish, God continues to question him (4:9, 11). Dialogue supplants distance.

i. Description and interpretation of the endings inspire a sweeping look at the way the external design unfolds the story. In scene one Yhwh commands Jonah once, indeed speaks only once. Yet however much Jonah disobeys, the deity thwarts the efforts through overwhelming power. As the scene concludes, with Jonah praying in the belly of the fish, the lesson holds firm. Though the deity does not address Jonah, the power of Yhwh prevails. Jonah has no exit. In scene two Yhwh commands Jonah a second time. He goes to Nineveh, ostensibly obeying Yhwh. With the repentance of Nineveh, the deity changes from threatening destruction to repenting of evil. This latter portrayal then expands at the conclusion where Yhwh talks to Jonah. Divine questions replace divine imperatives and divine power. The outcome remains open. Viewed from the

---

18. The imbalance of length between units 9 recalls comparable instances in units 6 and 7 (cf. subsections d and f above). Overall, the asymmetry of these units works in tandem to effect the symmetry of the whole. See below on asymmmetry.

19. The contrast reverberates inversely with the contrast set forth in units 3. In scene one Jonah disobeys the divine word (1:3); in scene two he obeys (3:3-4a). Symmetry of design in units 3 and 9 vies with asymmetry in the character portrayal of Jonah.

perspective of the whole, the juxtaposition of the endings shows theological movement from a god of distance to a god of dialogue; from a god of power to a god of persuasion, from a god of rigidity to a god of rhetoric. (Recall all the meanings of this last word and play with them.) Yhwh who controls Jonah in the fish counters Yhwh who seeks to persuade Jonah under the sun. But in striking contrast to the divine change, Jonah remains constant. As in the beginning, so in the end he holds fast to his own ideas. His last words confirm himself (4:9b). Yet Yhwh, not Jonah, has the last word in the story (4:10-11). It keeps the dialogue open. In form and content the endings of scenes one and two contrast even as they correspond. Asymmetry vies with symmetry.

j. This overview begins to enlarge the relationship between design and plot. (Remember that form [design and structure] and content [plot] must converge for appropriate interpretation.) When Aristotle discussed "the proper arrangement of the component elements within plots," he declared that "to be a whole," a story must "have a beginning and a middle and an end."[20] By "beginning" he meant that which is itself not after anything but after which something comes. By "middle" he meant that which comes after something and after which something comes. By "end" he meant that which itself comes after something but after which nothing comes. Well-constructed plots neither begin nor end by chance but conform to these principles. Within the Aristotelian framework one might chart the plot of Jonah as follows: The beginning is Yhwh's command and Jonah's response (1:1-3); the middle is the story of the sea (1:4—2:11) and of the city (3:1—4:5); the ending is Yhwh's appointments and Jonah's responses (4:6-11).[21] But this charting slights the function and effect of the symmetry. It slights the peculiarities of the book that the external design makes clear. They include double images of beginning, middle, and end. Scene one begins with the word of Yhwh to Jonah and his response (1:1-3). The middle contains the events at sea (1:4-16). The end comes with the fish incident that returns Jonah to dry land (1:17—2:10). But it is an unsatisfactory ending. The beginning has found no resolution;

---

20. *Aristotle's Poetics*, 14. Though his discussion specifies tragedy, the observation extends to other genres.

21. Cf. Licht, who sees the entire plot as three "episodes": chapters 1 (beginning), 3 (middle), and 4 (end). Accordingly, chapter 3 (Jonah's mission in Nineveh) is structurally and thematically the central episode. Chapter 1 (the futile voyage) prepares for this conflict, and chapter 4 (the story of the plant) resolves it. Note that Licht ignores chapter 2, calling it "a poetical intermezzo," counts the repetition between 1:1-2 and 3:1-2 only as marking two of three "episodes," and downplays sections of chapter 4 (*Storytelling in the Bible*, 121–23).

so the story resumes a second time. Scene two begins with the word of Yhwh to Jonah (3:1-2). The middle runs from Jonah's response through the events in Nineveh (3:4-10). The end comes with the dialogue between Jonah and Yhwh (4:1-11).[22] Thus double images of beginning, middle, and end shape the book.[23] Symmetrical design yields a well-constructed plot.

3. Commentary on Asymmetry

Throughout the commentary on symmetry, asymmetry threatened like a storm at sea: flaws, discrepancies, and gaps in the design. Appropriating insights of Kuhn,[24] one might argue that all such phenomena work against the paradigm of symmetry to break it down from within. Appropriating the strategies of Derrida, one might argue that symmetry proceeds from asymmetry.[25] The chart is not stable and so undermines itself. Appropriating an observation made by the early twentieth century biblical scholar George Adam Smith, one might argue that asymmetry belongs to the warp and woof of symmetry. When exploring the rhythm of Hebrew poetry, Smith noted "frequent irregularities" that occur in the number and proportion of stresses.[26] To account for them he turned to a feature of oriental art that he dubbed "symmetrophobia: an instinctive aversion to absolute symmetry, which, if it knows no better, will express itself in arbitrary and even violent disturbances of the style or pattern of the work."[27] Citing similar tendencies in Shakespearean blank verse as well as in modern Arabic poetry, he maintained that such deliberate irregularities constitute artistry within a larger whole. Rather than destroying symmetry,

---

22. Note the correlation with the rhetorical units. The beginning contains units 1, 2, and 3; the middle, units 4 through 8; and the end, units 9.

23. Canonical criticism might posit another variation on the Aristotelian categories. The opening word of Jonah, "and-it-came-to-pass," suggests continuation; the last words, a question without an answer, suggest incompletion. These features situate Jonah as the "middle" between Obadiah and Micah in the Book of the Twelve Prophets. Cf. Childs, *Introduction to the Old Testament as Scripture*, 421–27. On intertextual readings, see also Alan Cooper, "In Praise of Divine Caprice: The Significance of the Book of Jonah," *Among the Prophets*, ed. Philip R. Davies and David J. A. Clines, JSOT Suppl. Ser. 144 (Sheffield: JSOT Press, 1993), 144–63; Paul R. House, *The Unity of the Twelve* (Sheffield: The Almond Press, 1990), 137–39 and *passim*.

24. See chapter 3, note 8.

25. See chapter 3, note 65.

26. George Adam Smith, *The Early Poetry of Israel in its Physical and Social Origins*, The Schweich Lectures 1910 (London: Oxford University Press, 1927).

27. Ibid., 17.

they confirm it. Difference enhances similarity. The concept of "symme-trophobia" offers, then, another way to understand asymmetry in the de-sign of Jonah.

One major category of symmetrophobia concerns gaps, places in the design where a unit lacks a match in whole or in part.[28] Units 5 contain a prime example. The response to impending disaster by Jonah in scene one has no counterpart in scene two. The gap fits the contrast between the situations. In the first, the storm sent by Yhwh threatens both the sailors and Jonah. But in the second, Jonah himself announces the im-pending disaster of Nineveh. It threatens only the Ninevites, not him. So the narrative keeps the focus on them as it moves from the response of the citizens (3:5) uninterruptedly to the response of their king (3:6). Be-sides, the gap subtly prepares for the delayed focus on Jonah in chapter 4.

In this connection verse 5 of chapter 4 assumes special interest. It re-ports, "But-went-out Jonah from the-city and-he-sat-down from-the-east to-the-city and-he-made for-himself there a-booth and-he-sat-down under-it in-the-shade until he-should-see what would-happen in-the-city." For several reasons the report has intrigued medieval rabbis and modern historical critics.[29] First, it appears after Jonah already knows "what would-happen in-the-city." The repentance of Nineveh has saved it from destruction. Second, nothing subsequent to 4:5 warrants a watch by Jonah. The outcome for the city remains unaltered.[30] Third, the booth Jonah makes for shade conflicts through proximity with the plant Yhwh makes to shade Jonah in the very next verse (4:6). The conclusion drawn from these observations is that 4:5 has been misplaced. It belongs after 3:4, immediately following the announcement of impending disaster.

Although the proposal for transposition has virtually no adherents to-day,[31] it merits rhetorical play. If 4:5 were transposed to follow 3:4, then

28. Cf. Sternberg's definition: "A gap is a lack of information about the world . . . contrived by a temporal displacement." The gap may be filled later or not at all. Cf. also his distinction between "gaps" and "blanks." The former designate lacunae of relevance, omis-sions for the sake of interest. They require closure; the reader fills the gaps. The latter designate lacunae of irrelevance, omissions for the lack of interest. They do not require closure. (Sternberg, *Poetics of Biblical Narrative*, 235–37).

29. Cf. Sasson for a summary of positions (*Jonah*, 287–90).

30. *Contra* Cooper, who argues for 4:11 as a declarative rather than an interrogative sentence. In that case, the outcome for Nineveh would be altered: "I will not have pity." ("In Praise of Divine Caprice," 158). For a critique of this view, see chapter 9, note 48.

31. But see Day, who has recently reaffirmed the proposal ("Problems in the Inter-pretation of the Book of Jonah," 42–43).

there would be no gap in the external design. Instead, a chiasm would enhance the symmetry:

Scene One	Scene Two
5. Response to impending disaster – by the sailors (1:5ab) – by Jonah (1.5c)	5. Response to impending disaster – by Jonah (4:5) – by the Ninevites (3:5)

In scene one Jonah responds to disaster just after the sailors. He retreats to the innards of the vessel, lies down, and goes to sleep. In scene two, with 4:5 now transposed to follow 3:4, Jonah responds to disaster just before the Ninevites. He withdraws from the city, sits in the east, constructs a booth, sits in its shade, and awaits the outcome. In both cases he seeks shelter.[32] The chiastic juxtaposition of his narrated responses makes sense for symmetry, content, and context. Moreover, the removal of 4:5 from its present location improves the symmetry of units 9. In scene one, after Jonah's prayer (2:2-10), Yhwh replies by word (Yhwh spoke, 2:11a) and by nature (the fish, 2:11b). In scene two, after Jonah's prayer (4:2-3), Yhwh replies by word (Yhwh questions, 4:4). But then, as the text now reads, the report of Jonah's leaving the city intervenes before Yhwh replies by nature (the plant, 4:6a). The proposed transposition would eliminate this intervention to leave a design corresponding more nearly to scene one:

Scene One	Scene Two
9. Yhwh and Jonah (2:1-11) – Yhwh's action and its result (2:1) – Jonah's prayer (2:2-10) – Yhwh's response and its result • by word (2:11a) • by nature: fish (2:11b)	9. Yhwh and Jonah (4:2-11) – Jonah's prayer (4:2-3) – Yhwh's response and its result • by word (4:4) • by nature: plant (4:6a)

Though one can never argue that 4:5 be transposed for the sake of symmetry, one can show that symmetry itself argues for transposition. Rhetorical analysis plays with the proposal while shrinking from promoting it.[33]

---

32. On the image of shelter, see James S. Ackerman, "Satire and Symbolism in the Song of Jonah," *Traditions in Transformation*, ed. Baruch Halpern and Jon D. Levenson (Winona Lake, Ind.: Eisenbrauns, 1981), 240–43.

33. Lack of textual or redactional evidence weakens the argument for transposition. Yet a skilled editor may well have left no traces. But then the question why 4:5 ever became misplaced remains unanswered.

In addition to gaps, lack of verbal or formal links between units constitutes a second category of symmetrophobia. Units 4 supply an example (cf. b above). In scene one the narrator reports that Yhwh hurls a great wind upon the sea, a storm ensues, and the ship thinks itself about to break up (1:5). In scene two Jonah proclaims the overturn of Nineveh (3:4b). The two accounts show no parallels in characters, vocabulary, grammar, or type of discourse. Nevertheless, the units that surround them (1, 2, 3, and 5) abound in verbal and formal links, thereby securing the juxtaposition of units 4 in the total design. This juxtaposition allows the shared theme of impending disaster to emerge. Asymmetry nestles within symmetry.

A third category of symmetrophobia pertains to major variations in length between juxtaposed passages. In units 6, for example, a glance at the captain (1:6) vies with an extended look at the king (3:6-9). Obversely, in units 7 an extended look at the deeds of the sailors (1:7-15b) vies with a glance at the deeds of the Ninevites (3:10ab). And in units 9 the balance shifts again. Even with the inclusion of the psalm, the ending of scene one (2:1-11) does not match in length the extended ending of scene two (4:2-11). The alternating contrasts provide a delicate pattern of overall balance even as they keep symmetrophobia alive and well.

✿   ✿   ✿   ✿   ✿   ✿   ✿

Summary. In the external design symmetry produces rhythm, contrast, emphasis, and continuity. It also serves a mnemonic function. (Recall the rhetorical faculty of *memoria.*) Asymmetry disrupts rhythm to give contrast and emphasis through discontinuity. It keeps memory alert. Within symmetry, asymmetry flourishes. All in all, an exquisitely designed story begins to disclose its treasures for the reader.

C. CONCLUSION

The chart presenting the external design resembles what the FOTL series calls Structure.[34] So the disciplines of form and rhetorical criticism share a common procedure even as they diverge on its nomenclature. For rhetorical criticism design can be shown through paraphrases and abridgements; structure only through verbatim content.[35] Further, because outlining and thematic analysis can too easily manipulate the text

---

34. Cf. chapter 3, section D.
35. This use of the words "design" and "structure" is neither engraved in stone nor written in sand, but it does make an important distinction. In so defining the words, the writer must continue to use them only in this way for the sake of clarity and consistency.

to say what readers want, validity of design depends upon verification by structure. Verification comes at two levels. The first selects parts of the verbatim text to show how they substantiate the design and what meanings result. The second moves deeply into the whole text with word by word analysis to show how the particularities work and what meanings result. Both levels involve identifying sufficient verbal anchors in structure to validate design.[36] The explication thus far operates at the first level.

What in general does this study of external design teach about the practice of rhetorical criticism? Like a detective, the student looks for clues to unravel the text. She has no set plan but wanders up and down, pursuing hints and guesses, hunches and questions. The wandering may turn back upon itself, digress, and jump around. The process parallels in classical rhetoric the faculty of *inventio*, the gathering of materials suitable for the occasion. Most often the phenomenon of repetition captures attention first. It signals structure and emphasis. This clue leads to other features: e.g., the distinction between narrated and direct discourse, the portrayal of characters, the development of plot, and the placement of words, phrases, and sentences. "Search and check and discard," advises Alonso-Schökel. "Follow your intuition. . . ." Throughout the search one assumes that the text is "com-posed," put together, and that its arrangement comes with literary-theological intent. Out of myriad movements the student eventually chooses an ordered procedure for reporting the results. The process parallels the faculty of *dispositio*, arranging the material in a way suitable for the occasion. Then the student describes and interprets her discoveries, using a clear, common, and consistent vocabulary. The work parallels the faculty of *elocutio*, choosing the style suitable for the material and the occasion.

In assembling, arranging, and offering clues, the student draws upon classical rhetoric, literary-critical theory, the literary study of the Bible, and form criticism. She also consults other biblical disciplines. One major advantage the seasoned reader has over the novice is the knowledge that the work does not get easier the more one does it. "With the sweat of your forehead you shall produce fruit." Particularities continually challenge expertise. They also excite wonder and invite play. Therein comes

---

36. The indeterminate adjective "sufficient" places the burden of judgment upon the reader. To determine sufficiency, various factors come into play; e.g., key words and phrases, their number, location, and use. The weight given these factors varies according to the particularities of a text.

the sharing of the fruit, not the sweat. Guiding the entire labor, from its elusive beginnings to its ordered end, is the Muilenburg rubric: an appropriate articulation of form-content yields an appropriate articulation of meaning. But the heart of the practice is yet to come. Explication moves from the first to the second level of verification: word by word analysis.

6
Internal Structure
of Scene One (1 : 1-16)

Analysis of external design begins to show how the text is put together and what it means; analysis of internal structure completes the endeavor. It uses the criterion of form-content to discern the limits of literary units and the configuration of their parts.[1] The process involves reading word by word, phrase by phrase, and sentence by sentence, but it does not presume that every word, phrase, and sentence has equal value.[2] The particularities of a text unfold the emphases. Appropriate articulation yields the meanings.

Among the basic tools needed for close reading is knowledge of rhetorical devices and structural divisions. A standard vocabulary based on classical rhetoric governs the devices[3] but not the divisions. They require explanation. The relatively short length of Jonah influences the decision to deem it a single act with two scenes. Each scene contains episodes and each episode contains incidents. Another critic might prefer to view the two scenes as two acts and so the episodes as scenes and the incidents as episodes. In any case, major clues for delineating the divisions, large and small, remain the same: shifts in discourse, setting, time, characters, and

---

1. See Muilenburg, "Form Criticism and Beyond," 9–10.
2. This process of close reading has affinities with interpretive interests far and wide. In the medieval world, for instance, it characterized both Jewish and Christian exegesis. In the twentieth century, it characterizes objective theories and deconstruction. Cf. the relevant discussions in Part One.
3. See, e.g., Lanham, *Handlist of Rhetorical Terms;* C. Hugh Holman and William Harmon, *A Handbook to Literature* (New York: Macmillan Publishing Co., 1992). Cf. Lentricchia and McLaughlin, eds., *Critical Terms for Literary Study.*

subject matter.[4] Whatever the particular terminology used, clarity and consistency are the virtues. The author holds responsibility for informing the reader.

Scene one (chapters 1–2) comprises four episodes. Episode one (1:1-3) sets the plot in motion. It reports Yhwh's command and Jonah's disobedient response. Episode two (1:4-6) begins with Yhwh's counter to disobedience and continues with the effect of the storm upon the sailors, Jonah, and the captain. Episode three (1:7-16) recounts the sailors' efforts to avert disaster, concluding with the expulsion of Jonah and their deliverance. Episode four (2:1-11) follows Jonah into the belly of a fish where he prays to Yhwh before being vomited upon dry land. This chapter discusses episodes one, two, and three; the next chapter discusses episode four.

A. EPISODE ONE (1:1-3)

Two incidents fill this episode: Yhwh's command (1:1-2) and Jonah's response (1:3).[5]

1. Command of Yhwh (1:1-2)

Narrated discourse opens the story: "And-was [or came] the-word-of Yhwh to Jonah, son-of Amittai, saying."[6] The sentence fits the form-critical category of the prophetic word formula. It prefaces a private communication from the deity to a prophet.[7] Yet no other prophetic book opens just this way.[8] The distinction recalls the familiar observation that Jonah differs from all other prophetic books in being a story about a

4. Cf. Bar-Efrat, *Narrative Art in the Bible,* esp. 93–140. Note that the clues embrace form and content.

5. Note that episode one corresponds to units 1, 2, and 3 of the external design. True to the principle of the inseparability of form-content, episodic divisions and unit divisions correlate within each scene, *and* they do not necessarily correlate between scenes. For example, though here in scene one units 1, 2, and 3 constitute episode one, in scene two units 1, 2, 3, and 4 constitute episode one. See chapters 8 and 9.

6. The single word *way(ye)hî* (and-was, and-came, or and-came-to-pass) suggests continuation rather than beginning. On Jonah as a part of the twelve minor prophets, see House, *The Unity of the Twelve, passim.*

7. See Burke O. Long, *2 Kings* FOTL 10, ed. Rolf Knierim and Gene M. Tucker (Grand Rapids, Mich.: William B. Eerdmans, 1991), 323. Note, however, that Jonah is not called a "prophet" in this story. But 2 Kings 14:25 does refer to a "Jonah, the son of Amittai, the prophet."

8. Variations of the formula introduce Hosea, Joel, Micah, Zephaniah, Haggai, and Malachi; on the word *way(ye)hî,* cf. Ezek. 1:1. See Sasson, *Jonah,* 66–68.

prophet rather than words (oracles) by a prophet.[9] At the beginning, then, conventional language bespeaks the unconventional.[10] Is it an earnest of things to come? The words name the principal characters and establish their relationship. The syntax encloses Jonah with divine speech, thereby securing the dominance of the deity: "word-of Yhwh to Jonah, son-of Amittai, saying." Structure and content show that Yhwh prevails over Jonah to initiate the plot.

What the prophetic word formula announces, direct discourse specifies (1:2). Three divine imperatives address Jonah: "arise," "go," "call." The first imperative stands alone; a prepositional phrase joins the second; a longer clause of indirect discourse completes the third. The progression moves from general command to specification of place to statement of purpose:[11]

> Arise
>> go to Nineveh the-city the-great
>> and-call to-her because has-come-up their-evil before-my-presence. (1:2)

By consulting a concordance, one can identify the double construction, "arise, go" as conventional speech. It occurs numerous times throughout the Bible, often as a divine command to a prophet.[12] Not separated by a conjunction, the combination illustrates the rhetorical device of asyndeton (literally, "unconnected"). It produces a hurried rhythm that here elicits a prompt response.[13] Accompanying this convention may come a third imperative prefaced by the conjunction *we* (and).[14] So in Jonah "and-call" follows the command "arise, go." Form criticism calls the total speech the

---

9. Cf., e.g., Eissfeldt, *The Old Testament*, 404; Sellin and Fohrer, *Introduction to the Old Testament*, 441; Rolf Rendtorff, *The Old Testament: An Introduction*, trans. John Bowden (Philadelphia: Fortress Press, 1986), 225.

10. Cf. the relationship between form criticism (the conventional) and rhetorical criticism (the particular); cf. also deconstructionist insights about discourse undermining itself.

11. The indentation of the second and third lines in the diagram indicates that all three lines constitute a single unit.

12. See, e.g., 1 Kings 17:9; 21:18; 2 Kings 1:3; Jer. 13:4-6; 49:28; Ezek. 3:22.

13. Cf. grammarians who hold that the imperative "arise" (*qûm*) functions as an auxiliary verb to aid the second imperative "go" (*hlk*). From a rhetorical perspective the use of *qûm* apart from *hlk* in the indicative that follows in 1:3 as well as the contrast in the use of the two verbs in 3:3 suggests nuances not accounted for in the grammatical observation. See chapter 8; cf. Sasson, *Jonah*, 69f.

14. E.g., in 1 Kings 17:9, the third imperative is "dwell"; in Jer. 13:4, "hide"; in Jer. 13:6, "take." On such repetitions, cf. Bar-Efrat, *Narrative Art in the Bible*, 212–15.

commissioning formula.[15] Rhetorical criticism explores its particular use in Jonah.

The prepositional object of the imperative "go," namely "to Nineveh the-city the-great," continues the movement of the divine word. Narrated discourse reporting Yhwh's word "to" (*'el*) Jonah (1:1) becomes direct discourse ordering Jonah "to" (*'el*) Nineveh (1:2). Using the same preposition of direction, the first movement connects the main characters Yhwh and Jonah and the second connects Jonah to the introduction of a third character, "Nineveh the-city the-great." As the identity "son-of Amittai" appears in apposition to Jonah, similarly the identity "the-city the-great" appears in apposition to Nineveh. The former occurs but once (a typical feature of an introduction); the latter occurs repeatedly to stress the gravity of Nineveh.

The third imperative completes the verbal movement: "and-call to-her because (*kî*) has-come-up their-evil before-my-presence." The particle *kî*, translated "because," performs a major role in Hebrew rhetoric. Playing on the sound of the Hebrew word (pronounced as the English "key"), one can pun that *kî* is the key.[16] Of its many meanings and functions, the causal and the asseverative interlock here. *Kî* introduces reason or motivation and can be translated "because" or "for"; it signals emphasis and can be translated "surely," "indeed," or the like. A deconstructionist might observe that it unlocks indeterminate meaning. Though the translator must inevitably choose a single English word, she cannot argue for its stability and exclusivity.

"And-call to-her (*'ālêhā*)[17] because has-come-up their-evil (*rā'ātām*) before-my-presence." A feminine singular reference, "to-her," and a

15. Long incorporates the commissioning formula and the prophetic word formula under the genre commission (*2 Kings*, 295f, 320).

16. Rhetorically this clause indulges in bilingual paronomasia, a play on the sound and meaning of a Hebrew and an English word. On the particle *kî*, see the bibliography in chapter 4, note 44. The rhetorical device of paronomasia constitutes one type of pun. Pun is a generic term for a play on words. It comes in several types: antanaclasis (literally, "bending back"), use of a single word in two different senses; paronomasia (literally, "play upon words that sound alike"); syllepsis (literally, "taking together"), a verb that bears a different relationship to two or more words that it governs. For a classic study, see I. M. Casanowicz, *Paronomasia in the Old Testament* (1894); cf. J. J. Glück, "Paronomasia in Biblical Literature," *Semitics* 1 (1970): 50–78. In Jonah puns play major roles; see Baruch Halpern and Richard Elliot Friedman, "Composition and Paronomasia in the Book of Jonah," *HAR* 4 (1980): 79–92.

17. The preposition "to" (*'al*) in the phrase "to-her" differs from the preceding preposition (*'el*) translated "to" in "to Jonah" and "to Nineveh." Though Sasson argues that *'al*

masculine plural possessive pronoun, "their-[evil]," depict Nineveh as one and many (and as gender inclusive). The singular refers to the city as city. The plural exemplifies metonymy (literally "change of name"), a rhetorical device that substitutes one name or word for another suggested by it. In this case, "their" substitutes for the citizens.[18] The complete construction "their-evil" suggests further the substitution of a quality for the people, a quality unacceptable to Yhwh. Prodded by the verb "has-come-up," the last two words of the sentence produce a sharp antithesis through juxtaposition of subject matter: "their-evil before-my-presence." Syntactically the word "their-evil" comes up before the word "before-my-presence." The antithesis cannot hold. Indeed, structure and content have already designated Jonah the mediator between the opposing characters (Yhwh to Jonah to Nineveh). Whether he is to mediate doom or a warning remains uncertain. Though much later the narrator says that the deity intended evil to Nineveh (3:10), such interpretation is not set here.[19] The imperative "call to-her kî has-come-up their-evil before-my-presence" might just as readily warn of potential doom, either in the presence of evil (the asseverative) or because of evil (the causal). Even as the kî clause leaves open the meaning of the message, a warning would leave open the outcome for Nineveh and Yhwh.[20] At the beginning uncertain meaning requires the reader to await developments.

Summary. Traditional speech dominates the opening of the story. The prophetic word formula (1:1) and the commissioning formula (1:2) belong to the genre designated commission. It brings narrator, characters, and readers into familiar realms of discourse. At the same time, particularities modify the conventions to indicate emphases and stir up meanings. In the next incident particularities, not conventions, dominate. The opportunity for rhetorical analysis deepens as the plot thickens.

2. Response of Jonah (1:3)

In a typical situation divine imperatives lead to indicatives that repeat them. For example, Yhwh commands Elijah to "arise, go to Zarephath." So he "arose and went" (1 Kings 17:9-10). Yhwh commands Jeremiah to

---

carries the special meaning of "imposing an (unpleasant) fate upon something," other scholars view the two prepositions as interchangeable (Sasson, *Jonah,* 72–75).

18. See Sasson, *Jonah,* 75f.

19. Neither is it nailed down by Yhwh's words in 3:2 nor by Jonah's in 3:4.

20. The later response of the Ninevites to Jonah's announcement aligns itself with this interpretation.

"arise, go to the Euphrates and hide." So Jeremiah declares, "I went and hid by the Euphrates as Yhwh commanded me" (Jer. 13:4-5; cf. 13:6-7). Continuity of vocabulary and change of grammar show the divine word finding fulfillment in the prophetic response. This typical situation informs through confirmation and contrast the particular response of Jonah. Divine imperatives impel him to act. His first act obeys the first command. The imperative "arise" becomes the declarative, "And-arose (*way-yāqom*) Jonah . . . ." The pattern leads the reader to expect the remaining imperatives, "go" and "call," to follow as declaratives: and he went and he called. But that does not happen. Rather than the third person declarative of "go," the infinitive "to-flee" (*librōaḥ*) appears, accompanied not by the phrase "to Nineveh" (*'el nîneweh*) but instead "to-Tarshish" (*taršîšâ*). Even the preposition *'el* that signaled direction to Nineveh (and to Jonah) is replaced by an alternative construction, the locative *-â*. City counters city. Nineveh is east; Tarshish west. Nineveh specifies Yhwh's direction; Tarshish signifies "from-the-presence-of Yhwh" (*millipnê*).[21] This prepositional phrase opposes Yhwh's phrase "before-my-presence (*lepānāy*)" (1:2). Jonah, the potential mediator between Yhwh and Nineveh, arises to flee to Tarshish from the presence of Yhwh and thereby to sever his connection to Nineveh. Numerous grammatical and verbal changes break continuity between the divine imperatives and the human indicatives. They alert the reader to an atypical situation.

The antithetical relationship between Yhwh's commands and Jonah's response affects understanding of the initial conjunction *wa-* in 1:3.[22] Prefixed to the verb "arose," it at first projects continuity with the imperative "arise" and so encourages the translation "and." Viewed from the end of the clause, however, *wa-* signals discontinuity and so encourages the translation "but." The ambiguity of *wa-* leads and misleads (or misleads and leads) the reader from command to disobedient response. A deconstructionist takes delight as the conjunction undermines its meaning.

"And/but-arose Jonah to-flee to-Tarshish from-the-presence-of Yhwh." The independent clause begins a chiasm. Repetition of words and phrases

21. The specific location of Tarshish remains uncertain; cf. Wolff, *Obadiah and Jonah,* 100–102; Sasson, *Jonah,* 79. For Tarshish as a place that does not know Yhwh, cf. Isa. 66:19.

22. On antithesis as a rhetorical form in classical and biblical sources, see Jože Kra-šovec, *Antithetic Structure in Biblical Hebrew Poetry* (Leiden: E. J. Brill, 1984), esp. 1–18, 126. Like rhetorical criticism, Krašovec's method stresses as primary the particularities of

in comparable positions defines the boundaries and produces the structure.[23]

    A   And/but-arose Jonah to-flee <u>to-Tarshish</u> from-the-presence-of Yhwh

        B   and-he-went-down to-Joppa

           C and-he-found a-ship

              D returning (to) Tarshish
                   x x x x x x x

           C' and-he-paid her-fare

        B' and-he-went-down in-it

    A' to-return with-them to-Tarshish from-the-presence-of Yhwh. (1:3)
       x x x x x x x

The diagram presents verbatim the structure of the sentence.[24] The letters A, B, and C identify the first three clauses and C', B', A' their counterparts. The prime (') to the right of each letter distinguishes different sections of the same variable.[25] D, the center of the chiasm, has no counterpart. Overall, the structure balances in the length of its corresponding sections and in the placement of key words and phrases.

Repetitions and grammatical forms relate the parts. Setting the boundaries, the phrase "to-Tarshish from-the-presence-of Yhwh" occurs at the end of the first and last lines (A and A').[26] They contain the only two infinitives in the chiasm, "to-flee" and "to-return." The second line (B) continues the action of Jonah begun in the first (A): "and-he-went-down" (*wayyēred*). The corresponding line B' also continues his action with the identical verb occurring in the identical place, "and-he-went-down" (*wayyēred*). The third line (C) reports another action by Jonah. Though its vocabulary is not repeated in C', the two lines conform syntactically, thematically, and structurally. Both have a third person masculine singular

---

individual texts and authors. He lists four antithetic units in Jonah: 1:2/3; 1:5ab/5c; 2:5-7a/7b; 4:10/11.

23. See Norbert Lohfink, "Jona ging zur Stadt hinaus (Jon 4,5)," *BZ* 5 (1961): 200–201. By showing structure in the *ipsissima verba* of the text (1:3), Lohfink exemplifies rhetorical critical analysis (though he does not so identify it). But his subsequent argument for a "structure" in 1:4-16 diverges from rhetorical critical analysis; see the Excursus at the end of the chapter.

24. See the explanation given in chapter 4 about the use of indicators to identify repetitions.

25. On the prime, see the extended note 2 at the end of chapter 2.

26. Note that the last line (A') differs grammatically from the first (A) in not being an independent clause (shades of symmetrophobia).

indicative verb (imperfect with *waw* consecutive in Hebrew), and both have single direct objects related to each other: "and-he-found a-ship"; "and-he-paid her-fare."[27] The content moves sequentially, and the surroundings secure the structure. At the center of the chiasm (D), the participial phrase "returning (to) Tarshish" centers the disobedience of Jonah. The word "(to) Tarshish" forges a verbal link with A and A', and the participle "returning" (*bā'â*) appears again as the infinitive (*lābô'*)in A'.[28] In addition to its repetitions, the last line obliquely introduces new characters and so anticipates the next episode. The phrase "with-them," minus an antecedent, is a metonym for the sailors (even as "their" functioned for the Ninevites in 1:2). At the end, the disobedience of the one man Jonah involves an unnamed nautical community "returning to-Tarshish."

Summary. Yhwh has commanded Jonah directly (1:2); Jonah has responded indirectly (1:3). If speech gives the divine character immediacy and authority, narration gives the human character distance and diminishment. What the narrated discourse indicates, the content substantiates. Jonah sets distance; he runs away. The distancing first becomes apparent when his ostensibly obedient response, "and-arose," leads not to "and-went" but "to-flee." The process continues with the directive "to-Tarshish" opposing the directive "to Nineveh." The occurrence of "to-/ (to) Tarshish" in the beginning (A), middle (D), and end (A') of the chiasm underscores the antithesis. In fleeing "to-Tarshish" Jonah is not going to Nineveh according to the word of Yhwh.[29] Nevertheless, the phrase "from-the-presence-of Yhwh" encircles Jonah's flight (A and A'). It adds emphatic irony.[30] The divine presence from which he flees

---

27. The Hebrew possessive signifies feminine gender, "her-fare" (*sekārāh*), and thus refers to the ship (also feminine gender). Translations ignore this reference by reading "the fare" (RSV, NJV, NAB) or "his fare" (NRSV, NEB, JB). Yet the nuance may underscore the magnitude of Jonah's action; he has financed an entire ship for disobedience. See Sasson, *Jonah*, 83. Moreover, the nuance attributes life to the ship itself, in keeping with her animated responses in 1:4, and it contributes to feminine (and female) imagery in the story; cf. the fish as feminine gender (2:2).

28. Translating the Hebrew verb *bô'* in 1:3 as "return" rather than the usual "go" (e.g., RSV, NRSV, NJV, NAB) avoids confusion with the Hebrew verb *hlk* (go) in 1:2; cf. Sasson, *Jonah*, 82–84, and the translation "bound" in JB and NEB. Yet to translate *bô'* as "return" sets up possible confusion with the verb *šûb* (return) in 1:13; 3:8, 10. See below.

29. Whether accidental or not, the center occurrence of the phrase "(to) Tarshish" has no directional construct. The preposition "to" is supplied in translation. The grammatical difference from the occurrences at the beginning and end resonates with the structural singularity of the center.

30. For irony in Jonah, cf. Good, *Irony in the Old Testament*, 39–55.

encloses him. What the words proclaim, the structure subverts. Jonah is trapped in flight, and his action implicates innocent sailors.

Throughout this handsome chiasm generous repetitions produce regularity, rhythm, and emphasis. Ample variations add nuances and enable movement. Together repetition and variation disclose meaning. They produce antithesis and irony. Thereby structure and content redirect the plot. But the redirection incorporates a gap: the failure to explain Jonah's flight. For that explanation the reader must wait.

B. EPISODE TWO (1:4-6)

Three incidents fill this episode: Yhwh's hurling of a storm upon the sea (1:4), the effect upon the sailors and Jonah (1:5), and the efforts of the captain to avert disaster (1:6).[31]

1. Storm upon the Sea (1:4)

In reporting Yhwh's counter to Jonah's disobedience, the incident opens with verbal overlap. The last word in the preceding verse (1:3) becomes the first word in this verse: ". . . Yhwh. Yhwh. . . ." The arrangement employs the rhetorical device of anadiplosis (literally, "repetition") to place end stress and initial stress upon the deity: "But-arose Jonah to-flee . . . from-the-presence-of Yhwh; but-Yhwh hurled. . . ."[32] By repeating the ending of verse 3, the beginning of verse 4 departs from usual Hebrew syntax in which verb precedes subject. Emphasis and contrast result. Divine activity begins to erode the distance that Jonah sought to put between himself and Yhwh, even though narrated discourse continues to thwart direct communication.

Changes in structure, style, and substance highlight the juxtaposition of Yhwh's action to Jonah's disobedience. From a handsome chiasm (1:3) the narrator turns to a modest sentence of three independent clauses, each with a different subject and verb:

> But-Yhwh hurled a-wind great to the-sea,
>
> and-there-was a-tempest great in-the-sea,
>
> and-the-ship thought to-break-up. (1:4).

---

31. Note that episode two corresponds to units 4, 5, and 6 of the external design.

32. The decision to translate the ambiguous particle *wa-* in the combination *waYhwh* as contrast ("But-Yhwh") derives from the content of the whole; cf. the discussion of *w-* above in 1:3.

The parallel adjectives "great" and the nouns "sea" join the first two clauses. The third clause has no verbal connections with these two but a syntactic link with the first. As the subject "Yhwh" precedes the verb "hurled," so the subject "ship" precedes the verb "thought." The beginning accents Yhwh; the end accents the ship. Three rhetorical devices sustain the attention given the ship: prosopopoeia, onomatopoeia, and assonance. Prosopopoeia attributes a human category to an inanimate object: "the-ship thought." Onomatopoeia uses words that sound like their meaning, namely boards cracking from the force of water: ḥiššebâ lehiššābēr (thought to-break-up).[33] Assonance identifies similar or identical sounds between the internal vowels of proximate words: the vowels i, e, a and i, a, e in ḥiššebâ lehiššābēr.[34] Focused on the ship, these devices underscore the terror of the storm hurled by Yhwh. They paint an unusual picture. Hence, a modest sentence acquires immodest proportions.

In verse 4, as in the preceding verse, the article wa (or we), generically translated "and," introduces each of the independent clauses. Such coordinate constructions exemplify the rhetorical device called parataxis: the placing side by side of clauses (or other grammatical elements) without regard to subordinate connections. The opposite device, called hypotaxis, subordinates clauses or phrases one to another. As I write this sentence, it illustrates hypotaxis. I write this sentence; it illustrates parataxis.[35] A common feature of Hebrew syntax, parataxis leaves open the exact relationship between clauses. Rhetorical critics do the same when they submit formal correspondent translations. So the rendering above of 1:4 demonstrates the principle to beg the question of how the three clauses interrelate. By contrast, a look at several "dynamic" equivalent translations shows the possibilities for hypotactic connections.[36] Sasson subordinates the second clause to the first but keeps the third independent:

---

33. Sasson, *Jonah*, 96.
34. See P. P. Saydon, "Assonance in Hebrew as a Means of Expressing Emphasis," *Biblica* 36 (1955): 36–50, 287–304.
35. See M. O'Connor, "Parataxis and Hypotaxis," *NPEPP*, 879–80; cf. Alter, *Art of Biblical Narrative*, esp. 5, 26, 118, 121, 135, 142; also Lanham, *Handlist of Rhetorical Terms*, 87–88, 108.
36. On formal correspondence versus dynamic equivalence, see chapter 4, note 46. The adjective "dynamic" appears throughout this book in quotation marks because, without a specified context, the word regrettably privileges one type of translation.

> The Lord, however, hurled such furious winds toward
> the sea that a powerful storm raged upon it; the ship
> expected itself to crack up.[37]

Allen keeps the first and second clauses independent but subordinates the third to the second:

> But Yahweh hurled a strong wind onto the sea; so vio-
> lent was the storm at sea that the ship thought it would
> break up.[38]

The NAB keeps the first and third clauses independent but subordinates the second to the third:

> The Lord, however, hurled a violent wind upon the sea,
> and in the furious tempest that arose the ship was on
> the point of breaking up.

These translations show the inevitable subjectivity involved in making hypotactic connections out of paratactic syntax.[39] Nevertheless, all the translations posit a principle of cause and effect. Yhwh's action in hurling a great wind (itself the effect of Jonah's disobedience) causes a storm at sea.[40] In turn, the storm, the effect of Yhwh's action, causes the ship to

---

37. Sasson, *Jonah*, 89.

38. Allen, *Books of Joel, Obadiah, Jonah and Micah*, 205; also NJV and NRSV.

39. See further the translation by Wolff. It begins by subordinating the second clause to the first: "Then Yahweh threw a (great) wind upon the sea, so that great waves sprang up in the sea." Next, it subordinates the third clause to the opening clause of the following verse (1:5): "When the ship threatened to break up, the seamen became afraid" (Wolff, *Obadiah and Jonah*, 105f).

40. As the parenthesis "(itself the effect of Jonah's disobedience)" notes, the causal pattern in 1:4 begins earlier. Jonah's disobedience (1:3) causes Yhwh's action (1:4). Yet his disobedience is itself the effect of Yhwh's imperatives; they cause him to flee. In turn, these imperatives are the effect of Yhwh's word (1:1); that word causes the imperatives. Yet that word is itself the effect of the narrator's discourse. This reasoning returns to the beginning of the narrative where cause and effect, effect and cause contend. Similarly, the reasoning moves forward from 1:4. The effect of the ship breaking up causes the fear of the sailors (1:5; cf. Wolff's translation), and on and on. From a deconstructionist perspective, the concept of cause and effect undermines itself continuously to leave indeterminate meanings. The process belongs to the rhetoric of metonymy (change of name). Cf. Culler, *On Deconstruction*, 86–88.

anticipate disintegration. Vocabulary supports the principle, linking verse 4 to what precedes and follows. The name "Yhwh," the adjective "great," and the noun "ship" carry over from earlier incidents (1:1, 2, 3). The noun "ship," the noun "sea," and the verb "hurl" carry over to the next incident (1:5).

2. Effect upon the Sailors and Jonah (1:5)

Another narrated incident continues the story as the sailors and Jonah respond to impending disaster. Six independent clauses divided in two sets of three each build contrast. Content and grammatical construction delimit the boundaries.[41]

> And-feared the-sailors,
>   and-they-cried, each-man to his-god(s),
>   and-they-hurled the-wares that (were) in-the-ship
>   to the-sea to-lighten from-upon-them.
> But-Jonah went-down to the-innards-of the-vessel,
>   and-he-lay-down,
>   and-he-slept. (1:5)

In 1:2 three commands of Yhwh initiate the plot. In 1:3 two matching sections of three clauses, each around a center, give the response of Jonah. In 1:4 three independent clauses report the activity of Yhwh and its consequences. Now in 1:5 three verbs describing the sailors (feared, cried, hurled) balance three describing Jonah (went-down, lay-down, slept).[42] The first two verbs about the sailors, "they-feared" and "they-cried," occur for the first time; the third, "they-hurled," carries over from 1:4 where it was used for Yhwh. The verbs about Jonah work inversely in relationship to their surroundings. The first, "he-went-down," carries over from 1:3 where it was used for Jonah. The last two, "he-lay-down" and "he-slept,"

---

41. For a different view, cf. the analysis of Jonathan Magonet, *Form and Meaning: Studies in Literary Technique in the Book of Jonah* (Sheffield: Almond Press, 1983), 57. It disregards internal coherence to divide 1:5 into three parts belonging to different sections of a proposed concentric scheme. On this scheme, see the Excursus.

42. According to the classic work of Axel Olrik (upon which Gunkel relied), the structural pattern of three clauses typifies folk narrative ("Epic Laws of Folk Narrative," *The Study of Folklore*, ed. Alan Dundes [Englewood Cliffs, N.J.: Prentice-Hall, 1965], 132f). One must be cautious, however, about applying Olrik's laws universally. For a discussion with reference to biblical narratives, see, e.g., John Van Seters, *Abraham in History and Tradition*, 131–34; 160–61; cf. Niditch, *Folklore and the Hebrew Bible*, 15.

appear for the first time. Such artistic shaping lends rhythm and logic to the developing story.

Within the symmetry, asymmetry takes over. Length, syntax, and content provide the contrasts. The first set of three clauses describing the sailors starts with a simple verb and subject: "and-feared the-sailors." The second clause lengthens somewhat. A phrase that specifies individual action accompanies the verb: "and-they-cried, each-man to his-god(s)." The third clause lengthens extensively. The object of its verb is followed by a relative clause plus an infinitive clause of purpose: "and-they-hurled the-wares that (were) in-the-ship to the-sea to-lighten from-upon-them." The second set of three clauses returns to Jonah to pose another antithetic relationship.[43] A syntactic change in which the subject "Jonah" precedes the verb "went-down" (cf. 1:4) immediately opposes him to the sailors. Five words reporting his descent constitute the first clause: "But-Jonah went-down to the-innards-of the-vessel."[44] Single words constitute the second and third clauses: "and-he-lay-down," "and-he-slept." Differences in length and content between the two sets of clauses yield differences in meaning. On the deck the sailors move from inner emotion to outward cry to vigorous action; below the deck Jonah moves from action to inaction to total withdrawal. As they increase, he decreases. Offsetting the symmetry of the sets, the asymmetry sharpens the antithesis between the sailors and Jonah.

The portrait of Jonah contains still other contrasts. First, the syntactic change in which the subject "Jonah" precedes the verb "went-down" recalls the same arrangement when the subject "Yhwh" preceded the verb "hurled" (1:4). The parallel suggests increasing opposition between the major characters; they have entered a power struggle.[45] Second, Jonah asleep during the storm contrasts with the alert ship that thinks itself to be breaking up (1:4). The animate and the inanimate reverse to diminish him yet again. Third, by going to sleep in the innards of the vessel, Jonah has in effect reduced himself to an object. He has replaced the wares that the sailors hurled to the sea.

---

43. Cf. the antithetic relationship between Yhwh's command (1:2) and Jonah's response (1:3), see note 22 above.

44. In his marvelous study of Hebrew rhetoric, Messer Leon referred only once to Jonah. He cited 1:5 as exhibiting a type of synecdoche in which a plural form carries a singular meaning. The text says Jonah went down into the "sides" (or innards) of the vessel. Messer Leon comments, "that is, had descended into one of the two sides of the ship" (*The Book of the Honeycomb's Flow*, 509).

45. See Magonet, *Form and Meaning*, 21.

The vocabulary of the incident mixes the old and the new. The verb "went-down" (*yrd*), first used for Jonah's physical flight to Joppa (1:3), now applies to his psychological escape in the innards of the vessel (1:5). The noun "ship" (*'oniyyâ*), first the inanimate object of Jonah's finding (1:3) and then the personified subject of the verb "think" (*hiššebâ*, 1:4), now figures as the repository of the wares (1:5a). The parallel noun "vessel" (*sepînâ*), new to the story, performs a similar service for Jonah. Its innards hold him. The verb "hurl" (*twl*) with the phrase "to the sea," already used for Yhwh's activity (1:4), now describes the sailors' behavior. They emulate the deity as they seek to counter the effects of the great wind. The infinitive "to lighten" (*lehāqēl*), new to the story, appears without a specified object. Translators usually add the pronoun "it,"[46] leaving the reader to supply the antecedent. Commentators often identify "it" as the ship (or its load) that is to be lightened from upon the sailors.[47] Yet the nearest antecedent is not "ship" but "sea" (*yām*): "to-the-sea to-lighten from-upon-them." Thus syntax implies that the sailors try to appease the sea (a deity?) by sacrificing their wares. This interpretation resonates with the line, "they-cried, each-man to his-god(s)."

Unlike the preceding narration (1:3, 4), verse 5 contains no internal repetitions. Subject matter does not account altogether for the difference. For instance, the word *'oniyyâ* (ship, 1:5a) might well have been repeated for Jonah's sleeping place (1:5b) instead of the new word *sepînâ* (vessel). A rhetorical critic ponders this total lack of repetition. Perhaps it sharpens the antithesis between the sailors and Jonah. They do not even share words. Whatever the reason, asymmetry in vocabulary joins asymmetry in length, syntax, and content to skew the symmetry of structure. Disjunction characterizes the incident.

3. Efforts of the Captain (1:6)

The appearance of a new character, the captain of the ship, sets the boundaries and content of the third incident. Introduced by the narrator, he enters Jonah's space below deck to bridge the separation from the sailors on deck. Two verbs and the repetition of the phrase "to-him" underscore his direct encounter with Jonah:

---

46. E.g., RSV, NRSV, and NJV.
47. E.g., Sasson, *Jonah*, 89; Wolff, *Obadiah and Jonah*, 112; Allen, *Books of Joel, Obadiah, Jonah and Micah*, 206.

And-drew-near to-him the-captain-of the-mariners[48]
and-he-said to-him.

The captain is the first human character to speak. Three kinds of sentences organize his speech: exclamatory, imperative, and declarative. They progress in length, a development comparable to Yhwh's command in 1:2 with which they share vocabulary.

What to-you, sleeping!
Arise, call to your-god.
Perhaps will-favor the-god to-us so-not we-perish. (1:6)

Particles introduce the first and third sentences. The interjection "what" (*mah*) indicates surprise, even indignation, at Jonah sleeping. It bids the hearers (Jonah and the reader) to pay heed. The particle "perhaps" (*'ûlay*) conveys hope in the presence of danger. A possibility, but not a guarantee, exists that Jonah's deity will save all the threatened characters. That possibility depends, however, upon obedience from (disobedient) Jonah.[49] Between the surprise and the hope, the exclamation and the declarative, lies the imperative. It ironically echoes Yhwh. Using the device of asyndeton, the captain orders Jonah to "arise, call" to the god whose own command, "arise . . . call," Jonah has already spurned. In the words of a foreign captain Jonah hears again the divine command. But he remains silent and the captain disappears. Though his cameo appearance has not relieved the crisis, it has awakened Jonah.

C. EPISODE THREE (1:7-16)

Four incidents fill this episode: a decision by the sailors (1:7), a conversation between them and Jonah (1:8-9), their continuing efforts to avert disaster (1:10-13), and their resolution of the crisis (1:14-16).[50]

1. Decision by the Sailors (1:7)

A unique vocabulary about casting lots delimits the first incident. After the introductory line, the discourse divides between direct and narrated,

---

48. The translation "mariners" (*hōbēl*) signifies a different Hebrew word from that translated "sailors" (*mallāhîm*) in 1:5.

49. The adjective "disobedient" in parentheses suggests an imbalance of knowledge between the captain and the reader. The latter knows what the former does not and so perceives the irony.

50. Note that episode three corresponds to units 7 and 8 of the external design.

the latter confirming and advancing the former. The content focuses upon the sailors until the end where it switches to Jonah.

> And-they-said, each-man to his-neighbor:
>> "Come and-let-us-cast lots
>>
>> and-let-us-know
>> on-whose-account the-evil the-this (is) to-us."
>
> And-they-cast lots
>> and-cast the-lot upon Jonah. (1:7)

The sailors once "cried, each-man to his-god" (1:5); now "they said, each-man to his-neighbor." This time their very words are recorded. With hortatory speech they propose to one another the casting of lots to determine the culprit of the evil. Following their speech, the narrator reports that they carried out their exhortation. As once they hurled wares into the sea after they cried to the god, so now they cast lots after they speak to one another.

Repetition of the verb "cast" (*npl*) and its subject "lot(s)" (*gôrālôt*) unites the direct and narrated discourse. The first hortatory, "Let-us-cast lots," leads to the declarative "and-they-cast lots." The second hortatory, "Let-us-know on-whose-account the-evil . . ." leads to the declarative "and-cast the-lot upon Jonah."[51] Along the way, the sailors' choice of the word "evil" (*rā'â*) to connote their experience plays off its use by Yhwh to describe the Ninevites (1:2). The shift in usage indicates how successfully Jonah has diverted the plot. Yet ironically upon him now falls accountability for the evil. At the end of the incident the objective phrase "upon Jonah" stands apart from the repetition "cast the-lot" to single out the culprit. The climactic phrase lays end-stress "upon Jonah."[52]

2. Conversation between the Sailors and Jonah (1:8-9)

Having identified Jonah as the culprit, the sailors begin to question him. In this second incident he answers them, thereby producing the first

---

51. Many translations lose the threefold repetition of the Hebrew verb *npl* by rendering the first two occurrences as "cast" and this third one as "fell" or "singled" (e.g., NJV, RSV, NRSV, NEB, NAB).
52. On end-stress, cf. Olrik, "Epic Laws of Folk Narrative," 136.

dialogue in the story.[53] The questions and answers relate inversely.[54] The sailors ask about the culprit (A) and about Jonah's identity (B). He answers with his identity (B') and hints at his culpability (A'). The arrangement traps Jonah within the evil he has wrought and the god he fears.

And-they-said to-him,

> **A** "Tell, please, to-us
>   on-whose account the-evil the-this (is) to-us?
> **B** What (is) your-occupation
>   and-from-where have-you-come?
>   What (is) your-land
>   and-where from-this people (are) you?"

And-he-said to-them,

> **B'** "A-Hebrew (am) I.
> **A'** And-Yhwh, God-of the-heavens,
>   I (am) fearing
>   who made the-sea and-the-dry-land. (1:8-9)"

The sailors' first question repeats almost verbatim the second half of their hortatory speech:

1:7	1:8
and-let-us know	Tell, please, to-us (*lānû*)
on-whose-account (*bešellemî*)	on-whose account (*ba'ašer lemî*)
the-evil the-this (*hārā'â hazzō't*)	the-evil the-this (*hārā'â hazzō't*)
(is) to-us (*lanû*).	(is) to-us (*lānû*)?

A few Septuagintal manuscripts omit in 1:8 the section repeated from 1:7. They move directly from, "Tell, please, to-us," to the second question, "What is your-occupation"? Some critics follow suit.[55] They reason that with the casting of lots the sailors already know that Jonah is the culprit. Yet the two occurrences of the words belong to different settings. The first time the sailors speak to one another before they know the identity

---

53. Bar-Efrat observes that in biblical narrative virtually all dialogue is duologue. A group such as the sailors constitutes a collective figure (*Narrative Art in the Bible*, 96). On dialogue, see further Alter, *Art of Biblical Narrative*, 63–87.

54. George M. Landes discerned this relationship.

55. E.g., Wolff, *Obadiah and Jonah*, 105, 107; Julius A. Bewer, *Jonah*, ICC (Edinburgh: T. & T. Clark, 1912), 35.

of the culprit. Their query has a general referent. The second time the sailors speak to Jonah after the lot casting has identified him as the culprit. Their query has a specific referent. Rather than being a gloss, the repeated words in 1:8 link incidents as they advance the plot.[56]

The repetitions lead to new speech that seeks new information:

> What (*mah*) (is) your-occupation
>> and-from-where (*ûmē'ayin*) have-you-come?
>
> What (*māh*) (is) your-land
>> and-where from-this (*we'ê mizzeh*) people (are) you? (1:8b)

Alternation of the particles *mah* and *m* in the four questions forms a litany of alliteration. Its staccato effect achieves force and urgency. The sailors pile questions upon Jonah; they press him for an answer. Their words speak their panic.

Three times Jonah has been addressed. The command of Yhwh led to his flight (1:2). The command of the captain met with his silence (1:6). But this time he is trapped, and the interrogative mood accomplishes what the imperative has not.[57] Jonah speaks. As "they-said to-him" (1:8a), so now "he-said to-them" (1:9a). The taciturn, recalcitrant, enigmatic character begins to reveal himself. Or does he? His first answer addresses the last of the four questions, a rhetorical device known as *hysteron proteron* (literally, "the latter as the former").[58] Five syllables form each set; a pronoun at each end gives the stress. The sailors ask:

	a		**b**
(*we'ê*)	*mizzeh*	*'am*	*'āttâ*
(and-where)	from-this	people	you

Jonah answers:

	a'	**b'**
	'ibrî	*'ānōkî*
	a-Hebrew	I

---

56. This issue shows rhetorical criticism interacting with textual criticism and historical criticism. Cf. also Sternberg's study on repetition (*Poetics of Biblical Narrative*, 365–440).

57. The effect of the interrogative mood upon Jonah foreshadows developments in Jonah 4. See chapter 9.

58. See Sasson, *Jonah*, 115.

The rhyme (*'ibrî 'ānōkî*) pleases the ear as it sounds Jonah's national identity. Yet two words hardly suffice to answer four questions.
Jonah continues, turning from the sailors' questions about his identity
(B') to their question about his culpability (A'). Obliquely he answers.

> "And-Yhwh, God-of the-heavens,
>   I (am) fearing
> who made the-sea and-the-dry-land." (1:9b)

The answer abounds in ironies of genre, setting, content, and structure.
Jonah makes a confession of faith in a noncultic setting to non-Yhwhistic
sailors.[59] He utters conventional speech in an unconventional situation.
The concepts heaven, sea, and dry land identify Yhwh as god of the cosmos. They constitute a merism (literally, division"), a rhetorical device
whereby the whole is divided into its parts.[60] Jonah proclaims the all-
encompassing power of Yhwh even while seeking to flee from the divine
presence (cf. 1:3). But rather than tell the sailors he is fleeing Yhwh, he
uses the ambiguous verb "fear" in a first person participial construction:
"I (am) fearing" (*'anî yārē'*). The narrator has already used this verb to
connote the fright of the sailors (1:5; cf. 1:10) and later will use it to report
their worship (1:16). On the lips of Jonah the verb sounds an uncertain
note. Tucked between cosmic descriptions of Yhwh, the report "I (am)
fearing" obscures Jonah's culpability.[61] Nevertheless, the structure of his
own sentence traps him. In splitting the theological formula "Yhwh God-
of the-heavens . . . who made the-sea and-the-dry-land," Jonah surrounds
himself with the God he is fearing. The splitting illustrates the rhetorical
device *hyperbaton* (literally "transposed"), the separation of words that
usually belong together. The arrangement recalls the narrator's surrounding of Jonah's flight from Yhwh with the presence of Yhwh (1:3).
But how much stronger is the irony now because Jonah's own words
undercut him.

---

59. On the genre "confession of faith," see Erhard S. Gerstenberger, *Psalms: Part 1
with an Introduction to Cultic Poetry*, FOTL 14 (Grand Rapids, Mich.: William B. Eerdmans, 1988), 246.
60. See Jože Krašovec, "Merism—Polar Expression in Biblical Hebrew," *Biblica* 64
(1983): 231–39. Note the difference between the devices of merism (Latin, merismus) and
synecdoche. Merism means the division of the whole into its parts; synecdoche means the
substitution of parts for the whole. For examples of the latter, see the discussion of 1:5
above. For the two devices used in tandem, see the discussion of 3:7 in chapter 8.
61. Cf. Alter's observation that direct speech "may be more a drawn shutter than an
open window" (*Art of Biblical Narrative*, 116f).

3. Continuing Efforts to Avert Disaster (1:10-13)

Interrupting the dialogue, the narrator plays off the verb "fear" (*yr'*) to relate that the situation has worsened for the sailors. If before the lot casting "they-were-afraid" (1:5), after Jonah's confession "and-were-afraid the-men a-fear great" (1:10a). As the verb and its cognate object with the intensifying adjective "great" encircle the subject "men," so emphatically fear captures them. The form and content of the sentence encloses the meaning to introduce a tightly constructed third incident. Repetition seals the structure and the stress.

And-were-afraid the-men a-fear great.

And-they-said to-him:
    "What (*mah*) (is) this you-have-done!"
        for (*kî*) knew the-men
        that (*kî*) from-the-presence-of Yhwh he (was) fleeing
        for (*kî*) he-told to-them. (1:10)

And-they-said to-him:
    "What (*mah*) shall-we-do to-you
        and-may-be-quiet the-sea from-upon-us?"
        ×
Indeed (*kî*) the-sea (was) going and-storming. (1:11)
        *

And-he-said to-them:
    "Pick-up-me and-hurl-me to the-sea
    and-may-be-quiet the-sea from-upon-you,
    ×
        for (*kî*) knowing (am) I
        that (*kî*) on-account-of-me
        the-storm the-great the-this (is) upon-you." (1:12)
And-digged the-men to-return (*šûb*)[62] to the-dry-land,
    and-not were-they-able.
Indeed (*kî*) the-sea (was) going and-storming upon-them. (1:13)
        *

The abundance of markers requires description and interpretation. "Once you have demonstrated structure in the very words of the text itself, then describe in clear prose what the diagram shows and interpret both diagram and description."[63]

---

    62. Note that the Hebrew verb *šûb* translated "to return" is not the same as the verb *bô'* translated "returning" in 1:3.
    63. See the guideline in chapter 4.

a. Narrated and direct discourse alternate in the incident. The narrated forms the limits (1:10a and 1:13); it also provides introductions and commentary throughout. Twice the formula "and-they-said to-him" prefaces the sailors' words (1:10b, 11a), with the second occurrence indicating continuation of a single speech broken by narrated explanation. The formula "and-he-said to-them" prefaces Jonah's reply. The extensive direct discourse continues the dialogue (cf. 1:8-9) between the sailors and Jonah.

b. The sailors' speech and Jonah's reply involve three kinds of sentences. They use the exclamatory and the interrogative (1:10c, 11b); he uses the imperative (1:12b). By position and content the interrogative mediates between the other two. The particle "what" (*mah*)[64] and the verb "do" ('*śh*) connect it to the exclamation. "What (is) this you-have-done!" leads to "what shall-we-do to-you?" Jonah's deed spurs the men to seek action. The remaining half of their question states the desired outcome: "and-may-be-quiet the-sea from-upon-us." The words lead to Jonah's imperative that begins, "pick-up-me . . . ;" it concludes, "and-may-be-quiet the-sea from-upon-you." Repetition and placement link three kinds of sentences.

c. Repetition also obtains between the narrated discourse in the middle (1:11) and in the end (1:13). Both report, "Indeed the-sea (was) going and-storming." The participles "going" and "storming" form an hendiadys (literally, "one through two"), a rhetorical device in which two words are joined by a conjunction to express a single idea that would otherwise be expressed by a qualifier and substantive. Rather than saying the sea was "storming greatly," the narrator gives parallel images, "going and storming." The device and its repetition underscore the intensity of the situation.

d. The particle *kî* figures prominently in the structure and the meaning.[65] Its first occurrences in each of the four verses form a pattern that alternates between the deictic or demonstrative use and the emphatic or asseverative use (a b a b). "For (*kî*) knew the-men" (1:10) is deictic; "indeed (*kî*) the-sea" (1:11) is emphatic; "for (*kî*) knowing I" (1:12) is deictic; "indeed (*kî*) the-sea" (1:13) is emphatic. The deictic uses precede the verb "know" (*yd'*) to accent vital information and account for motivation. They introduce the reason for the men's exclamation (1:10) and for Jonah's imperative (1:12). Regular syntax (verb preceding subject) presents the first

---

64. *Mah* in 1:10c and 1:11b continues the staccato effect of the sailors' first words to Jonah in 1:8.

65. On *kî*, cf. note 16 above; cf. esp. A. Schoors, "The Particle כי," 242–48.

reason: "for knew the-men." Alternate syntax (participle preceding pronoun, cf. 1:9) presents the second: "for knowing (am) I." Besides fashioning an order parallel to the regular syntax, the alternate calls attention to Jonah's taking the blame for the evil inflicted upon the sailors.[66]

e. The emphatic uses of *kî* introduce the refrains that stress the crisis: "Indeed, the-sea (was) going and-storming." Though identical in vocabulary, the refrains may or may not be identical in discourse. For certain the second occurrence (1:13) is narrated discourse. The first (1:11) may be either narrated or direct.[67] If it belongs to the men, a pattern of inverted discourse (a b b' a') results among the four *kî* clauses (in addition to the alternating pattern of the deictic and the emphatic). The inversion begins (a) with narrated discourse about what the men knew (1:10). It moves (b) to direct discourse as the sailors report on the raging sea (1:11). It continues (b') with direct discourse as Jonah says he knows (1:12). It ends (a') with narrated discourse about the raging sea (1:13). On the other hand, if the first occurrence of the phrase "indeed, the-sea (was) going and-storming" belongs to the narrator, then no distinctive pattern of discourse emerges among these *kî* clauses. But then the refrains about the sea form exact parallels in discourse and in vocabulary.

f. The particle *kî* appears three more times. The first instance (1:10) follows the verb "know" to introduce an objective or subordinate clause: "that (*kî*) from-the-presence-of Yhwh he (was) fleeing."[68] The content repeats information and vocabulary from episode one (1:3). The second instance, which follows immediately (1:10), directs attention to vital information: "for he-told to-them." The content fills a gap in the story.[69] Nothing Jonah or the narrator has said heretofore informs the reader that the men know of his flight from Yhwh. Indeed (*kî!*), in his confession of faith Jonah has sounded an ambiguous note by using the participle "fear-

---

66. Citing Norman Snaith and Masoretic accents, Sasson develops this point (*Jonah*, 125). Note further that the reversal of pronoun and participle here in 1:12 sets up a chiastic relationship with the participle and pronoun in 1:9: "I fearing" (*'anî yārē'*, 1:9); "knowing I" (*yôdēa' 'anî*, 1:12). This structural relationship tied to the content suggests that Jonah is at cross purposes with himself.

67. For interpretation of the phrase as narrated discourse, see, e.g., RSV, NRSV, NJV, NAB, NEB; also Wolff, *Obadiah and Jonah*, 106. For interpretation as direct discourse, see Allen, *Books of Joel, Obadiah, Jonah and Micah*, 206, who does not explain his choice; see also Sasson, *Jonah*, 123f, who does explain.

68. On this common usage, see A. Schoors, "The Particle כִּי," 253–56.

69. On gaps see the discussions of Iser and Sternberg in chapter 3; also see chapter 9, pp. 203, 221f.

ing" rather than "fleeing" (1:9). Now in clarifying the situation, the narrator also accounts for the fear of the men (1:10a). The third instance of *kî* (1:12) functions as the first. It follows the verb "know" to introduce an objective or subordinate clause whose content repeats information: "that (*kî*) on-account-of-me the-storm the-great the-this (is) upon-you." The word "on-account-of-me" plays on the sailors' word, "on-whose-account" (1:7a, cf. 8a). In all three instances the content of the *kî* clauses tidies up the story. As they join the other four appearances of the particle, the resulting seven form a concatenation that builds a constant refrain. Ordered repetitions of *kî* in every verse produce rhythm, rhyme, and reason. This rhetorical device persuades the eye, the ear, and the heart.[70] A little word harbors a multitude of meanings.

g. Pronominal objects dot the wordscape. Of the twelve instances, three perform a conventional task. They identify objects of the verb "say" to introduce direct discourse: "to-him" (1:10), "to-him" (1:11), "to-them" (1:12). Two other instances of the pronoun "them" occur in narrated discourse at the ends of verses: "to-them" (1:10) and "upon-them" (1:13). The latter receives double stress. It stands outside the exact repetition of the sentence, "Indeed the-sea (was) going and-storming" (1:11), and it concludes the entire incident. In both respects it parallels the phrase "upon Jonah" at the close of 1:7. The pronoun "them" calls attention to the sailors. Within direct discourse come seven more pronominal references. The sailors pit "to-you" against "from-upon-us" (1:11). Jonah answers by pitting "me" against "you" in pairs: first, "pick-up-me and-hurl-me" and "from-upon-you" (1:12a); second, "on-account-of-me" and "upon-you" (1:12b). The extensive roster of pronominal objects produces rhythm in Hebrew sounds. For example, the sound "e" characterizes words translated "them": *lāhem* (to-them), *'alêhem* (to-them), and *'alêhem* (upon-them). It also appears in words translated "you": *mē'alêkem* (from-upon-you) and *'alêkem* (upon-you). The sound "i" characterizes words translated "me": *śā'ûnî* (pick-up-me), *wahatîlunî* (and-hurl-me), and *bešellî* (on-account-of-me). Overall, the sounds, positions, juxtapositions, and preponderance of twelve pronominal objects dot the wordscape as they interrelate the characters.

h. A play on the consonants l, h, s, y, b and l, h, y, b, s in the phrase "to-return (*lehāšîb*) to-the-dry-land (*'el hayyabbāšâ*)" (1:13) draws attention to the infinitive and its object. Together they stress the goal of the

---

70. Note that the phrase "the eye, the ear, and the heart" is a merism signifying the reader.

sailors to seek refuge from the tempestuous sea. Each word sends and receives meanings from the larger narrative. The root *šûb* (to-return) anticipates its theological use for the Ninevites (3:8, 10) and for God (3:10). The root *ybš* (dry) recalls Jonah's confession (1:9) that Yhwh controls not only the sea in which the sailors "dig" but also the dry land for which they aim. Though they do not reach it, Jonah himself will eventually be vomited upon it (2:11). And still later the root *ybš* will reappear to dry up the plant under which Jonah finds shade (4:7). The consonantal play in the phrase "to-return to the-dry-land" accents words that send thematic signals into the larger story.[71]

i. The noun "sea" (*yām*) and the verb "hurl" (*twl*) play pivotal roles. They evoke past actions: "And/but-Yhwh hurled a-wind great to the-sea and-there-was a-storm great in-the-sea. . . ." (1:4); the sailors "hurled the-wares that (were) in-the-ship to-the-sea to-lighten [the sea] from-upon-them" (1:5). When the mariners tell Jonah that they seek to quiet the sea (1:11), he picks up on their words. "Pick-up-me, and-hurl-me to the-sea . . . ," he says (1:12). Once when he slept in the innards of the vessel, he became in effect a substitute for the discarded wares. Now he insists that this ware, namely himself, be hurled to the sea "and-may-be-quiet the-sea from-upon you."[72] Having confessed that Yhwh made the sea (1:9), Jonah proposes appeasement through sacrifice. As culprit and human offering, he can accomplish what inanimate sacrifices have not. Crucial to the incident, the verb "hurl" and the noun "sea" flow from earlier events as they prepare for things to come (cf. 1:15).

j. Mirroring in miniature the structure and movement of the entire episode, this incident features the sailors over Jonah. They set the boundaries. The narrated framework describes first their feeling and last their action: "they-were-afraid" (1:10) and "they-digged" (1:12). The boundaries do not bode well because they move from fear to failure. The imagery of "digging" oars into the water "to-return to the-dry-land" (hardly good nautical procedure) depicts desperation. Succinctly the narrator reports their impotence: "and-not were-they-able." Nothing the sailors have said or done has alleviated their great fear. Though they surround Jonah, his disobedient behavior continues to control their lives. Within this nar-

---

71. Cf. Sasson, *Jonah*, 131; also Halpern and Friedman, "Composition and Paronomasia in the Book of Jonah," 83, who deem this play "clever" but "thematically inconsequential."

72. On Jonah's ironic use of the verb "hurl" (*twl*), cf. Good, *Irony in the Old Testament*, 45.

rated framework they press him for a solution. "What shall-we-do to-you . . . ?" His reply (1:12) fits the complexities of his character. The one who has disobeyed the commands of Yhwh and ignored the commands of the captain issues his own. "Pick-up-me and-hurl-me to the-sea. . . ." Acknowledging his own culpability, "for on-account-of me . . . ," Jonah seems willing to pay the price. He offers himself as sacrifice to save the sailors. The solution appears magnanimous, courageous, and altruistic. But appearance masks continuing disobedience. If neither flight nor sleep has saved Jonah from the divine imperatives, then perhaps drowning will. Concern for the sailors camouflages self-concern. Altruism discloses, even as it hides, egocentricism. Deception and irony abound in Jonah's character to entrap the sailors who surround him.[73]

Summary. Though not exhaustive, these observations about the third incident of episode three suffice to demonstrate rhetorical analysis as they illuminate treasures in Jonah. Description and interpretation of the diagram—its structure, substance, and style—has yielded abundant meanings.

4. Resolution of the Crisis (1:14-16)

The fourth incident resolves the crisis. The sailors are in dire straits. Having failed in their efforts to reach dry land, they try another way: "And-they-called (*qr'*) to (*'el*) Yhwh." The action and the language recall their first appearance when they "cried (*z'q*), each-man, to (*'el*) his-god" (1:5). It also echoes the captain's command to Jonah, ". . . call (*qr'*) to (*'el*) your-god" (1:6). The sailors do what Jonah did not. They pray. So another genre enters the story, the communal complaint song.[74] Its setting presumes an occasion of misfortune for a group. Addressed to God, the song may come from either the innocent or the penitent. The content covers petition, complaint, confession, reason, motivation, vow, description of distress, expression of confidence in God, reference to sacrifice, and

---

73. Jonah traps even scholars. Cf. Allen, who thinks that here Jonah "realizes his guilt before God" (*Books of Joel, Obadiah, Jonah, and Micah,* 210f); also Sternberg, who thinks that the story "starts by opposing a compassionate Jonah to a wrathful God . . ." (*Poetics of Biblical Narrative*), 56. On the latter, see chapter 9 on 4:2.

74. See Gerstenberger, *Psalms,* 245. Cf. Hermann Gunkel, *Einleitung in die Psalmen* (Göttingen: Vandenhoeck & Ruprecht, 1933), 117–39; A. R. Johnson, "The Psalms," *The Old Testament and Modern Study,* ed. H. H. Rowley (Oxford: The Clarendon Press, 1956), 166f; Aage Bentzen, *Introduction to the Old Testament I* (Copenhagen: G. E. C. Gad, 1958), 154–59.

thanksgiving for deliverance. These conventional features (the interest of form criticism) join the study of particularities (the interest of rhetorical criticism) to explicate the prayer.[75]

The introduction leads to the three components of invocation, petition, and motivation.

And-they-called to Yhwh and-they-said:

> *Invocation:* "Ah! (*'ānnâ*) Yhwh,
>
> *Petition:* Not (*'al-*), pray (*nā'*), let-us-perish
> for-the-*nepeš*-of the-man the-this;
> and-not (*we'al*) give upon-us blood innocent.
>
> *Motivation:* For (*kî*) you (*'attâ*), Yhwh,
> as (*ka'ašer*) you-wish you-do." (1:14).

Particles structure the sections and subsections. The invocation commences with the strong interjection *'annâ*, and the first petition with *'al*, adverb of negation, followed by *nā'*, word of entreaty.[76] The second petition repeats *'al*. A different sound, the particle *kî*, opens the motivation. Within it the particle *ka'ašer* lends alliteration and assonance.

Following the invocation, the petition makes two negative requests: that the sailors not perish because of Jonah and not be held responsible should he be innocent. They view their plight as double jeopardy. They perish if Jonah stays on board; they perish if they throw an innocent man overboard. In this bind they protest misfortune and plead for acquittal. And they do more. They recognize the power of Yhwh as motivation for their petition. Two of the verbs they use, "perish" and "do," have a history. Petitioning that they not "perish" (*'bd*), the sailors repeat the sentiment of the captain, "and-not we-perish" (*'bd*, 1:16).[77] Giving the motivation, they appropriate the verb "do" (*'śh*) that Jonah introduced when he described Yhwh as "God-of the-heavens . . . who made (*'āśâ*) the-sea and-the-dry-land" (1:9). The sailors first applied the verb to Jonah, "What (is) this you-have-done (*'āśîtā*)?" (1:10), but later shifted its power to themselves, "What shall-we-do (*mah na'aśê*) to-you?" (1:11). Now they return

---

75. On *ad hoc* prayers embedded in texts, see Moshe Greenberg, *Biblical Prose Prayer: As a Window to the Popular Religion of Ancient Israel* (Berkeley: University of California Press, 1983), 1–18, esp. 15–17.

76. On the particle *nā'*, see Sasson, *Jonah*, 132.

77. Cf. the discussion of the verb "perish" (*'bd*) in the external design (chapter 5, subsections d and e).

the power to Yhwh, "as you-wish you-do (*'āśîtā*)" (1:14). The placement of the Tetragrammaton likewise shapes their theology. "Yhwh" as vocative in the invocation and in the motivation surrounds the petition. Unlike Jonah, who flees from the presence of Yhwh (1:3, 10), the sailors beseech the deity, "Ah! Yhwh."[78] At the close, the independent pronoun increases the emphasis: "You (*'attâ*), Yhwh."

After their prayer the sailors speak no more; narrated actions conclude their appearance. Two sentences, each with three independent clauses, match structurally verses in episode two (cf. 1:4, 5). Within each sentence a single repetition links two of the three clauses. In 1:15 the word "the-sea" links the second and third, but not the first, clause. In 1:16 the divine name "Yhwh" links the first clause and the second, but not the third. The extremities of the combined sequence match in their singularity (A and A′) and the internal clauses match in their similarity (B and B′).

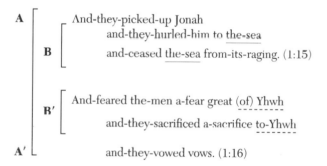

A
B
   And-they-picked-up Jonah
   and-they-hurled-him to the-sea
   and-ceased the-sea from-its-raging. (1:15)

B′
   And-feared the-men a-fear great (of) Yhwh
   and-they-sacrificed a-sacrifice to-Yhwh

A′
   and-they-vowed vows. (1:16)

The crisis is resolved. In Aristotelian terms change of fortune comes through reversal and recognition. Reversal is the change to "the opposite state of affairs."[79] The storm ceases (1:15). Recognition "is a change from ignorance to knowledge."[80] The sailors acknowledge Yhwh (1:16).

---

78. The contrast in meaning between the phrase "from-the-presence-of Yhwh" surrounding Jonah (1:3) and the vocative "Yhwh" surrounding the petition of the sailors (1:14) prompts a rhetorical reminder about the interpretation of structures. The first *inclusio* signifies the incongruity between what Jonah wants and what form and content ironically give. The second *inclusio* signifies the congruity between what the sailors seek and what form and content give. The difference in meaning illustrates the guideline that "a specific structure or device does not mean the same everywhere."

79. *Aristotle's Poetics*, 19.

80. Ibid, 20. Aristotle also mentions suffering, the result of "destructive or painful action," as a third element in plot. That element fits the plight of the sailors.

Rhetorical analysis explores further the particularities of this reversal and recognition.

The reversal (1:15) culminates a sequence of events beginning just after Jonah's attempted flight. It builds on the principle of cause and effect.[81] Throughout the sequence, repetition with variation forges links and propels change. The verb "hurl" (*twl*) and the noun "sea" (*yām*) remain constant images.

> But-Yhwh hurled a-wind great to-the-sea
> > and-there-was a-storm great in-the-sea. (1:4ab)

> And-they [the sailors]-hurled the-wares . . . to the-sea
> > to-lighten from-upon-them. (1:5c)

> Pick-up-me and-hurl-me to the-sea
> > that-may-be-quiet the-sea from-upon-you. (1:12b)

> And-they-picked-up Jonah and-they-hurled-him to the-sea
> > and-ceased the-sea from-its-raging. (1:15)

The double action by the sailors in 1:15 collects meanings from the preceding events. First, it counters the action by Yhwh (1:4ab). Hurling Jonah to the sea negates Yhwh's hurling of the wind upon the sea. Second, the hurling substitutes Jonah for the wares that the sailors once hurled to the sea to lighten from upon them (1:5c). By changing the object of their verb, the sailors achieve their goal. Third, their action fulfills the command and receives the promise made by Jonah (1:12b). Picking him up and hurling him to the sea stops the storm: "and-ceased the-sea from-its-raging." With various words the narrator, the sailors, and Jonah have all depicted the sea in an active state of raging and storming (1:11, 12, 13). Now the narrator reports that the sea returns to a passive state.[82] The personified sea loses its power to inflict danger, a loss signaling that the power was never its own but Yhwh's. In summary, the double action by the sailors, picking up and hurling, reverses the situation to "the opposite state of affairs."

81. Cf. Magonet, *Form and Meaning*, 16f.
82. Sasson shows that the verb '*md* (cease) connotes an involuntary state (*Jonah*, 136–37).

150

Reversal effects recognition. The sailors turn from their own gods (1:5) and from the divinity of the sea (1:5, 11) to worship Yhwh. Like the reversal their action effected, the recognition culminates a sequence of events. Repetition with variation again forges links and propels change. Throughout the sequence the sailors remain subjects of the verb "fear" ($yr^{^{,}}$).

    <u>and-feared</u> the-sailors (1:5a)

    <u>and-feared</u> the-men a-fear great (1:10a)

    <u>and-feared</u> the-men a-fear great (of) Yhwh. (1:16a)

True to its position, the middle clause mediates in content between the other two. In 1:10a the cognate object "fear" with the adjective "great" intensifies the fear first reported only in the verb at the beginning (1:5a). Object and adjective then reappear in the end (1:16a), but the addition of the objective phrase "(of) Yhwh" dramatically alters the meaning. Though in both 1:10a and 1:16a fear surrounds the men to control them, in the latter that fear changes from a negative emotion to a positive affirmation, from fright to worship of Yhwh. According to Aristotelian concepts, the sailors recognize "a change from ignorance to knowledge."

    The next lines specify the change. They make concrete the worship (fear) of Yhwh with activities that fit the *Sitz im Leben* of the communal complaint song (1:14). The use of cognate objects in all three lines reinforces the recognition, the change from ignorance to knowledge:

        And-feared the-men a-fear great (of) Yhwh
          and-they-sacrificed a-sacrifice to-Yhwh
          and-they-vowed vows. (1:16)

The clauses shrink from five to three to two words. So the sailors fade.[83] Narrated discourse and its brevity distance them even while touting their Yhwhistic credentials and assuring the reader that all is well for them. The sailors form but a subplot. Important as a foil to Jonah throughout episode three, they have at last overturned his controlling actions. Now they disappear from the story as he disappears into the sea. But given his failure so far to flee from the presence of Yhwh, the reader has reason to think Jonah might fail again. That thought moves into episode four.

    83. Cf. the shrinkage to two verbs when Jonah tries to disappear into the innards of the vessel (1:5).

EXCURSUS

Muilenburg cited two tasks for the rhetorical critic: delineating the boundaries of a literary unit and discerning the structure and configuration of its component parts. Jonah 1 has been used to teach these tasks. To assume, however, that the analysis set forth is the only valid one would be an injustice to the method, the riches of the text, and the reader. Not unlike music and art, a work of literature may embody numerous patterns and meanings. A single reader sees some at one time and others at another; multiple readers increase the possibilities. The resulting situation does not mean, however, that all readings are valid or that all valid readings are equally valid. The criterion of form-content adjudicates proposals. In general, proposals that account for all the *ipsissima verba* take precedence over those that attend to selected words, larger units, or themes. Accounting for all the words does not necessarily mean that each of them requires or invites commentary, but it does mean that no word(s) or larger unit(s) is passed over in order to impose a structure that would not otherwise be there. If several different proposals account for all the words, then one might decide to let them stand without further judgment. Another choice is to discern the one (or those) that best account for the *ipsissima verba*. But "best" is a slippery word—at best.[84]

Three proposals about sections in Jonah 1 illustrate differences among readings and ways of choosing among them. The first proposal I originally intended to offer. Rather than viewing 1:1-3 as episode one, I instead designated 1:1-2 as the prologue giving the command of Yhwh and so setting the plot in motion. Then 1:3-5 became episode one. It began with Jonah's disobedient response, continued with Yhwh's hurling the storm, and ended with the effect of the storm upon the sailors and Jonah. Narrated actions by Jonah marked the boundaries. At first, "and-arose Jonah" (1:3a); at last, "and-he-slept" (1:5h). Within these boundaries only narrated discourse occurred. By contrast, direct discourse surrounded the boundaries (1:2 and 1:6), thereby lending additional support to the perceived structure. The overall arrangement brought forth a pleasing interpretation. Opposite movements at opposite ends, "arose" and "slept," converged in meaning: physical and psychological flight from Yhwh. Moreover, three well-defined incidents filled the episode. A chiasm of six independent clauses about Jonah composes the first (1:3); a report in

---

84. The criterion of the "best" recalls the principle of Dworkin appropriated by Patrick and Scult; see chapter 2.

three independent clauses about Yhwh, the second (1:4); a set of three independent clauses about the sailors and three about Jonah, the third (1:5). This internal arrangement allowed yet another pleasing interpretation. Within the circle of Jonah's behavior (1:3a and 1:5h) Yhwh threatened disaster and the sailors worked to avoid it. If the crisis was to pass, then the encircling power of Jonah must be broken.

Though I continue to think this reading valid, I judge it less satisfactory than the one eventually chosen. In it, 1:1-3 constitutes episode one and 1:4-6 episode two. Several reasons tip the balance for the latter reading. First, Jonah's response (1:3) belongs with Yhwh's commands (1:2) rather than in a separate episode. Second, the hurling of the storm (1:4) initiates new action that brings responses from the sailors, Jonah, and the captain (1:5-6). His words engage the report about Jonah asleep. Third, the plot next turns away from the captain and Jonah to the sailors talking among themselves (1:7). Such considerations of content and structure moved me away from the reading just sketched to the analysis earlier offered. It takes precedence because it accounts more satisfactorily for all the parts and angles of the text.

A second proposal that gives a different reading begins with Lohfink's discovery of the chiasm in 1:3. This analysis is itself a model of rhetorical criticism, though not so named.[85] On the other hand, his view that 1·4-16 forms a similar concentric structure diverges sharply from rhetorical analysis. By resorting to themes and summaries, Lohfink posited the following structure:

A Framework (1:4-6)
B Two speeches by the sailors (1:7-8)
Center Confession of Jonah (1:9-10a)
B' Two speeches by the sailors (1:10a-11)
A' Framework (1:12-16)

He also cited parallel themes in the framework:

A	**A'**
beginning of the storm	end of the storm
storm hurled to the sea	Jonah hurled to the sea
sailors crying to God	sailors crying to Yhwh
sailors in fear	sailors in fear of Yhwh

85. Lohfink, "Jona ging zur Stadt hinaus (Jon 4:5)," 201.

Though these themes show parallels, they fail to encompass the content of what Lohfink calls the framework. The themes cited for A (1:4-6) cover only parts of the verses. Unaccounted for are the ship thinking to break up, the hurling of wares to the sea, the descent of Jonah to sleep, and the arrival of the captain to arouse him. Similarly, the themes cited for A' (1:12-16) cover only parts of the verses. Unaccounted for are the instructions of Jonah to the sailors, his explanation of their calamity, their effort to return to dry land, and its ineffectiveness. Besides, Jonah's answer to the sailors (1:12) belongs not in the framework but with their question to him (1:11). By removing his answer from B', however, Lohfink could claim a concentric "structure" for B C B'. It puts Jonah's confession in a center surrounded by two speeches of the sailors, each with two parts (1:7a and 8; 1:10b and 11ab). Like the framework (A and A'), this arrangement also leaves portions of the text unaccounted for: the narrated discourse about the casting of lots (1:7b), the sailors' fear (1:10a), their knowledge of Jonah (1:10c), and possibly the rage of the sea (1:11c). Lohfink's concentric structure passes over sections of the text in order to impose a structure not otherwise present. Rhetorical analysis it is not.

A third proposal offers another contrast among ways of reading. Inspired by Lohfink, Magonet held that 1:4-16a forms a concentric structure beginning with a narrative containing the word "fear" (1:4, 5a), centering in Jonah's confession of "fear" (1:9), and ending with a narrative containing the word "fear" (1:15, 16a).[86] To achieve this "structure" he relied upon themes, mixed genres, isolated words, and omitted what does not fit. He called both 1:5b and 1:14 "Prayer of the Sailors," though the former is but a narrative report and only the latter an actual prayer. For the center (1:9, 10a) he threw together direct speech by Jonah (1:9) and narrated report about the sailors (1:10a). Then he dropped the last two-thirds of 1:16, the narrated report of the sailors' sacrifice to Yhwh and their vows, deeming them a "necessary omission . . . to maintain the pattern."[87]

Magonet perceptively sees interplays on the verb "fear," but they do not sustain the concentric structure he proposed for 1:4-16a. Like Lohfink, he tended to impose or invent structure by themes, summaries, and omissions. In the process many insights emerged, and yet the

---

86. Magonet, *Form and Meaning*, 56f, 133. This study also builds on the analysis by Rudolf Pesch, "Zur konzentrischen Struktur von Jona 1," *Biblica* 47 (1966): 577–81.

87. Ibid., 56.

particularities of the text suffered. The inseparability of form-content in the *ipsissima verba* failed to receive its due.

Setting these three proposals alongside the rhetorical analysis given above serves didactic aims. The juxtaposition shows the complexities of the literature, eschews a single interpretation, cautions against claims for objectivity, and accents the role of the reader in making choices. Keeping these lessons in mind, the reader returns to the task at hand: rhetorical analysis of episode four in scene one.

7
Internal Structure
of Scene One (2:1-11)

EPISODE FOUR (2:1-11)

Episode four follows Jonah into the belly of a great fish where he prays to Yhwh before being vomited upon dry land.[1] A splendid chiasm of narrated discourse joins setting, vocabulary, and subject matter to delimit the boundaries. But the presence of a psalm within the narrative complicates structure and meaning, a matter of no small consequence for rhetorical analysis. A derivative issue affects the parts of the narrative. Does the movement into the fish (2:1a), in the fish (2:1b-10), and out of the fish (2:11) constitute three incidents, suggested by the expanded middle in contrast to the brevity of the beginning and end? Or, as set forth here, does the narrative constitute a single incident equivalent to the episode? This matter is of small consequence, though the psalm aggravates it.

A. A CHIASM OF NARRATED DISCOURSE (2:1, 2, 11)

Correspondences in repetition, location of words, and pairing of grammar shape the chiasm.

A   And-appointed Yhwh a-fish great to-swallow Jonah,

$$\overbrace{\text{and-was Jonah}}^{a} \overbrace{\text{in-the-belly-of the-fish}}^{b} \overbrace{\text{three days and-three nights.}}^{c}$$

B   and-was Jonah in-the-belly-of the-fish three days and-three nights.
     ×××××××××××××××

$$\overbrace{\text{And-prayed Jonah}}^{a'} \overbrace{\text{to Yhwh his-God}}^{d} \overbrace{\text{from-the-belly-of the-fish.}}^{b'}$$

B′   And-prayed Jonah to Yhwh his-God from-the-belly-of the-fish.
     ×××××××××××××××××××

A′   And-said Yhwh to-the-fish and-it-vomited Jonah to-the-dry-land. (2:1,2,11)

---

1. Note that this episode corresponds to unit 9 of the external design.

In the external segments (A and A') Yhwh as the subject of active verbs returns to the story for the first time since the hurling of the storm (cf. 1:4). "And-appointed Yhwh"; "and-said Yhwh." The verbs act upon the fish as object. In turn, the fish becomes subject, acting upon Jonah as object of the infinitive "to-swallow" and of the indicative "it-vomited." In the internal segments (B and B') Jonah becomes the subject of the verbs "was" and "prayed." The fish is an object in parallel prepositional phrases: "in-the-belly-of the-fish" and "from-the-belly-of the-fish."[2] These impressive relationships secure the structure within which variations appear. In A, but not in A', the adjective "great" modifies the fish. In B, but not in B', occurs the phrase "three-days and-three nights;" correspondingly, in B', but not in B, occurs the phrase "to Yhwh his-God." At the end of A', the phrase "to the-dry-land" lies outside the parallelism to A.

Throughout the chiasm an interchangeable sequence of cause and effect operates (cf. 1:5, 15).[3] It begins with Yhwh causing a fish to swallow Jonah, though that divine action is itself the effect of his having been thrown into the sea. The sequence continues with the effect of the swallowing, which is his residence in the belly of the fish. This effect causes him to pray. As effect, the prayer causes Yhwh to speak to the fish. As effect, the fish causes the vomiting up of Jonah. And that effect causes the scene to end—but the story to continue.

The noun "fish" (*dāg* or *dāgâ*) catches several meanings. In the extremities (A and A') it occurs between the words "Yhwh" and "Jonah." Placement matches function. The fish mediates divine action while keeping Yhwh and Jonah apart. As the tool of Yhwh, it relates to Jonah by the countermovements of ingestion and ejection: "to-swallow" (*liblōaʿ*) and "and-it-vomited (*wayyāqēʾ*)." They contrast death and life.[4] On the insides (B and B'), the function of the fish alters. No longer the mediator between Yhwh and Jonah, it becomes the repository for Jonah. As the belly lies within the fish, so the phrase "belly-of the-fish" lies within the belly of the chiasm. The images of descent (B) and ascent (B') fill the

2. Yet the grammatical gender of the noun "the-fish" inexplicably switches from the masculine (*haddāg*) in B to the feminine (*haddāgâ*) in B'. The latter form suggests a womb-like enclosure. Though traditionally translated here as "belly," the noun *mēʿeh* (plural, *mēʿîm*) designates a variety of internal organs, including the womb. Cf., e.g., Gen. 25:23; Num. 5:22; 2 Sam. 20:10; Job 20:14; Song of Sol. 5:14; Ruth 1:11.

3. Cf. the deconstructionist undermining of the hierarchical opposition between cause and effect; see Culler, *On Deconstruction*, 86–89. Cf. chapter 6, note 40.

4. The verb "swallow" (*blʿ*) has exclusively a negative meaning: e.g., Num. 16:28-34; Exod. 15:12; Job 20:15.

belly. They are similar to the countermovements of ingestion (A) and ejection (A'). The elusive phrase "three days and-three nights" indicates a complete time span, a long residence for Jonah.[5] It anchors his abode, thereby completing the motif of descent that began when he "went-down" to Joppa (1:3) and continued when he "went-down" to the innards of the vessel to sleep (1:5), and when he was "hurled" into the sea (1:15). Now he resides in the belly of the fish. Descent bespeaks death. But the reverse image follows immediately. Jonah praying "to Yhwh his-God[6] from-the-belly-of the-fish" signals a return to the presence of Yhwh (cf. 1:3). Ascent bespeaks life. The belly of the fish contains the polarities of death and life without digesting them. No wonder the fish vomited.

The opposing movements of ingestion and ejection and of descent and ascent produce another set of relationships: thematic correspondence between A and B and between B' and A'. The destructive message of the verb "swallow" (A) extends itself for "three days and three nights" (B). By contrast, the prayer to Yhwh (B') results immediately in the restorative message of the verb "and-it-vomited" (A'). In these relationships irony lurks. Structurally and theologically, Yhwh as subject encloses the episode. Every movement happens within the divine confines. So the ingestion and descent of Jonah signify not destruction but appointment. By the same token, the ascent and ejection signify not restoration to resolution but to continuing conflict. Thwarted in his efforts unto death to flee from the divine presence, Jonah returns to life on dry land, still under the control of Yhwh.

Nuances contribute special meanings in the closing line (A'). The absence of the adjective "great" for the fish (cf. A) diminishes its appearance to suggest that its job is done.[7] The noun "dry-land" appears for the third and last time (cf. 1:9, 13). It leaves behind fish and sea to ground the

---

5. Cf. the interpretation of George M. Landes, "The Three Days and Three Nights' Motif in Jonah 2:1," *JBL* 86 (1967): 446–50, adopted by Ackerman, "Satire and Symbolism in the Song of Jonah," 223, note 11. For critique, see Sasson, *Jonah*, 153–54, 158. Note the potential juxtaposition of this time span to the reference about Nineveh as "a-journey-of three days" (3:3).

6. Cf. the captain's plea that Jonah call "to your-god" (1:6) and Jonah's confession that he fears "Yhwh . . . God-of the-heavens" (1:9); cf. also Jonah's prayer to "Yhwh . . . God" (4:2).

7. Heretofore the adjective "great" (*gādôl*) has modified "city" (1:2), "wind" (1:4), "storm" (1:4, 12), and "fear" (1:10, 16). Sasson notes that its use in 2:1 with the noun "fish" produces a wordplay through the reversal of two Hebrew consonants, *dg* and *gd*: *dāg gādôl* (a-fish great).

story. Lying outside the ichthyic parallelisms between A and A', the single phrase "to the-dry-land" serves a triple function. It concludes the chiasm, episode four, and scene one.

Close reading of this narrated incident illustrates the guiding rubric: appropriate articulation of form-content yields appropriate articulation of meaning. But the task is far from over. The presence of the psalm between B' and A' poses a major challenge for the rhetorical endeavor.

B. THE PSALM (2:3-10)

For more than a century source critics have argued that the psalm was neither composed nor included by the author of the narrative. An editor added it later. Evidence for the argument abounds.[8] First, details within the psalm diverge from the narrative. For example, the psalmist claims that Yhwh threw him into the sea (2:4), but the story reports that the sailors hurled Jonah at his own request (1:15). The psalmist locates his activity in "the-womb-of Sheol" and in the holy temple (2:3, 5, 8); he says nothing about "the-belly-of the-fish." Second, the vocabulary of the psalm differs from the narrative. Rather than using the word "hurl" (*twl*) from the story, it introduces two other verbs for the same idea: *šlk* (2:4) and *grš* (2:5). Rather than using the phrase "from-the-presence-of Yhwh" (1:3, 3, 10), it says "from-before your-eyes" (2:5). Further, the psalm never uses the adjective "great," the word most often repeated in the narrative. Third, the genre of the psalm conflicts with the setting. It requires a complaint song; instead, a song of thanksgiving appears.[9] Fourth, the narrative and the psalm describe different characters. The psalmist thanks Yhwh and performs cultic acts; Jonah defies Yhwh to the end. Over time these and other arguments have spawned refutations that have brought scholarship back to the dry land of traditional formulation, to the view that the

8. Consult the commentaries for extended discussion of the evidence. An alphabetical listing of scholars adopting this view includes such impressive names as Bentzen, Bewer, Budde, Cornill, Driver, Eiselen, Eissfeldt, Gunkel, van Hoonaker, Marti, Nowack, Oesterley and Robinson, Pfeiffer, Rowley, Sellin, Smart, von Rad, Weiser, Wellhausen, and Wolff.

9. On the genre of thanksgiving, see Gerstenberger, *Psalms*, Part 1, 14–16. For critics who prefer the description "declarative psalm of praise," see Landes, "The Kerygma of the Book of Jonah," *Int* 21 (1967): 4, who follows Claus Westermann, *The Praise of God in the Psalms*, trans. Keith R. Crim (Richmond: John Knox Press, 1965), 25–30, 102-16. On the genre of the complaint song (or lament), cf. the discussion in chapter 6; also Gerstenberger, *Psalms*, Part 1, 11–14. Note that the *hithpaʿel* form of the verb "pray" in 2:2 argues for a complaint song; see Ackerman, "Satire and Symbolism in the Song of Jonah," 221.

psalm belongs to the original story whether or not the author composed it.[10] Round and round has swum the debate, and on its circuit the debate returns. The inevitable subjectivity of research characterizes arguments pro and con.[11]

1. Rhetorical Beginning

Within this fluid setting rhetorical criticism engages source criticism.[12] The isolation of the chiasm in 2:1, 2, 11 has already shown the rhetorical method at work on a putative earlier text. That analysis has demonstrated how structure, content, and meaning cohere apart from the psalm.[13] But the matter does not rest because rhetorical analysis must always wrestle with the final form.[14] The question becomes how the psalm functions in the present story, not if the psalm was added to an earlier story. Function neither requires nor disavows harmony, though many critics seem to assume the former. They interpret the psalm as genuine piety of Jonah, and they seek continuity between it and the narrative.[15] By contrast, this study ponders dissonance.[16]

---

10. The return to the traditional view dates from two studies: Landes, "Kerygma of the Book of Jonah" (1967), and Gabriel H. Cohn, *Das Buch Jona im Lichte der biblischen Erzählkunst,* Studia Semitica Neerlandica 12 (Assen: Van Gorcum, 1969). See later Ackerman, "Satire and Symbolism in the Song of Jonah," 214, note 1; John C. Holbert, "'Deliverance Belongs to Yahweh!': Satire in the Book of Jonah," *JSOT* 21 (1981), 70–75.

11. The sociology of knowledge, constantly overturning itself, tends to make first one way of thinking, and later another, more attractive.

12. Remember that though rhetorical analysis focuses on the final form, it is not limited to that form; cf. the discussion in chapter 4.

13. Data elsewhere in Jonah support this finding. No other broken chiasms appear (cf. 1:3, 5); no other narratives binding cause and effect have poetic interruption (cf. 1:4, 15); and other references to calling upon the deity occur without specific content (cf. 1:5; 3:8).Yet the parallel reference in 4:2 to calling upon the deity does use the same two introductory verbs as in 2:2, "pray" *(pll)* and "say" *('mr)*, with Jonah as the subject and with the content of his prayer included.

14. Recall how rhetorical criticism worked on the issue of transposing 4:5 to follow 3:4; see chapter 5.

15. E.g., Cohn, *Das Buch Jona,* 84; Landes, "Kerygma of the Book of Jonah," 22–25; Magonet, *Form and Meaning,* 49–54.

16. On dissonance, cf. Ackerman, "Satire and Symbolism in the Song of Jonah," esp. 216f.

Dissonance surfaces in three kinds: disruption, delay, and irony. The psalm disrupts the narrative structure. Locked within the confines of an exquisite chiasm, it provides a glaring instance of symmetrophobia.[17] The poetry occurs not in the center of the chiastic narrative (after B) but between two lines (B' and A') whose counterparts (A and B) are not so divided. Thus the psalm throws the episode off balance. It also delays the movement of the plot. Whether reporting Jonah's activity throughout three days and three nights or just at the end, it extends time to postpone the outcome of the ichthyic ingestion. In effect Jonah and the reader bog down in the belly of the fish. Irony marks their sojourn. The negative meaning of the verb "swallow" (bl'), the descent of "three days and three nights," and the hithpa'el form of the verb "pray" (pll) combine to prepare the reader for complaint, cry, or plea. Features within the psalm reinforce the expectation. A 3/2 rhythm characteristic of lament governs the stress pattern.[18] The opening word, the verb "call" (qr'), repeats the same vocabulary that the captain (1:6) and the sailors (1:14) used in seeking help from danger.[19] (And the sailors' call did produce a proper complaint.) The second word, "distress" (ṣārâ), anticipates lament. Despite these signs, however, Jonah delivers a thanksgiving song. It describes a devout worshiper saved from misfortune, one who prays in the temple, makes a sacrifice, and acknowledges deliverance from Yhwh. Genre and Sitz im Leben clash. Irony joins disruption and delay to sound dissonance between the psalm and the narrative.

17. How this instance relates to the overall symmetry of the book remains a moot issue. Sasson rightly observes that the symmetrical argument cannot decide the source critical question. If the psalm supports symmetry, it does not necessarily follow that the psalm belongs to the original story. "[I]nterpolators also have strong stakes in neatly balanced books" (Jonah, 203). Conversely, if the psalm detracts from symmetry, it does not necessarily follow that the psalm is an insertion. Authors have their reasons for skewing balance.

18. But 3/2 rhythm is not limited to lament. Cf. Frank M. Cross, "Studies in the Structure of Hebrew Verse: The Prosody of the Psalm of Jonah," The Quest for the Kingdom of God; Studies in Honor of George E. Mendenhall, ed. H. B. Huffmon, et al. (Winona Lake, Ind., Eisenbrauns, 1983), 158-67. For critique, see Sasson, Jonah, 208–13.

19. The Hebrew perfect tense of the verb "call" (and of the other verbs in the psalm) can connote present meaning. Cf. Pss. 120:1; 130:1, 2a; also Sasson, Jonah, 160, 163. Given the context, one begins by so interpreting the tense: "I-call." But as the content of the psalm unfolds, a shift to past meaning becomes arguable: "I-called"; so, e.g., NJV, RSV, and NRSV.

2. Rhetorical Exegesis

Close reading of the psalm increases the dissonance. To pursue this task requires explication of poetic terminology.[20] The words "colon," "line," "strophe," and "stanza" designate divisions from small to large.[21] Two or three cola constitute a line.[22] Two or more lines constitute a strophe. One or more strophes constitute a stanza, which consists, in Muilenburg's words, of "a beginning and ending, possessing unity of thought and structure. The prosody group must coincide with the sense."[23]

Scholarly analyses find three, four, five, or seven stanzas in the Jonah psalm, with no consensus on the beginnings and endings of units.[24] This study works with a chiasm of four stanzas.[25] Stanza A consists of one strophe with two lines (2:3); stanza B of two strophes (2:4 and 2:5), each with two lines; stanza B' of two strophes (2:6-7b and 2:7c-8), each with three lines; stanza A' of one strophe with three lines (2:9-10). In the following translation indentations denote a second (and a third) colon within a single line.

A
    "I-call from-the-distress to-me
       to Yhwh and-he-answers-me.
    From-the-womb-of sheol I-cry.
       You-hear my-voice. (2:3)

20. The subject of poetic terminology is much debated, commensurate with the larger debate on the nature of Hebrew poetry. For a major contribution, see Wilfred G. E. Watson, *Classical Hebrew Poetry* (Sheffield: JSOT Press, 1984); cf. David L. Petersen and Kent Harold Richards, *Interpreting Hebrew Poetry* (Minneapolis: Fortress Press, 1992); also the studies by Kugel (note 47, chapter 2), Berlin (note 116, chapter 3), and O'Connor (note 118, chapter 3).

21. See Watson, *Classical Hebrew Poetry*, 11–15; cf. Petersen and Richards, *Interpreting Hebrew Poetry*, 49–63.

22. "Cola" is the plural of the Greek word *colon*, literally meaning "limb" or "clause." "Colon" designates a half-line (or less) of poetry: the shortest independent section that relates in meaning to the remainder of the unit.

23. Muilenburg, "Form Criticism and Beyond," 12, who does not distinguish between "strophe" and "stanza" but prefers the former word. Cf. Muilenburg, "Biblical Poetry," *Encyclopaedia Judaica*, vol. 13 (Jerusalem: Keter Publishing House, 1971), 670–81.

24. On the diversity, see Michael L. Barré, "Jonah 2, 9 and the Structure of Jonah's Prayer," *Biblica* 72 (1991): 237–38.

25. Cf. Jerome T. Walsh, "Jonah 2, 3-10: A Rhetorical Critical Study," *Biblica* 63 (1982): 219–29. Though his study treats the psalm separate from the narrative setting, many of his insights inform this reading.

B

You-cast-me toward-the-depths,
into-the-heart-of the-sea,
and-the-current surrounds-me.

All your-waves and-your-breakers
over-me pass. (2:4)

But-I, I-said, 'I-have-been-driven-out
from-before your-eyes,'
Nevertheless I-continue to-look
to the-temple-of your-holiness. (2:5)

B'

Enclosed-me waters up-to the-neck (*nepeš*);

deep surrounds-me.

Weeds entwine to-my-head
to-the-roots-of the-mountains I-go-down.
The-earth [netherworld], its-bars about-me forever. (2:6-7b)

But-you-bring-up from-the-grave my-life,
Yhwh my-God.

When-ebbing-away to-me myself (*napšî*)

Yhwh I-remember.

And-comes to-you my-prayer
to the-temple-of your-holiness. (2:7c-8)

A'

Those-obeying idols empty
their-loyalty forsake.
But-I with-a-voice-of thanksgiving,
I-shall-sacrifice to-you.
What I-vow I-shall-pay.
Deliverance to-Yhwh!" (2:9-10)

Though of unequal length, the stanzas balance in vocabulary and subject matter. The words "Yhwh" and "voice" in stanza A (2:3) recur inversely in A' (2:9-10). The psalm begins with entreaty to Yhwh and the report of an answer; it ends with thanksgiving to Yhwh and the exclamation of deliverance. Similarly, stanzas B (2:4-5) and B' (2:6-8) balance. The first lines of their first strophes close with the corresponding pair "the-current surrounds-me (*yesōbebēnî*)" and "deep surrounds-me (*yesōbebēnî*)." The last lines of their second strophes close with the identical phrase: "to the-temple-of your-holiness." Verbal parallelisms sustain thematic links.

Stanza B describes the psalmist cast into the sea (2:4, strophe one) and his thoughts about the temple (2:5, strophe two). Stanza B' describes his life under water (2:6-7b, strophe one), his rescue and his prayer coming to the temple (2:7c-8, strophe two).

Stanza One (A). The first and last words of the stanza form an alliterative, rhyming, and conceptual *inclusio.* Both begin with the consonant *qōp* (q) and end with the vowel sound *i: qārā'tî* (I-call) and *qôlî* (my-voice). Jonah's first person references to his speech enclose his description of distress and deliverance.[26] Other sound patterns throughout the two lines please the ear and the eye. The opening colon repeats the "a" sound four times: *qārā'tî miṣṣārâ* (I-call from-the-distress). The second line accents the consonant *šîn* (š) in three consecutive words: *šᵉ'ôl šiwwaʿtî šāmaʿtā* (sheol I-cry you-hear). The "i" sound in the first word *qārā'tî* and thereafter at the end of each colon joins its respective consonants to form a rhyming scheme of a b c a' b': *-tî, -lî, -nî, -tî, -lî.* All the sounds focus on Jonah as subject and object.

Congruent with the sounds, parallels between the syntax of each line constitute the structure. They play with corresponding images.

a	b	b'	a'
I-call (*-tî*)	from-the-distress to-me (*-lî*)	to Yhwh	and-he-answers-me (*-nî*).

c	d	d'	c'
From-the-womb-of sheol	I-cry (*-tî*)	You-hear	my-voice (*-lî*). (2:3)

The opening line begins with a first person verb reporting the action of the penitent, "I-call" (a), and closes with an answering verb in which the penitent becomes object, "and-he-answers-me" (a'). Between the verbs prepositional phrases indicate direction inward and outward: "from-the-distress to-me" (b) and "to Yhwh" (b'). Jonah speaks about rather than to Yhwh. Caller and answerer keep distance through the kind of discourse used, though structurally they meet at the center: "to-me (*lî*) to (*'el*) Yhwh." The next line overcomes the distance. Jonah places matching verbs together in the middle, and he addresses Yhwh directly: "I-cry" (d); "you-hear" (d'). Cryer and hearer meet. Surrounding this intimate juxtaposition, the words "from-the-womb-of sheol" (c) and "my-voice" (c') complete the thought. Interrelationships between the two lines invert images: first, verbs and prepositional phrases; second, objects and verbs.

---

26. To fit the context, I merge the voices of Jonah and the psalmist.

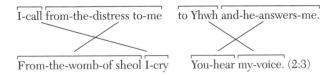

I-call from-the-distress to-me   to Yhwh and-he-answers-me.

From-the-womb-of sheol I-cry   You-hear my-voice. (2:3)

At every turn, within lines and between lines, Jonah and Yhwh meet and crisscross. Subject vies with object, distance with proximity, and distress with deliverance.[27]

The vocabulary and imagery of stanza one plays off the narrative. First, the verb "call" (*qr'*) is the same used by Yhwh (1:2) and by the captain (1:6). Though their calling to Jonah did not bring the desired results, his calling to Yhwh does. Belatedly following the captain's imperative, he calls from his distress to his God. And he receives from Yhwh what he himself refused to give the deity, namely an appropriate answer. Second, use of the preposition "from" (*mi-*) with the objects "distress" and "womb" recalls the phrase "from-the-belly-of the-fish" (*mimme'ê haddāgâ*).[28] Though the imagery of womb (*beten*) may evoke the belly (*me'îm*) of the fish, and possibly also the innards (*yārēk*) of the vessel (1:5), the entire phrase "from-the-womb-of sheol" depicts a more deadly residence.[29] Jonah has descended not only beyond them but indeed beyond the earth and the sea. His abode in "the-womb-of sheol" fits his effort "to-flee . . . from-the-presence-of Yhwh" (1:3). Yet from this abode he cries to Yhwh. From his distress, indeed from the womb of Sheol, irony undermines disobedience.[30]

Stanza Two (B). Returning in theme to the opening line of the poem, the first strophe of stanza two recapitulates distress and the second turns to contrasting thoughts. Rhyme accents the plight of Jonah. Two "i" sounds in strophe one climax in three "i" sounds in strophe two to high-

---

27. Note that the inverse relationships discerned in 2:3 contain no repetitions in vocabulary. For that reason, I have refrained from calling them chiasms. Note, however, that Hebrew poetry in general is replete with chiastic repetitions of key words; cf. Anthony R. Ceresko, "The Chiastic Word Pattern in Hebrew," *CBQ* 38 (1976): 303–11; Ceresko, "The Functions of Chiasmus in Hebrew Poetry," *CBQ* 40 (1978): 1–10.

28. See Wolff, *Obadiah and Jonah,* 134.

29. See Sasson, *Jonah,* 171-73. On the belly of the great fish as a type of sheol, cf. Frye's discussion of the metaphor of the cave in mythical descent themes (*Words With Power,* 229–71, esp. 231).

30. This reading of 2:3 presents numerous possibilities for rhetorical analysis of Hebrew poetry. Though close reading of the remaining verses continues, it involves fewer details.

light him as object and subject: "you-cast-me (-*nî*)," "surrounds-me (-*nî*)"; and "but-I (*we'anî*)," "I-said (-*tî*)," "I-have-been-driven-out (-*tî*)." Yet counter rhyme begins to shift emphasis as he begins to shift vision. Four times, twice in each strophe, the "ka" sound directs attention to Yhwh: "your-waves (-*kā*)," "your-breakers (-*kā*)," and "your-eyes (-*kā*)," "your-holiness (-*kā*)." These two sounds, "i" and "ka," echo the struggle between Yhwh and Jonah. Throughout this first strophe Jonah experiences Yhwh as perpetrator of disaster (2:4).

The experience continues emphatically in the second strophe, in the first colon of the first line: "but-I, I-said, 'I-have-been-driven-out'" (2:5a). Three first person pronouns accent Jonah in distress. The first and the second begin with the Hebrew letter *'ālep* ('); the second and the third end with the syllable -*tî*. The second colon (2:5b) completes the thought with visual language: "from-before your-eyes." But then, in the second line (2:5c) the change comes. At the beginning of the first colon the particle *'ak* (nevertheless) signals the reversal. Immediately in the verb *'ôsîp* (I-continue) comes another first person reference, followed by the infinitive *lehabbît* (to-look). Like the first two words of line one (but-I, I-said), the first two words of line two (nevertheless, I-continue) begin with the letter *'ālep* ('). Located in exact parallel positions, the two pairs of words produce double alliteration as they stress the "I" of Jonah in his first thought and then in his reversal of thought. The third word in the first colon of line two, the infinitive "to-look," picks up on and begins to play off the visual language at the end of the first line (from-before your-eyes). The imagery is then completed in the second colon (2:5d): "to the-temple-of your-holiness." Within the intricacies of the structure the precise meaning of the particle *'ak* remains ambiguous.[31] Though it signals the reversal of Jonah's thoughts, it may work as either an asseverative or an adversative. The former would signify a humble gesture; the latter, a defiant stance. Given Jonah's desperate situation, the asseverative reading makes sense. Given his recalcitrant demeanor, the adversative makes sense. Perhaps Jonah engages Yhwh on both levels.

The content of stanza two bears an uneasy relationship to the narrative. Does the information fill a presumed gap between the hurling of Jonah into the sea (1:15) and his swallowing by the fish (2:1)? If the two events be understood as separated by time, then here Jonah describes his harrowing experience in the sea. But if that is the case, either his memory is

---

31. On *'ak*, see T. Muraoka, *Emphatic Words and Structures in Biblical Hebrew* (Jerusalem: The Magnes Press, 1985), 129–30.

faulty or his interpretation skewed. He accuses Yhwh of casting him into the sea when in fact the sailors hurled him at his own request. Is Jonah now blaming Yhwh to put himself in a favorable light? Overcome by the waves of God, he "nevertheless" harbors noble thoughts about the holy temple. And yet even these thoughts contain a false assertion. He continues to insist that his flight from Yhwh was not of his own doing: "I-have-been-driven-out." And rather than using the language of the narrative, "from-the-presence-of Yhwh," he uses the phrase "from-before your-eyes." Besides these discrepancies, the cultic piety avowed hardly fits Jonah's demeanor. Such dissonance drives wedges between the psalm and the narrative—or it makes grotesque the developing portrait of Jonah.

Stanza Three (B'). Playing off stanza two, the first strophe of stanza three continues to describe Jonah's plight in the water and the second strophe continues with the theme of reversal. The descent deepens. Jonah goes down beyond "the-heart-of the-sea" and beyond "the-current [that] surrounds" him (2:4) to the bars of the netherworld (2:6-7b). He is totally self-absorbed. The rhyming sound "î" appears in every colon to designate the first-person pronoun as object, possessive object, or subject: "enclosed-me (-*nî*)," "surrounds-me (-*nî*)," "my-head (*rō'šî*)," "I-go-down (-*tî*)," "about-me (*ba'adî*)." Of particular importance is the verb *yāradtî* (I-go-down) because spacially it completes the journey begun in episode one. As the third person form of the verb took Jonah down to Joppa (1:3), down in the ship (1:3), and down in the innards of the vessel (1:5), so now the first person takes him down to the netherworld.[32] Appearing on either side of the verb are two descriptions of the place: "the-roots-of the-mountains" and the bars of the earth. The abode of death encloses the descent.[33] If the poetic language resonates with his narrative descent to death (cf. 2:1), nevertheless the setting of waters, deep, weeds, and mountains hardly fits the belly of a great fish.

At the nadir of the netherworld (2:7) comes the dramatic reversal of fortune.[34] The first word in the second strophe, "but-you-bring-up" (*wat-ta'al*) counters the verb "I-go-down" (*yāradtî*). As in the narrative (1:5), so here antithetic movements meet.[35] Unlike the descent, which is re-

---

32. On the verb *yrd,* cf. Magonet, *Form and Meaning,* 17, 43.

33. For descriptions of the netherworld, see Sasson, *Jonah,* 187–90.

34. On this Aristotelian concept, cf. chapter 6, p. 149f. Sasson calls 2:7 "the psychological center of the psalm" (*Jonah,* 182).

35. Cf. Krašovec, *Antithetic Structure in Biblical Hebrew Poetry,* 1–18, 126.

ported in sixteen words spanning three lines, the ascent happens quickly. Five words in the opening line bring swift deliverance: "But-you-bring-up from-the-grave my-life, Yhwh my-God." They reverse both Jonah's descent and his experience of Yhwh. "You-bring-up . . . my-life" overturns "you-cast-me toward-the-depths" (2:4). Addressing Yhwh by name, Jonah avers that the destroyer has become the deliverer. The particular verb "bring-up" (*'lh*), like its counter, the verb "go-down" (*yrd*), resonates beyond the psalm. The evil of Nineveh "has-come-up" (*'āletâ*) before the divine presence (1:2); a plant yet to be appointed by Yhwh will "come-up" (*wayya'al*) as shade over Jonah.

Reversal of fortune continues throughout the second strophe. Jonah recalls his calamity in order to remember his God: "When-ebbing-away to-me myself (*napšî*), Yhwh I-remember." He repeats the noun *nepeš*, which earlier specified his neck (2:6), but gives it here the larger meaning of his total self (cf. 1:14; 4:3, 8). Using the rhetorical device anastrophe,[36] he highlights the deity by placing the object "Yhwh" before the verb "I-remember." The positioning fashions another parallel to line one. "Yhwh" begins the second colon of both lines. Double emphasis results: "Yhwh my-God" and "Yhwh I-remember." Remembrance carries into the third line: "and-comes to-you my-prayer to the-temple-of your-holiness." References to Yhwh and to Yhwh's temple surround Jonah's prayer. It is secure (as is he) within the bounds of the sacred. And yet the Jonah of the narrative is far from secure. Though he does not reside in the waters or in the netherworld, neither has he come to the holy temple.

Like the first, the second strophe of stanza three shows Jonah struggling with Yhwh. Three times the rhyming sound "ay" occurs: "my-life" (*hayyay*), "my-God" (*'elōhāy*), "to-me" (*'ālay*). Three times the rhyming sound "î" follows: "myself" (*napšî*), "I-remember" (*zākārtî*), "my-prayer" (*tepillātî*). By contrast, the first two lines of the strophe climax in the divine name, and the last line uses the "ka" sound twice in reference to Yhwh: "to-you" (*'ēlêkā*), "your-holiness" (*-kā*). Paralleling the close of stanza two, the phrase "to the-temple-of your-holiness" advances the meaning.[37] First Jonah looks to the temple; this time his prayer arrives there. But all the while he stays in the belly of the fish.

36. On this device, cf. 1:4.
37. Tracking the reversal of movement uncovers a chiasm of key words that move into and then out of a dead center. On the one side come "temple" (2:5), *nepeš* (2:6), "I-go-down" (2:7). In the center is "netherworld" (2:7). On the other side come "you-bring-up" (2:7), *nepeš* (2:8), "temple" (2:8). How these seven words work within their surroundings

Stanza Four (A'). The verse that heads stanza four (2:9) lies uneasy in the psalm: "those-obeying idols empty their-loyalty forsake." Asseverative language about idol worshipers hardly fits the subject of Jonah and Yhwh.[38] Moreover, the location of the verse poses problems. Some critics judge it the end, some the inside, and some the beginning of a stanza.[39] The first and second views lose the parallelism between the phrases "to the-temple-of your-holiness" as the conclusions of stanzas. The third view skews the symmetry that would otherwise hold between the beginning (2:3) and the ending (2:10) of the psalm. Verse 3 reports Jonah's distress to "Yhwh," who then hears his "voice;" verse 10 reports Jonah's "voice" of thanksgiving to "Yhwh," who has delivered him. Verse 9 stands apart from this design. Uneasy lies this verse.

The decision to designate 2:9 the beginning of stanza four appeals to the rhetorical maneuver of contrast (cf. its use in stanzas two and three). By disparaging others, Jonah exalts himself before Yhwh.

> Those-obeying idols empty
> their-loyalty forsake. (2:9)
> But-I (*wa'anî*) with-a-voice-of thanksgiving,
> I-shall-sacrifice to-you.
> What I-vow I-shall-pay.
> Deliverance to-Yhwh! (2:10)

Verse 9 forms an inversion that itself contains a contrast.[40] Grammatically, two verbal forms surround two nominal forms; thematically, two contrasting attitudes, obeying (a) and forsaking (a'), surround two contrasting allegiances, empty idols (b) and loyalty (b').[41]

a	b	b'	a'
Those-obeying	idols empty	their-loyalty	forsake.

---

and what meanings result make a worthy assignment for the diligent student. On chiastic repetition of key words, see the references in note 27 above.

38. Cf. Sasson: Verse 9 "contains neither the language nor the construction of a petition" (*Jonah,* 194).

39. For 2:9 as the ending, see Barré, "Jonah 2,9 and the Structure of Jonah's Prayer"; for 2:9 as the inside, see Frank M. Cross, "Studies in the Structure of Hebrew Verse: The Prosody of the Psalm of Jonah," 166f; for 2:9 as the beginning, see Jerome T. Walsh, "Jonah 2,3-10: A Rhetorical Critical Study," 224–26, 28.

40. See Walsh, "Jonah 2, 3-10: A Rhetorical Critical Study," 224f.

41. The meaning of the second colon remains muddy; see Sasson, *Jonah,* 194–99.

Verse 10 also forms an inversion, but one of continuity rather than of contrast. Expressions of thanksgiving and of deliverance (a and a') surround affirmations about the cultic acts of sacrifice and vow (b and b').

a	b
But-I with-a-voice-of thanksgiving	I-shall-sacrifice to-you.

b'	a'
What I-vow I-shall-pay.	Deliverance to-Yhwh!

Verses 9 and 10 offer numerous juxtapositions. One line of poetry demeans idol worshipers; they have no voice (2:9). Two lines exalt Jonah; he has triple voice. He describes them, reports his own speech, and speaks it (2:10). Moreover, he accents the contrast by placing the first person independent pronoun at the beginning of the second line: "But-I" (*wa'anî*). Three verbs then confirm the accent: "I-shall-sacrifice," "I-vow," "I-shall-pay" (cf. 2:5). In numerous ways Jonah makes himself superior to "those-obeying idols empty." But who are they? Surely his description does not fit the sailors. They have become Yhwh worshipers, sacrificing a sacrifice and vowing vows (1:16). Nor does it fit the Ninevites who will display true piety (3:5-9). The contrast Jonah draws here exacerbates the tension between the psalm and the narrative. At the end a climactic utterance encapsulates the grand message: "Deliverance to-Yhwh!" The sacred name concludes the psalm. Yet all the while Jonah remains undelivered in the belly of the fish. A lament the reader expected; thanksgiving the reader hears. Dissonance triumphs.

3. Rhetorical Summary

a. *For the Psalm.* Someone, whether author or editor, has put in the voice of Jonah a beautifully constructed poem full of piety in the midst of adversity. His voice distorts the message. The first words signal trouble. "I call . . . to Yhwh." Though echoing the captain's command (1:6), the verb "call" (*qr'*) reminds the reader of the precise opposite. Jonah did not call to his God. Neither complaint nor petition came from his lips. Now when he does call, he misrepresents the situation. Yhwh has not cast him into the sea, driven him away from the divine sight, or brought up his life from the grave. Mouthing words of deliverance received, Jonah remains in mortal danger. The psalm shows his distorted perception of reality. Similarly, it proclaims his arrogance. He manipulates words of thanksgiving to boast about himself in misery and in piety. The first person singular as subject, object, or possessive occurs twenty-six times. Jonah avers that even when suffering unto death at the hand of Yhwh he has remained faithful, devout, and virtuous. As he remembered Yhwh in the past, so in the present he promises future sacrifice and vows. Self-righteous religiosity seeks to flatter the deity.

Distortion and arrogance peak when Jonah contrasts himself favorably with those who forsake loyalty to heed empty idols. The reference sends the reader in vain back to the sailors and forward to the Ninevites. Unlike Jonah, they model true piety. Thus his judgment in the psalm against idolaters becomes a judgment against himself in the narrative. He sought to flee from the divine presence; later he will berate God. Between the genuine worship of the sailors and the genuine repentance of the Ninevites comes counterfeit piety from loquacious Jonah. The closing line, "Deliverance to-Yhwh!" elevates the satiric tone. Though these words might deliver the message of the entire book, when spoken by Jonah they have a nauseous effect.[42] Immediately Yhwh spoke to the fish "and-it-vomited Jonah to the-dry-land" (2:11). Rather than a neutral term for bringing forth,[43] the verb "vomit" (*qî'*) underscores the repugnance that Jonah's words have elicited. Ironies of deliverance ensue. The fish, a potential instrument of death, has delivered Jonah from the sea even as it has been delivered of him. But Jonah, saved from death, has not been delivered from the command of Yhwh. His return to dry land means also that readers have not been delivered of him.[44]

b. *For the Method.* Scholars rage voluminously about the psalm, deconstructing it and their methods without end. Much labor becomes a weariness of the mind, though it may encourage informed judgements. Working on several compositional levels, this rhetorical analysis begins not with the psalm but with its narrative surroundings.[45] First, the analysis supports source critical findings that deem the psalm a secondary addition to the narrative. The chiastic structure and content of 2:1, 2, 11 form a complete literary unit; the omission of the psalm does not disrupt, much

---

42. Cf. Holbert, "Satire in the Book of Jonah," 74.

43. Cf. two other verbs that might have been used for "bringing forth": the *hiphil* of *yṣ'* as in, e.g., Gen. 1:12, 24; Exod. 8:18; Num. 20:8, 10; Isa. 40:26; 42:1, 3; Ps. 37:6; Job 38:32; or the *qal* of *plṭ* as in, e.g., 2 Sam. 22:44; Ps. 22:5, 9; 31:2; 37:40; 71:2.

44. Cf. Frye's claim that in "metaphorical thinking . . . the sea, the sea monster, and the foreign island [*sic*] he [Jonah] lands on are all the same place and mean the same thing" (*The Great Code*, 191). Such sweeping assertions build a chasm (not a chiasm) between archetypal criticism and rhetorical criticism. The two disciplines emphatically do not "mean the same thing."

45. Do not conclude from this study that rhetorical criticism always supports arguments for compositional levels. Cf. the discussion in chapter 4.

less destroy, the storyline.[46] Second, the analysis engages redaction criticism and canonical criticism to explore how the addition of the psalm affects the structure and theology of the whole.[47] The psalm disrupts symmetry, prolongs a focus on Jonah, delays the movement of the plot, exploits irony, and introduces perspectives at variance with the narrative. Third, the analysis works with the present form of the text. But even then it does not hold that the psalm harmonizes with the context. Instead, the method casts its lot with those who perceive dissonance between psalm and narrative.[48] Working on several compositional levels, rhetorical analysis plays with competing points of view. Each has persuasive power; the reader must evaluate "with knowledge and propriety."[49]

Extended focus on the psalm ironically becomes a victory of sorts for pious Jonah. It gains him prolonged attention, makes more complex the portrayal of him, and delays his journey to Nineveh. Evoking a great storm over centuries, the eight-verse poem threatens to swallow the forty-verse narrative. So let the argument stop even as the sea ceased from raging. This study has completed its two tasks: to explore rhetorical analysis of a poetic text; to illustrate interaction between rhetorical criticism and other disciplines. Now let the psalm with all its problems stay where it may not belong, in the belly of the fish. Meantime, Jonah has been vomited to the dry land. There Yhwh awaits him and rhetorical criticism awaits the reader.

46. Contra the literary analysis of Magonet, *Form and Meaning*, 51f.
47. Cf. Childs, *Introduction to the Old Testament as Scripture*, 422–25.
48. Cf. Landes, "Kerygma of the Book of Jonah," *passim* and esp. 30, and Ackerman, "Satire and Symbolism in the Song of Jonah," *passim*. Though both hold that the psalm belongs to the original story, Landes argues for harmony and Ackerman for dissonance.
49. See Brock, Scott, and Chesebro, *Methods of Rhetorical Criticism*, 12–19 on evaluation as a part of the critical impulse. Cf. chapter 3.

8
Internal Structure
of Scene Two (3:1-10)

With remembrance of things past, scene two (chapters 3–4) begins anew. It comprises four episodes. The first (3:1-4) sets the plot in motion with Yhwh's command and Jonah's obedient response. The second (3:5-10) relates efforts in Nineveh to avert disaster and gives God's repentant response. The third (4:1-5) tells of Jonah's angry reaction, Yhwh's reply, and Jonah's departure from the city. The fourth (4:6-11) offers an inconclusive ending as Yhwh and Jonah confront each other in deed and speech. Using the guiding rubric, rhetorical analysis makes its way word by word through scene two. This chapter discusses episodes one and two; the next chapter, episodes three and four.

A. EPISODE ONE (3:1-4)

Two incidents fill episode one: the command of Yhwh and the response of Jonah.[1]

1. Command of Yhwh (3:1-2)

As in scene one (1:1-2), the genre of commission opens the plot.[2] It includes the prophetic word formula (3:1) and the commissioning formula (3:2). Both differ from their first appearances. The prophetic word formula omits the paternal identification "son-of Amittai" and adds the particle šēnît (a-second-time) to signify continuation: "And-was the-word-

---

1. Note that episode one corresponds to units 1, 2, 3, and 4 in scene two of the external design.
2. See the comments in chapter 6; also Long, *1 Kings*, 246.

of Yhwh to-Jonah a-second-time, saying." The commissioning formula
turns away from the evil of Nineveh to make a different emphasis:

Arise
　go to Nineveh the-city the-great
　and-call (*qr'*) to-her the-calling (*qr'*) that I (am) wording to-you. (3:2)

The command "call (*qr'*) to-her" leads not to a *kî* clause but to a cognate
object of the verb: "call . . . the-calling (*qr'*)" (cf. 1:10, 16). In turn, the
object leads to a relative clause that gives no particular message but
stresses divine authority over Jonah: "that I (*'ānōkî*) (am) wording to-you."
This time Jonah must await the word about Nineveh. Meanwhile, the pronominal prepositional phrases *'ēlêhā*[3] (to-her) and *'ēlêkā* (to-you) relate
the city and him through alliteration, assonance, and rhyme. Between the
phrases the divine *'ānōkî* (I) mediates. The arrangement contrasts with
the prophetic word formula (3:1) in which Jonah mediates between Yhwh
and Nineveh.[4] The structuring strength of Yhwh's words changes relationships. In the structure of the entire commission, however, the cognate
terms "word-of Yhwh" and "wording" bind the two parts. The narrated
"word" occurs second from the beginning of the incident; the direct
"wording" second from the end. What the narrator accents Yhwh confirms. With every word in place, the command calls Jonah forth again to
word the word. Despite the differences between this commission and that
in scene one, the basic plot remains the same: "Arise, go . . . call." Yhwh
persists. The story begins a second time; divine imperatives await the response of Jonah.

2. Response of Jonah (3:3-4)

　Narrated discourse culminating in prophetic speech shapes the incident
of response. It relates Jonah's arrival in Nineveh, describes Nineveh, reports his walk there, and closes with his words to the city. The first two
clauses begin to fulfill the commands. Ending with the phrase "the-word-
of Yhwh," they revert to the opening of incident one. The resulting *inclusio*
exemplifies structures that form across incidents within the same episode:

3. In 1:2, '*al-* denotes "to"; in 3:2, '*el* denotes "to." Though many scholars view the
prepositions as interchangeable, Sasson proposes that when joined with the verb "call" (*qr'*),
they signify different idioms. *Qarā' 'āl-* (1:2) signifies a death warrant; *qarā' 'ēl-* (3:2) commissions a specific message (*Jonah*, 72–75, 226). On use of the verb *qr'* in Jonah, cf. Halpern
and Friedman, "Composition and Paronomasia," 82f.
　4. Cf. the comments on 1:1.

And-was the-word-of Yhwh to Jonah a-second-time, saying,
"Arise

go to Nineveh the-city the-great

and-call to-her the-calling that I (am) wording to-you." (3:1-2)

And-arose Jonah

and-he-went to Nineveh according-to-the-word-of Yhwh. (3:3ab)

Within "the-word-of Yhwh" balance and imbalance contend. The two imperatives, "arise, go," become two indicatives, "and-arose Jonah and-he-went." The oracle fulfillment formula, "according-to-the-word-of Yhwh," seems to confirm obedience.[5] Yet absence of the third indicative, "and-he-called," to answer the third imperative "call," leaves the response incomplete. The first time around, Jonah obeyed but one imperative: "he-arose to-flee" (1:3). Though now he obeys two, by analogy with the beginning, his total obedience is not assured. Suspense lingers. The narrator exploits it by a delaying tactic.

Even as the clauses, "and-arose Jonah and-he-went to Nineveh according-to-the-word-of Yhwh," close an *inclusio*, they also open a chiastic structure. In it Jonah and Nineveh meet. The following diagram shows the interconnections of the parts and the whole.

a
And-arose Jonah

b
and-he-went [walked] to Nineveh according-to-the-word-of Yhwh.

b'	**c**	**d**	**e**

And-Nineveh was a-city great to-god, a-walk-of three days,

a'		**c'**	**d'**	**e'**

And-began Jonah to-enter into-the-city a-walk-of day one. (3:3-4a)

5. On the formula, see Long, *1 Kings*, 265.

Repetition of words in inverse and parallel arrangements delineates boundaries, structure, and emphases. Occurrences of the nouns "Jonah" and "Nineveh" in the first two clauses and of "Nineveh" and "Jonah" in the second two clauses bind the unit (a, b, b', a'). The verb "he-went" ["walked"] (wayyēlek) in the second clause prepares for the noun "walk" (mahalak) in the third and fourth clauses (d and d').[6] In addition, the three nouns "city," "walk," and "day" appear in synonymous parallelism (c, d, e, c', d', e'). Standing outside all these inverted and parallel arrangements, the oracular fulfillment formula "according-to-the-word-of Yhwh" mediates between Jonah and Nineveh on the one side (a and b) and Nineveh and Jonah on the other (b' and a'). In contrast to scene one, where the formula never appears, the prominence here indicates, but does not guarantee, the power of Yhwh's word to achieve its purpose. After all, though the first two clauses fulfill two divine commands, the last two clauses walk away from the third command.

Within the last two clauses other emphases unfold. Once again (cf. 1:4, 5) Hebrew syntax places subject before verb: "And-Nineveh was." The description "a-city great to-God, a-walk-of three days," extends meaning beyond size. The preposition in the adjectival phrase "great lē-God" lends itself to various interpretations.[7] Accordingly, the complete phrase can suggest divine perspective: the greatness of Nineveh impresses even God (great before-God). It can suggest divine favor: God has ordained the greatness of Nineveh (great to-God). And it can suggest divine abode: the greatness of Nineveh qualifies as a residence for God (great for-God). These and other possibilities resonate with Yhwh's repeated description of Nineveh as "the-city the-great" (1:2; 3:2; 4:11).[8]

Emphasis on Nineveh puts Jonah's action in perspective. Unlike scene one, when his response focused on himself (1:3), he now begins "to-enter into-the-city a-walk-of day one." This infinitive phrase plays off the opposite, "to-flee to-Tarshish." Moreover, the infinitive itself (lābô', translated

---

6. Though sense and convention argue here for translating *hlk* variously as "go" and "walk," the translations obscure a concatenate design: *lēk* (go, 3:2), *wayyēlek* (he went, 3:3), *mahalak* (a walk, 3:3), and *mahalak* (a walk, 3:4). Note that the verb occurs also four times in scene one (1:2, 7, 11, 13). It contributes to overall symmetry; see Magonet, *Form and Meaning*, 29f. On the problem of translation, see below.

7. BDB, 510–18.

8. *Contra* scholars who reduce the idiom "great to-God" to a superlative; e.g., D. W. Thomas, "A Consideration of Some Unusual Ways of Expressing the Superlative in Hebrew," *VT* 3 (1953): 109–224. Cf. Sasson who rejects the superlative while finding the meaning unstable (*Jonah*, 228–30).

"to-enter") echoes from the participial phrase "returning (*bā'â*) to-Tarshish" and repeats the infinitive in the phrase "to-return (*lābô'*) with-them to-Tarshish." The plot reverses but the verb endures. Jonah begins to enter into the city a walk of one day. Repetitions of the words "city," "walk," and "day" accent Nineveh as the appointed place.

Repeated uses of the verb *bô'* in different contexts (e.g., 1:3 and 3:4) present a problem for rhetorical analysis because the verb can be variously translated as "go," "come," "return," and "enter."[9] Different translations for the same verb prevent readers from seeing repetition. The difficulty may seem to be eliminated if *bô'* is consistently rendered as "go": "a-ship going to-Tarshish"; "to-go with-them to-Tarshish"; "to-go into-the-city." But this rendering produces another problem. It makes the verb indistinguishable in translation from the verb *hlk*, "go": "go to-Nineveh" (1:2; 3:2) and "he-went" (3:3).[10] The same translation for different verbs misleads readers to assume nonexistent repetition. Again, the difficulty may seem to be eliminated if *hlk* is consistently rendered by another of its connotations, namely "walk," but that translation would introduce difficulties of awkwardness and meaning. For example, the sailors use the verb *hlk* when they speak each to his neighbor, and so a third connotation surfaces: "Come (*lekû*) and-let-us-cast-lots" (1:7). These problems permit no satisfactory solution. In all cases where a single word acquires or requires different translations or different words acquire or require a single translation, rhetorical analysis suffers (and so does the reader).[11]

In returning to the incident at hand, the reader enters the realm of direct discourse. The introduction to it relieves the suspense about Jonah's response to Yhwh's third imperative "call." Before the common idiom, "and-he-said," the narrator places the particular vocabulary, "and-he-called" (*qr'*). It clinches perfect obedience between commands and responses: "arise," "go," "and-call" (3:2); Jonah "arose" (3:3), "and-he-went" (3:3), "and-he-called" (3:4b).

And-he-called and-he-said:

"Yet forty days and-Nineveh will-be-overturned (*nehpāket*)
[or] overturns." (3:4b)

---

9. BDB, 97–99.

10. Translations tend not to recognize the problem. E.g., the NRSV translates both verbs as "go."

11. On this annoying problem, see guideline 5b in chapter 4 on p. 102f.

This five word "calling" by Jonah abounds in unstable properties. The particle "yet" ('ôd) leaves open the exact timing. Does it mean "within" or "at the end of"? The conventional idiom "forty days" ('arbā'îm yôm) signifies an unspecified time of trial and testing that does not forecast the outcome.[12] "Nineveh" as emphatic subject (cf. 3:3b) precedes a mercurial verbal form: nehpāket may be passive or reflexive, indeed deliberately ambiguous.[13] The verb hpk holds the opposite meanings of destruction and deliverance.[14] The "calling" by Jonah lacks a standard prophetic formula such as "the word of Yhwh," "thus says Yhwh," or "oracle of Yhwh." Though from the perspective of Nineveh, a Yhwistic formula may well be incomprehensible, from the perspective of Hebrew prophecy its absence may challenge the authenticity of the utterance.[15] Nowhere in the story has Yhwh given Jonah these exact words to speak. Is his prophecy, then, true or false? A contrast by omission also feeds doubt about the authenticity of the utterance. The storyteller declares that Jonah "arose and-went to Nineveh according-to-the-word-of Yhwh" (3:3a) but then does not use the phrase "according-to-the-word-of Yhwh" when reporting what Jonah "called and-said" (3:4b). Overall, the "calling" abounds in unstable properties. They invite characters and readers to exploit meanings.

B. EPISODE TWO (3:5-10)

Following Jonah's indeterminate words, three incidents occupy episode two.[16] They feature popular, royal, and divine responses: efforts by the Ninevites to avert disaster, efforts by their king, and the resulting repentance of God.[17] The setting, the human characters, the animals, and the genre of a royal edict are all new to the story.

---

12. See Sasson, Jonah, 233.
13. Ibid., 234–37.
14. For the predominant meaning "destruction," see, e.g., Gen. 19:21, 25, 29; Deut. 29:22; Jer. 20:16; Lam. 4:6; for the meaning "deliverance," see, e.g., Deut. 23:5; Jer. 31:13; Ps. 66:6.
15. Note that the divine name Yhwh never occurs in the report about Nineveh. Only the generic 'elōhîm is used. Use of "Yhwh" in the episodes about the sailors might well have set a precedent, but it did not.
16. Note that episode two corresponds to units 5, 6, and 7 of scene two in the external design.
17. Critics who transpose 4:5 to follow 3:4 would, however, precede the efforts by the Ninevites with the activity of Jonah. On this issue, see chapter 5.

1. The Popular Response (3:5)

Upon arrival in Nineveh Jonah does not go to the throne of power but walks in the city for a day. Then he makes his proclamation. The Ninevites hear it and respond independently of their king. The narrator's first word about them signals a turn in the plot: "and-believed" (*wayya'amînû*). Coming from the root *'mn*, this verb puns on the name of Jonah's father, Amittai (1:1). Yet the verb is new in the narrative. Never was it used for the sailors, even though it would have been appropriate.[18] To hear that the Ninevites "believed" alerts the reader to a radical turning. The unstable "calling" of the son of Belief (Amittai) elicits belief in God.

What the first word promises, the incident fulfills. Using the familiar sentence structure of three independent clauses, the narrated popular response moves from description through announcement to action.

> And-believed the-people-of Nineveh in-God,
>   and-they-called a-fast,
>   and-they-put-on sackcloth, from-their-great and-to their-small. (3:5)

In contrast to the solo appearance of the verb "believe," the verb "call" plays on preceding events. Twice Yhwh has instructed Jonah to "call" (*qr'*) to Nineveh (1:2; 3:2) and, on the second occasion, even to "call . . . the-calling." The captain has urged him to "call" to his God (1:6). In the psalm Jonah himself has "called" to Yhwh (2:3). And just now (3:4) he has "called" his five indeterminate words. The Ninevites in turn "call" a fast. Their belief in God leads to their penance. They put on sackcloth, "from-their-great and-to their-small." This idiom constitutes a merism. "Great" and "small" signify the total population. Yet it has already been identified as a whole in the phrase "the-people-of Nineveh." Thus the idiom "from-their-great and-to their-small" also qualifies as pleonasm (literally, "excess"), a rhetorical device employing more words than necessary. Merism and pleonasm add nuance and emphasis. Embracing male and female, the combination "from-their-great" (*miggedôlām*) and "and-to-their-small" (*we'ad-qetannām*) suggests the riches of inclusivity: from royalty to commoners, nobility to peasants, age to youth, powerful to powerless— indeed, all sorts and conditions of folk. As end-stress, the idiom "from-their-great and-to their-small" augments the subject "people-of Nineveh"

---

18. The single verb *yr'* (fear) denotes both the fright of the sailors and their belief in Yhwh. It contributes to artistic and thematic unity in scene one (1:5, 9, 10, 16).

at the beginning. Most emphatically, the entire population believes in God, calls a fast, and puts on sackcloth. They ask no questions; they seek no explanation.

Why the Ninevites so readily believe in God the story never explains. Unlike the sailors facing imminent death from a storm at sea, they have no immediate threat of danger. Unlike the sailors who requested and heard Jonah's confession about Yhwh (1:9), they hear only his ambiguous pronouncement that does not even mention God. Unlike the sailors who experienced deliverance from the raging sea, they have no evidence for divine mercy. Jonah neither gives them his credentials nor explains his words. Nevertheless, the Ninevites respond immediately. They believe in God. Why remains unknown.

This permanent gap in information has led commentators to invent reasons.[19] They range from the assumption that Jonah persuaded the Ninevites by telling them his full story to the speculation that his repulsive flesh, altered by the gastric juices of the fish, was enough to convince them.[20] Rather than inventing reasons, a rhetorical critic asks how this gap works within the story. One answer concerns implied comparisons. The developing portrait of the sailors gives ample reasons for their conversion; the nondeveloping portrait of the Ninevites gives no reason for their conversion. Juxtaposed, the portraits disallow stereotypical thinking about foreigners. Each depiction complements and reinforces the other.[21] A related answer observes the gap working proleptically to prepare for a different sort of contrast (4:1-11). So readily the Ninevites believe in God; no explanation complicates the outcome. So doggedly[22] Jonah will argue

19. Cf. Sternberg's three types of omissions in narratives: (1) Blanks signify irrelevancies, information omitted for lack of interest. (2) Temporary gaps signify information delayed for the sake of interest. (3) Permanent gaps signify information omitted for the sake of interest (*Poetics of Biblical Narrative*, esp. 235–63). Jonah contains all three types. (1) Blanks occur, e.g., in 1:1 and 2:11. Where Jonah was when the word of Yhwh came, what he was doing, and upon what dry land the fish vomited him are irrelevancies. (2) A temporary gap occurs in 1:3. No reason is given for Jonah's flight to Tarshish; Jonah fills the gap in 4:2. A less obvious example occurs in 4:7; see the discussion in chapter 9. (3) A permanent gap occurs here in 3:5. Exploration of it relates rhetorical criticism to poetics.

20. For the reasons, see Sasson, *Jonah*, 244.

21. Cf. ibid., 340–42.

22. The word "doggedly" is another instance of bilingual paronomasia. (Cf. chapter 6, note 16). As noted, the Hebrew words for "a-fish great" (*dāg gādôl*) produce a wordplay through the reverse of the consonants *dg* and *gd*. In English these consonants cling doggedly to Jonah.

with God; elaborate explanation will complicate the outcome. Juxtaposed, the portraits disallow stereotypical thinking about the foreigners and the Hebrew. In these and perhaps other ways, the lack of information about why the Ninevites immediately believe in God serves artistic and theological interests.

2. The Royal Response (3:6-9)

Only after the Ninevites have responded does their king enter the story. The incident begins, "And-reached the-word to the-king-of Nineveh" (3:6a). The noun *haddābār* (the-word) appropriates a dominant motif. "The-word-of Yhwh" came to (*'el*) Jonah (1:1; 3:1, 2); he arose and went according to "the-word-of Yhwh" (3:3). Now "the-word," without reference to Yhwh, reaches to (*'el*) the king. He responds as individual and monarch.

a. Individual Response

The king's first act, "he-arose," recalls Jonah who twice made an identical response to Yhwh's word, first in disobedience (1:3) and then in obedience (3:3). Heir to ambivalent uses, the third appearance of the verb needs explication. It comes through a particular structure and content not dependent upon repetition for balanced configuration.

A   And-he-arose from-his-throne

   B   and-he-removed his-robe from-upon-him

   B'   and-he-covered-himself [with] sackcloth

A'   and-he-sat upon the-ashes. (3:6b)

Actions and counteractions produce an inversion of movement. The verb "arose" and its object "throne" (A) counter the verb "sat" and its object "ashes" (A'). The verb "removed" and its object "robe" (B) counter the verb "covered" and its object "sackcloth" (B'). These movements provide striking contrasts. From the king on his throne in a royal robe (A and B), the verse plummets to the man covering himself in sackcloth and sitting upon ashes (B' and A'). A wordplay between the phrase "from-his-throne" (*mikkis'ô*, A) and the verb "he-covered" (*wayekas*, B') enhances the transformation. As an individual like unto his people, the king has humbled himself. He has "overturned" in dwelling, dress, and dignity.[23] Whether his actions precede destruction or deliverance awaits the telling.

b. Official Response

Having identified with his people, the king as ruler addresses them. "And-he-cried and-he-said" (3:7a). The use of two verbs to introduce his speech parallels the use of two verbs to introduce Jonah's speech (3:4). In the earlier instance the particular verb "call" preceded the common verb "say" (*'mr*). In this instance the particular verb "cry" (*z'q*) precedes the common verb "say" (*'mr*). The verb "cry" has already been used for the sailors (1:5). Faced with destruction, they "cried," each to his god; faced with destruction, the king "cries" in issuing a decree. Though a "dynamic" equivalent translation might fittingly render the two royal verbs, "and-he-proclaimed and-he-published," it would lose the syntactic and verbal parallels that formal correspondence preserves. Yet these small parallels between introductory sentences evince literary and thematic sensitivities. The structure, vocabulary, and theology of the decree itself shows this crafting on a grand scale.

Authorization	In-Nineveh By-the-authority-of the-king and-his-great-ones, to-say:
Salutation	The-human and-the-animal, The-herd and-the-flock
Corpus	
Negative instructions	Let-not them-taste anything; Let-not them-graze; And-water let-not them-drink.

Positive
instructions
	But-let-them-cover-themselves (in) sackcloth,
	    the-human and-the-animal;
	And-let-them-call to God with-strength,
	And-let-them-turn, each-one,
	    from-his-way-of the-evil
	    from-the-violence that (is) in-their-hands.

23. Cf. the ambiguous meaning of *hpk* in 3:4b.

Conclusion   Who knows,

                    May-return
                    And-may-repent the-God
                    And-may-turn from-the-burning-of his-nostrils

                    And-not we-perish. (3:7b-9)

The decree institutionalizes repentance. Authorization replaces spontaneity. The word translated "authority" (*ṭa'am*) carries the concrete meaning of taste and the figurative meaning of judgment.[24] Its use prepares for a pun with the first instruction, "let-not them-taste (*'al-yiṭ'amû*) anything." The taste (judgment) of the king and his great ones is that the people not taste. The identification "great-ones" echoes one half of the merism "from-their-great and-to their-small" (3:5), thereby connecting the popular and royal responses. Following the authorization, the salutation addresses all the inhabitants of Nineveh. The first line employs merism; the whole population is divided into its parts, "the-human (*hā'ādām*) and-the-animal (*wehabbehēmâ*)." The second line employs synecdoche; a part of the animal(s), "the-herd and-the-flock," represents the whole.[25]

The corpus balances negative and positive instructions. Grammatically called jussives, they convey through the third person an indirect imperative meaning. Each set forms the characteristic three clause sentence. The negative instructions concern fasting. The first two appear to follow the order of addressees in the salutation. The people are not to taste and the animals not to graze. Parallel commands exhibit parallel syntax. The third clause departs from the parallelism; it appears to address people and animal together. The object "water," consumed by both, precedes the jussive "let-not them-drink." The contrasting set of positive instructions continues to address "the-human and-the-animal."[26] The first jussive, "but-let-them-cover-themselves (in) sackcloth," reiterates what the people and their king have already done (3:5, 6d).[27] Indeed, it employs the same verb (*ksh*, cover) used for the king. The monarch who emulates his subjects decrees that they emulate him. Whether the next two instruc-

24. Cf. BDB 381.
25. On merism and synecdoche, cf. above, chapter 6, note 60.
26. Cf. Sasson who effectively counters proposals to excise either one or both occurrences of this phrase (*Jonah*, 255).
27. Three times the noun "sackcloth" occurs. The plural form *ṣaqqîm* in reference to the people (3:5) and to the human and the animal (3:8) surrounds the singular form *ṣaq* in reference to the king (3:6).

tions include the animals remains a moot point. The jussive, "and-let-them-call (qr') to ('el) God," puns on the captain's imperative to Jonah (1:6) and the narrator's indicative about the sailors (1:14). But it adds the condition "with-strength," thereby preparing the Ninevites (and the reader) for the radical requirement of the last jussive.

"And-let-them-turn (weyāšubû), each-one. . . ." Whereas all the previous instructions concern external activity (not taste, graze, drink but cover, call), this one turns to inward change. The verb "turn" (šûb) calls for repentance. Its imagery plays on the verb "overturn" (hpk, 3:4). On the one hand, the turning of the Ninevites may counter the overturning of them. It may counter destruction. On the other, the turning of the Ninevites may correspond to the overturning of them. It may correspond to deliverance. Prepositional phrases extend the profundity, thereby stressing the climactic function of this jussive. They specify the direction and content of the turning:

| from-his-way-of | the-evil |
| and-from the-violence that (is) | in-their-hands. |

The lines may be read as synonymous parallelism, the second repeating with different words the meaning of the first. They may be read as synthetic parallelism, the second extending the meaning of the first. In either case their parts relate inversely. On the outsides, the pronominal suffixes "his" and "their" fix responsibility individually and corporately,[28] and the nouns "way" and "hands" signify the means. On the insides, the nouns "evil" and "violence" specify the ends. Structurally, the means converge on the ends; instrumentality encircles outcome. Yet the preposition "from," in parallel locations, turns the meaning of the phrases away from their content, away from evil and and away from violence. The turning derives from the power of the verb šûb (turn). It governs the sentence and the sentiments to signal the radical message of reversal. The whole and the parts of these well-wrought prepositional phrases reinforce one another to explicate the message. In position, vocabulary, structure, and length the third positive jussive climaxes the instructions. By shifting the requirements from conventional acts to radical repentance, it prepares for the conclusion.

The conclusion provides rationale and hope.

---

28. Translations often miss or dismiss this nuance. E.g., the RSV, NRSV, NAB, JB and NJV all convert the plural suffix "their" into a singular to match the suffix "his."

Who knows,

May-return (*šûb*)

And-may-repent (*nḥm*) the-God

And-may-turn (*šûb*) from-the-burning-of his-nostrils.

And-not we-perish. (3:9)

The phrase "who knows" (*mî-yôdēaʿ*) sets tone and theology.[29] It expresses possibility and uncertainty, both the premise of hope. Its position converges with its message. In the external design "who knows" corresponds to the "perhaps" (*'ûlay*) of the captain (1:6).[30] In the internal structure it comes after the ordered "turning" (*šûb*) of the Ninevites and before the wished for "turning" (*šûb*) of God, thus undercutting any idea of human manipulation effecting divine deliverance. The turning of "the human and-the-animal" does not itself guarantee the turning of God. Who knows?

The content of the hope follows. As the king directs the Ninevites to "turn" (*šûb*), so the same verb turns to God. Parallel occurrences of *šûb* surround a synonymous verb *nḥm*, "and-may-repent" [or "change-the-mind"] with God as subject and center. After the *inclusio* comes the prepositional phrase "from-the-burning-of his-nostrils" (*mēḥarôn 'appô*), a metaphor for divine anger.[31] Like the description about the Ninevites, "and-from the-violence that (is) in-their-hands," it comes at the end of a sentence and consists of a prepositional phrase whose object is body language for destructive action. The hands of the Ninevites convey violence; the nostrils of God convey anger. As the king instructs "the-human and-the-animals" to turn from violence, so he hopes that God may turn from anger. The last two words specify his hope: "and-not we-perish" (*welō' nō'bēd*). Matching exactly the outcome desired by the captain (1:6), they climax and conclude the well-crafted royal decree.[32]

3. The Divine Response (3:10)

The divine response comes quickly and decisively. Though similar in basic structure to the popular response, it exhibits a more complicated syntax: three independent clauses separated by two subordinate clauses.

29. See James L. Crenshaw, "The Expression MI YODEAʿ in the Hebrew Bible," 274–88.

30. See the pertinent discussions in chapters 5 and 6.

31. See Sasson, *Jonah,* 262; also M. I. Gruber, *Aspects of Nonverbal Communication in the Ancient Near East,* Studia Pohl 12 (Rome: Pontifical Biblical Institute, 1980) 491–502.

32. See the discussion in chapters 5 and 6.

a
And-saw the-God their-deeds,

b
kî they-turned from-their-way-of the-evil,

b'
and-repented the-God about the-evil

a'
that (*'ašer*) he-worded to-do to-them,

a''
and-not he-did. (3:10)

"The-God" (or the corresponding pronoun "he") is subject of the verbs in the independent clauses: "saw," "repented," and "did not." The deity controls the action. The subordinate clauses alternate the activity of the Ninevites, "they-turned," and the speech of God, "he-worded." The particle *kî* allows for different interpretations. It may introduce an objective clause in apposition to "their-deeds" and so be translated "that" or "how." This meaning reverts to the first five jussives of the royal decree. Not tasting, not grazing, not drinking but covering and calling are all "deeds" observed by God who saw "that" [or "how"] the Ninevites turned from their evil. But *kî* may introduce a causal clause and so be translated "because" or "for." This meaning reverts to the sixth jussive with which the clause shares the words "turn" (*šûb*), "way" (*derek*), and "evil" (*rā'â*). Accordingly, the Ninevites have done more than perform proper deeds of penance. They have changed inwardly; they have overturned (though not as Jonah intended). The particle *ki* calls attention to the genuine change that motivates their deeds: ". . . because they-turned from-their-way-of the-evil."[33]

A chiasm based on the key words "do" and "evil" organizes the incident. On the insides, references to "evil" pertain to the Ninevites (b) and to God (b'). The verbs "turned" and "repented" depict corresponding movement between the subjects. It appropriates the familiar principle of

---

33. Most translations and commentaries choose the first interpretation, with *kî* introducing an object clause in apposition; e.g., RSV, NRSV, NJV; Wolff, *Obadiah and Jonah*, 144; Allen, *Books of Joel, Obadiah, Jonah and Micah*, 226. But in a footnote Allen acknowledges a difficulty: "We are meant to assume that the Ninevites complied with the summons to true repentance" (ibid., 226, note 32). The second interpretation renders the assumption unnecessary by making it explicit; see Sasson, *Jonah*, 263.

cause and effect. Mutual turning eradicates evil.[34] On the outsides of the chiasm, variations of the word "do" (*'śh*) surround the turning away from evil. They pertain to "the-deeds" of the Ninevites (a) and to the action of God, "to-do" (a'). In repentance, human and divine, "doing" matters. It leads to the eradication of evil. The closing line of the passage doubles the emphasis: "and-not he-did" (a''). This two word clause embodies its own meaning by not containing the word "evil."

The overturning is complete; the divine response brings deliverance. In reporting the outcome, the narrator appropriates key words, phrases, and themes from the royal response. The king has urged:

> and-let-them-turn (*śûb*), each-one, from-his-way-of the-evil (3:8c).

The narrator confirms:

> because they-turned (*śûb*) from-their-way-of the-evil (3:10b).

The king has hoped:

> and-may-repent (*nḥm*) the-God (3:9a).

The narrator confirms:

> and-repented (*nḥm*) the-God. (3:10c)

The king has concluded:

> and-not we-perish (3:9c).

The narrator confirms in conclusion:

> and-not he-did (it). (3:10d)

Besides these resonances with the royal response, the divine draws upon other passages. The key words in the clause "the-evil that he-worded to-do to-them" return to scene one. There Yhwh spoke of "their-evil" in reference to Nineveh (1:2), and the sailors spoke twice of evil in reference to the storm (1:7, 8). The verb "worded" (*dbr*) evokes "the-

---

34. Cf. Magonet, *Form and Meaning,* 22.

word-of Yhwh" (1:1; cf. 3:1,2,3). The verb "do" ('*śh*) recalls the questions of the sailors to Jonah: "What (is) this you-have-done? What shall-we-do to-you?" (1:10-11). Repeated vocabulary builds emphasis, contrast, and coherence between the scenes.

Summary. a. *For episode two.* In its entirety episode two responds to Jonah's announcement, "Yet forty days and-Nineveh will-be-overturned." Though he never exegetes his words, they appear to declare irreversible disaster. They make no call for repentance and propose no conditions for change. But the Ninevites hear in the words what Jonah may not have intended: the possibility of deliverance. In this case, the audience within the story, and not the author outside, controls the meaning of the text. The verb *hpk* (overturn) contains the irony of reversal. Through acts of penance and repentance Nineveh overturns, as Jonah predicted but not as he intended. Paradoxically his prophecy is both true and false. Perspective and interpretation make the difference. From the Ninevites' perspective the prophecy offers the hope, though not the guarantee, of repentance human and divine. From God's perspective their repentance overturns divine evil to bring deliverance. From Jonah's perspective, the divine deliverance overturns his prophecy to discredit it. The reversal makes him angry and so leads to a confrontation with God in the next episode.

b. *For structure and plot.* In the design of Jonah the episodes focused on the sailors balance the episodes focused on the Ninevites. Both plots appropriate the Aristotelian pattern of reversal and recognition. Efforts to avert calamity lead to change of fortune. For the sailors, the storm ceases; for the Ninevites, God repents of evil. Yet the move from ignorance to knowledge happens differently. For the sailors, recognition comes in stages before and after the reversal. In their attempts to stop the storm, they recognize the power of Yhwh to whom they pray. Only after the cessation do they recognize Yhwh through worship, sacrificing a sacrifice and vowing vows. For the Ninevites, recognition comes full blown just after Jonah's announcement; all of it precedes the reversal of fortune. Immediately the people believe in God, call a fast, and put on sackcloth. Their king follows suit. His decree recognizes simultaneously the power and the worship of God.

c. *For the characters.* Comparisons between structures and plots involve the depiction of the characters: length of appearance, use of dialogue, use of prayers with responses, and status and activity. First, the sailors occupy center stage; the captain makes a brief appearance. The king occupies center stage; the Ninevites make a shorter appearance. Second, the sailors address each other, Jonah, and Yhwh; the Ninevites

190

address no one. The captain addresses Jonah but never the sailors; the king addresses the Ninevites but never Jonah. Yet the brief words of the captain and the longer words of the king share sentiments and vocabulary: expression of hope ("perhaps" and "who knows"), reference to the deity as *hā-'elōhîm*, and use of the clause "and-not we-perish." Third, the sailors pray directly to Yhwh (1:14); narration reports obliquely the response (1:15b). The king and the people pray obliquely to God (3:8); narration reports directly the response (3:10). Fourth, at the beginning the sailors are innocent victims; at the beginning the Ninevites are attached to "their-evil" (1:2). Both groups confront impending disaster. Before deliverance the sailors pray; before deliverance the Ninevites repent. After deliverance the sailors worship; after deliverance the Ninevites disappear. In worshiping, the sailors make a sacrifice and vow vows (1:16); in repenting, the Ninevites call a fast and put on sackcloth (3:5, 7, 8).

Throughout episode two the depiction of Jonah fits the portrait already developed. The crisis for the sailors happens because of his flight from the presence of Yhwh. As they work out a solution, they consult him. His helpful response but supports his own self-interest. The crisis for the Ninevites happens because of Jonah's announcement to them. As they work out a solution, they do not consult him. His concomitant lack of response still supports his own self-interest. Thus far Jonah remains a self-centered man. (What this episode hints, episodes three and four will make abundantly clear.)

Comparisons among the characters display the talents of the storyteller to present types while eschewing stereotypes, to balance parts for the sake of the whole, and to sound emphases through artistic and thematic motifs.

EXCURSUS

No text is an island unto itself.[35] In reference to the third chapter of Jonah and to the corresponding section in the first chapter, form criticism augments rhetorical analysis by collecting numerous parallels in other biblical texts. The parallels help to identify a type of literature (genre) and a setting (*Sitz im Leben*) in which a people faces disaster, responds in penitence, and receives deliverance. Comparison and contrast illuminate six features.

1. The situations typically involve an entire society. When the Philistines threatened destruction, "all Israel" assembled at Mizpah (1 Sam.

---

35. Recall Frye's corrective to the isolationist tendencies of New Criticism.

7:5). When pestilence followed David's census, Israel and Judah "from Dan to Beersheba" was afflicted (2 Sam. 24:1, 15). When God portended evil against Judah, Jeremiah insisted that "all the people" hear the words of his scroll (Jer. 36:6, 9, 10). When in the time of Ezra mixed marriages threatened loss of identity for the Jews, "all the returned exiles" assembled at Jerusalem to resolve the matter (Ezra 10:7-9). When the Persian king Ahasuerus decreed annihilation for the Jews, his edict specified "all Jews, young and old, women and children" (Esther 3:6, 13). When the warrior Holofernes set out to destroy Israel, the description included all men and "their wives and their children and their cattle and every resident alien and hired laborer and purchased slave" (Jdt. 4:9-10). So in Jonah 3 when disaster looms, it covers all Nineveh, "from-their-great and-to their-small," "the-human and-the-animal, the-herd and-the-flock" (Jonah 3:5, 7, 8). Similarly in Jonah 1 disaster threatens the entire ship: its inhabitants, its cargo, and itself.

2. Individual leaders emerge in the crises. The prophet Samuel met the Philistine threat (1 Sam. 7:5). The scribe Ezra brought order to the post-exilic community in Judah (Ezra 7–10). The citizen Mordecai stood up to king Ahasuerus (Esther 3:4), and the high priest Joakim led Israel in confronting Holofernes (Jdt. 4:8). So in Jonah 3, the king emerges from among the Ninevites to make his official decree (3:6). In Jonah 1, the captain emerges briefly and then the sailors themselves lead.

3. Cultic sites often provide the settings for the crises. Samuel gathered Israel for worship at Mizpah (1 Sam. 7:5). Jeremiah had his scroll read in the temple (Jer. 36:10). Ezra first assembled the people for worship at the river Ahava and later brought them to Jerusalem, to the house of their God (Ezra 8:21-36). The Israelites prostrated themselves in front of the temple as Joakim and other priests offered sacrifices and offerings within it (Jdt. 4:9-15). By contrast, Esther and Jonah do not identify cultic sites, though they do record cultic acts of penance.

4. Penitential acts characterize responses to potential disaster. On a fast day Baruch read Jeremiah's scroll calling for repentance (Jer. 36:5). Ezra proclaimed a fast to seek God's protection for the exiles who began the dangerous journey homeward (Ezra 8:21-23). When Haman sought to destroy the Jews, Mordecai rent his clothes, put on sackcloth and ashes, and wailed. In every province the Jews lamented and fasted, most of them in sackcloth and ashes (Esther 4:1-3). As Esther prepared to approach the king (a dangerous act punishable by death), she ordered Mordecai to have the people fast on her behalf (Esther 4:15-17). In taking on Holofernes, Joakim ordered "the whole people" to fast and "put ashes on their heads

and spread out their sackcloth before the Lord" (Jdt. 4:8-11). So in Jonah 3 all the Ninevites fast, cover themselves in sackcloth, and call to God (Jon 3:5-8). In Jonah 1 the sailors cry, each to his god (1:5) and call to Yhwh (1:14). They sacrifice a sacrifice and vow vows.

5. Penitential acts lead to deliverance. In Samuel, Yhwh "thundered with a mighty voice against the Philistines" (1 Sam. 7:10). In Ezra, God heard the entreaty of the people (Ezra 8:23). Though in Esther the Jewish people did not explicitly invoke God, they were saved from annihilation (Esther 9:20-22). In Judith, Yhwh heard the cry of the people and delivered them from the Assyrians (Jdt. 13-16). So in Jonah 3 God delivers Nineveh from destruction (3:10). In Jonah 1 the storm ceases (1:15).

6. Conventional vocabulary marks these conventional situations. For instance, the verb "cry" (z^cq) describes the anguish of people and their appeals to God. Mordecai "cried" bitterly when he learned of the Persian orders to annihilate all Jews (Esther 4:1). The Israelites bade Samuel not to cease to "cry" to Yhwh so that they might be saved from the Philistines (1 Sam. 7:8). The king of Nineveh "cries" his proclamation to the people (Jon 3:7; cf. 1:5) even as the sailors "cry" to their gods (1:5). The vocabulary of "evil" ($r\bar{a}'\hat{a}$), "do" ($'\acute{s}h$), "turn" ($\check{s}\hat{u}b$), and "repent" (nhm) also fits these occasions. In the aftermath of David's census, when the angel prepared to destroy Jerusalem, Yhwh "repented of the evil" (2 Sam. 24:16). Jeremiah reported on "the evil" Yhwh intended "to do" and pondered if everyone would "turn from his evil ways" (Jer. 36:3, 7). The king of Nineveh orders that everyone "turn . . . from his way of evil" (Jonah 3:9); the narrator reports that the people "turned from their way of evil" and that God "repented of evil" and "did not do" it (Jon 3:10). Several stories use the particle "perhaps" (*'ûlay*) or its parallel "who knows" (*mî yôdēa'*) to express hope. Yhwh said through Jeremiah that "perhaps" Judah would repent and then be forgiven (Jer. 36:3). In persuading Esther to appeal to the king, Mordecai said, "Who knows if you have not come into the kingdom for such a time as this?" (Esther 3:14). So in Jonah the king of Nineveh concludes his decree, "who knows, the god may repent" (3:9) even as the captain says, "Perhaps the god may think of us" (1:6).

     o   o   o   o   o   o   o

Jonah 3 and its parallels in Jonah 1 belong to a community of literature with conventional speech for crisis settings. Form criticism identifies and interprets these typicalities. It provides point and counterpoint for the particularities that rhetorical analysis emphasizes. Speaking in concert, the tongues of these disciplines articulate meanings without confusion.

9
Internal Structure
of Scene Two (4:1-11)

As the conclusion of scene two, Jonah 4 parallels Jonah 2 at the close of scene one.[1] Juxtaposed in the external design, the endings focus on Yhwh and Jonah to yield point and counterpoint. In the first ending, these characters do not talk to each other; in the second, they talk. In the first, a prayer (psalm) disrupts the narrative to give an ambiguous picture of Jonah; in the second, a prayer fits the narrative to give a forthright picture. In the first, a brief narrative surrounding the prayer fails to explore the character of Jonah; in the second, an extended narrative surrounding the prayer probes his character. In the first, Yhwh overpowers Jonah; in the second, Yhwh seeks to persuade Jonah.

Chapter 4 may be described as a single episode or as two episodes with an intervening verse or as two episodes. The exclusive focus on Jonah and Yhwh throughout suggests a single episode. Yet the change of venue in provocative verse 5, "But-went-out Jonah from the-city. . . ," argues for two episodes (episodes three and four).[2] The verse relates

---

1. Note that Jonah 4 corresponds to units 8 and 9 of the external design. In scene one, unit 8 (response of the sailors) concludes episode three (units 7 and 8), all of which focuses on the sailors and Jonah. Unit 9 then begins episode four in which the sailors are not present and the focus is on Yhwh and Jonah. But in scene two, unit 7 (disaster averted) concludes episode two (units 5, 6, 7), all of which focuses on the Ninevites and God without reference to Jonah. Unit 8 (response of Jonah) then begins episode three where the Ninevites are not present and the focus returns to Jonah who subsequently prays to Yhwh. These correlations of units and episodes *within* each scene and the resulting divergences of their placements in the symmetry *between* scenes fit the rubric of the inseparability of form-content. See above, chapter 6 note 5.

2. If 4:5 were transposed, however, to follow 3:4, the resultant narrative would constitute a single episode with two incidents (4:1-4, 6-11).

195

to them variously as conclusion (4:1-5), transition (4:5), and introduction (4:5-11).[3]

A. EPISODE THREE (4:1-4 AND 5)

Apart from verse 5, episode three constitutes a single incident that reports Jonah's reaction to events in Nineveh (4:1), his prayer to Yhwh (4:2-3), and Yhwh's question to him (4:4). If verse 5 is regarded as the conclusion, it becomes the second incident.

1. Jonah and Yhwh (4:1-4)

Parallel clauses using the verb "burn" (*ḥrh*) delimit the incident. At the opening the narrator reports "the burning" of Jonah; at the end, Yhwh questions him about his "burning." Surrounding Jonah's prayer, his burning anger provides the context for his text.

> And-it-was-evil to Jonah an-evil great and-it-burned-to-him.
> And-he-prayed to Yhwh and-he-said:
> "Ah! Yhwh,
> Was-not this my-word while I-was in-my-homeland?
> Therefore I-hastened to-flee to-Tarshish
> because I-knew that
> You God (are)
> gracious and-merciful
> long-of nostrils
> and-abundant-of faithfulness
> and-repenting about the-evil.
> And-now Yhwh,
> take, please, my-*nepeš* from-me
> for better my-death than-my-life."
>
> And-said Yhwh, "Is-it-good it-burns to-you?" (4:1-4)

---

3. Note how translations treat 4:5. E.g., the RSV and NRSV use it to close a paragraph; the NJV and NAB use it to open a paragraph; the JB and NEB use it within a paragraph that includes all of chapter 4. Cf. Sasson, who holds that the choice made about the function of 4:5 "can influence our very understanding of Jonah's denouement" (*Jonah*, 270–72); also Wolff, *Obadiah and Jonah*, 162f.

a. Jonah's Reaction (4:1)

At the beginning narrated discourse mediates between episodes two and three. The turning of God (3:10), effected by the overturning of the Ninevites (3:5-9), causes an adverse effect upon Jonah (4:1).[4]

> And-it-was-evil (*wayyēraʿ*) to Jonah an-evil (*rāʿâ*) great
> and-it-burned to-him. (4:1)

Two clauses appropriating familiar vocabulary give Jonah's reaction to the divine response (3:10). The structure of the first mirrors its content. "Evil" as verb and cognate object consumes Jonah. At the opening of the story, Yhwh attributes "evil" to the Ninevites (1:2), and then the sailors apply it twice to the storm (1:7, 8). Later the king uses it in exhorting repentance (3:8), and the narrator in confirming repentance human and divine (3:10). This time "evil" encloses Jonah. The second clause describes its effect: "it-burned" (*wayyiḥar*), a verb first used for the deity: that God may turn "from-the-burning-of his-nostrils" (*mēḥarôn appô*, 3:9). What God has turned from now inflames Jonah. Wordplay blazingly contrasts the characters. The external design provides a second contrast, this one between the sailors and Jonah. Verbs with cognate objects enhance the juxtaposition.[5] The sailors sacrificed a sacrifice and vowed vows; Jonah "eviled" evil. Narrative sequence builds a third contrast, this one between the Ninevites and Jonah. They "turned from-their-way-of the-evil" (3:10); he "burned" with evil.

The precise referent(s) of the pronoun subject "it" in the verbs "it-was-evil" and "it-burned" remains uncertain.[6] Five possibilities emerge. "It" refers to all that happened in 3:5-10; "it" refers only to what happened in 3:10; "it" refers to Jonah himself; "it" signifies two different referents, all that happened as subject of the first verb and Jonah as subject of the second; it signifies two different referents, only what happened in 3:10 for the first verb and Jonah for the second. The following "dynamic" equivalent translations illustrate the possibilities.

> All this [that happened in Nineveh] infuriated Jonah
> and it inflamed him.

---

4. In interchanging cause and effect (a deconstructionist move), the verse continues a pattern endemic to the story.

5. See units 8 of the chart in chapter 5.

6. For a parallel construction, see Neh. 2:10.

This [the repentance of God] infuriated Jonah and it inflamed him.

Now Jonah was furious and he burned with anger.[7]

All that happened infuriated Jonah, and he burned with anger.[8]

This [the repentance of God] infuriated Jonah, and he burned with anger.

Whatever the referent(s) of "it," the narrator begins to expose the inner Jonah. Form critical and literary insights aid the exposure. Gunkel observed that biblical characters seldom receive psychological probings.[9] Often but a single trait is ascribed, specifically that trait needed for plot development. So characters emerge more as types than individuals. Alter extended the discussion by extracting from the Bible a scale for revealing characters. At the lower end come actions or appearances. In the middle comes speech, by or about the characters. At the upper end comes "the reliable narrator's explicit statement of what the characters feel, intend, desire."[10] Bar-Efrat rendered a comparable judgment.[11] Though words spoken by characters command respect, only statements put forth by the omniscient narrator (like those by God) have "absolute validity."[12] All these observations illuminate the sentence, "and-it-was-evil to Jonah an-evil great, and-it-burned to-him." The brief description singles out only the emotion of anger to make Jonah one-dimensional. Yet coming from the narrator, the information is totally reliable. It helps the reader interpret the prayer that follows.

---

7. Cf. Allen, *Books of Joel, Obadiah, Jonah and Micah,* 227: "Jonah was terribly upset, and angry too." Similarly, see the NEB and JB.

8. Cf. Wolff, *Obadiah and Jonah,* 159: "But this brought a great displeasure over Jonah and he became angry." Similarly, see the NAB, RSV, NRSV, NJV, and Sasson, *Jonah,* 270. On the meaning of the expression *wayyihar lōʾ,* scholars debate between "he was angry" and "he was depressed" or "unhappy." See Gruber, *Aspects of Nonverbal Communication in the Ancient Near East,* 373; Sasson, *Jonah,* 273–75.

9. Gunkel, *Legends of Genesis,* 53–67.

10. Alter, *Art of Biblical Narrative,* 116f.

11. Bar-Efrat, *Narrative Art in the Bible,* 47–92.

12. Ibid., 54. Cf. Sternberg's observations about the omniscient narrator (*Poetics of Biblical Narrative,* 12f and *passim*).

b. Jonah's Prayer (4:2-3)

Juxtaposed to the psalm in the external design, the prayer has an identical introduction: "and-he-prayed to Yhwh." The *hithpaʿel* form of the verb, *wayyitpallēl*, connotes a complaint song or lament. Unlike the first prayer, this one matches the genre and fits the narrative setting.[13] Like the complaint of the sailors (1:14), it divides into invocation, corpus, and conclusion.

Invocation	"Ah! (*'ānnâ*) Yhwh!
Corpus	
Rebuke	Was-not (*halô'*) this my-word
	while I-was (*-tî*) in my-homeland (*-tî*)?
Justification	Therefore (*'al-kēn*) I-hastened (*-tî*) to-flee to-Tarshish
Motivation	because I-knew that (*kî yādaʿtî kî*)
	You God (are)
	gracious and-merciful
	long-of nostrils
	and-abundant-of faithfulness
	and-repenting about the-evil.
Conclusion	
Petition	And-now (*weʿattâ*), Yhwh,
	take, please (*qaḥ-nā'*), my-*nepeš* (*napšî*) from-me,
Reason	for (*kî*) better my-death than-my-life." (4:2-3)

(1) Internal Analysis

The emphatic particle *'ānnâ* (ah!) and the divine name Yhwh compose the brief invocation. The more lengthy conclusion begins similarly. Within Yhwh's presence Jonah seeks to explain his past. The corpus contains rebuke, justification, and motivation. Like the invocation and the conclusion, it opens with a particle, the interrogative *ha-* combined with the negative *lô'*. Signaling either a rhetorical question or an emphatic adverb, the particle introduces new information as Jonah rebukes Yhwh: "Was-

---

13. Cf. in chapter 6 the discussion of the genre; also Sasson, *Jonah*, 276.

not this my-word while I-was in my-homeland?"[14] To this point the reader has not been told that Jonah spoke a word in his homeland. The narrator uses the strategy of delaying information. Whether direct or inward speech,[15] that "word" now vindicates Jonah over against Yhwh's "word" (1:1; 3:1, 2). A second particle, *'al-kēn* (therefore), links the new information to a known event as Jonah justifies himself: "Therefore[16] I-hastened to-flee to-Tarshish."[17] Self-justification prepares for the motivation: "Because I-knew that . . ." Introducing this conventional clause of disclosure, a third particle, *kî*, makes a causal connection with the preceding sentence. Next comes the verb *yādaʿtî* (I-knew) followed by a second *kî* that introduces the object clause of information. The sequence *kî yādaʿtî kî* produces rhythmic emphasis.[18] In addition, the verb completes a rhyming scheme that runs from the rebuke through the justification to the motivation. The syllable *-tî* appears at the end of four words, all of which accent Jonah:[19] *heyôtî* (I-was), *'admātî* (my-homeland), *qiddamtî* (I-hastened), *yādaʿtî* (I-knew).

These self-justifying words ironically testify to divine mercy. The independent pronoun "you" (*'attā*) and the appellative "God" (*'ēl*) preface four rhythmic phrases that form an ancient confession of divine attributes.[20]

---

14. Cf. H. A. Brongers, "Some Remarks on the Biblical Particle *halō*," *Remembering All the Way . . .*, 184f. Brongers argues for an adverbial, not an interrogative, emphasis: "This, O Lord, is exactly what I feared. . . ." Sasson agrees: "Please, Lord, this certainly was my opinion . . ." (*Jonah*, 270, 277). For a similar expression, cf. Exod. 14:12.

15. Sternberg interprets "my-word" to mean "a genuine dialogue" between Jonah and Yhwh (*Poetics of Biblical Narrative*, 320). Cf. Alter's discussion on rendering thought (inward speech) as direct speech; he ranks the former more reliable for revealing character (*Art of Biblical Narrative*, 67–70; 116f).

16. On the syntactic functions of *'al-kēn*, see Pedersen, *Israel*, 116–18; more recently, R. Frankena, "Einige Bemerkungen zum Gebrauch des Adverbs *'al-kēn* im Hebräischen," in *Studia Biblica et Semitica Theodoro Christiano Vriezen . . . Dedicata*, eds. W. C. van Unnik and A. S. van der Woude (Wageningen: H. Veenam and Zonen, 1966), 94–99.

17. Cf. Aristotle's dictum that character comes through choices made (*Aristotle's Poetics*, 13).

18. Use of the phrase in other texts illustrates its deictic function in calling attention to climactic utterances; e.g., Gen. 22:12b; Exod. 18:11; 1 Kings 17:24.

19. Sasson, *Jonah*, 277f.

20. Cf. Exod. 34:6-7; also Num. 14:18; Deut. 4:31; Joel 2:13; Nahum 1:3; Pss. 86:5, 15; 103:8; 111:4; 112:4; 145:8; Neh. 9:17, 31; 2 Chron. 30:9. Cf. Joseph Scharbert, "Formgeschichte und Exegese von Ex 34:6f und seiner Parallelen," *Biblica* 38 (1957): 130–50; Gottfried Varoni, *Das Buch Jona* (St. Ottilien: Eos Verlag, 1978), 139–41; Sasson, *Jonah*, 279–83.

The pair "gracious and-merciful" (ḥannûn weraḥûm) speaks of divine succor and maternal love.[21] It gives emphasis through assonance and pleonasm. The anthropomorphic expression "long-of nostrils" ('erek 'appayim) signifies friendliness and graciousness.[22] The description "and-abundant-of faithfulness" (werab-ḥesed) connotes the fullness of benevolence.[23] The characterization "and-repenting about the-evil" (weniḥām 'al-hārā'â) undercuts its own malicious object. As the heart of Jonah's prayer, appearing between rebuke and justification on the one side and petition and reason on the other, this recital of divine attributes motivates his behavior in the past and his request for the present.

The adverb we'attâ at the conclusion signals immediacy and urgency as Jonah again addresses Yhwh by name: "And-now Yhwh." The particle nā' (please), echoing 'ānnâ in the invocation, joins the imperative qaḥ (take) to make the petition: "Take, please, my-nepeš from-me." In four words Jonah asks the God who has just restored life to the Ninevites to take his life away. In four more words he gives his reason: "for (kî) better my-death than-my-life." The "i" sound of the first person pronoun in napšî (my-nepes), mimmennî (from-me), and môtî (my-death) keeps the accent on Jonah. It recalls the similar use of the "ti" sound running throughout the corpus. Altogether Jonah surrounds a confession about God with vocabulary and sounds that exalt Jonah. "I" and "my" prevail unto death.

Summary. Internal analysis of the prayer shows how form-content shapes meanings. Particles play a major role. Introducing each section ('ānnâ, halô', we'attâ) and each subsection ('al-kēn, kî . . . ki, nā', kî), they order the sense, provide the stress, harmonize the sounds, and facilitate the movement. Divine appellatives, "Yhwh," "God," and "Yhwh," punctuate the beginning, middle, and end. The address to Yhwh in the invocation leads Jonah to justify his past. The address to Yhwh in the conclusion leads him to reject his present and seek to terminate his future. Nine self-centered references, either "I," "me" or "my," enclose the theological center of the prayer, a confession to God about God's merciful character. The enclosure subverts the center. Jonah's affirmations about himself un-

---

21. Cf. Limburg, *Hosea-Micah,* 154; Trible, *God and the Rhetoric of Sexuality,* 1–5; 31–59.

22. See Gruber, *Aspects of Nonverbal Communication,* 485, 503.

23. Cf. Katharine Doob Sakenfeld, *Faithfulness in Action* (Philadelphia: Fortress, 1985), 47–52; Gordon R. Clark, *The Word* Hesed *in the Hebrew Bible,* JSOT Suppl. Ser. 157 (Sheffield: JSOT Press, 1993), 247–55.

dermine his affirmations about God. Colossal egocentrism ensnares true faith. Context betrays text.[24]

(2) External Analysis

What internal analysis shows, external analysis augments. The prayer gives and receives meanings throughout the story. First, juxtaposition to the psalm puts a double focus upon Jonah. In both passages he highlights himself through pronouns, possessives, and rhyming schemes.[25] He also borrows speech: the psalm and the ancient confession. But he mocks the message he borrows. In the belly of the fish he manipulates a testimony of thanksgiving to boast about himself; in the city of Nineveh he manipulates a theology of repentance to justify himself. His words sound dissonance within their respective settings. The context of the psalm (2:1, 11) hardly accounts for the incongruity; the context of the prayer (4:1, 4) posits anger as the explanation. Juxtaposition of the prayer and the psalm develops the portrait of self-confirmatory Jonah.

Second, the prayer appropriates vocabulary and idioms appearing in the narrative and the psalm. The deictic phrase *kî yāda'tî kî* (because I-knew that) matches phrases in narrated discourse about what the sailors knew (1:10) and in direct discourse about what Jonah knew (1:12).[26] The description God "long-of nostrils" (*'erek 'appayim*) plays on God's turning "from-the-anger-of his-nostril" (*mēharôn 'appô*, 3:9). God "abundant-of faithfulness" (*werab hesed*) plays off those who forsake faithfulness (*hesed*, 2:9). God "repenting about the-evil" (*wenihām 'al hārā'a*) confirms the king's hope that God may "repent" (*nhm*, 3:9) and the narrator's report that "the-God repented (*nhm*) of the-evil" (*'al hārā'â*, 3:10).[27] In the conclusion the words *nepeš*, "life," and "death" sound themes from scene one. The sailors implore that they not "die" because of the *nepeš* of Jonah (1:14). Jonah describes the water enclosing his *nepeš* (2:6), the ebbing away of his *nepeš* (2:8), and Yhwh's restoring his "life" (2:7c). Now he prays, "Take, please, my-*nepeš* from-me, for better my-death than-my-life

---

24. Yet as the story progresses, the text may well betray the context. The merciful God continues to reach out to Jonah despite his egocentric affirmations. Thereby the center subverts the enclosure; gracious Yhwh subverts angry Jonah.

25. Cf. the discussion in chapter 7.

26. Cf. Schoors, "The Particle כִּי," 240–76.

27. Cf. other links to the vocabulary of evil in scene one; see Halpern and Friedman, "Composition and Paronomasia in the Book of Jonah," 85.

(*mehayyay*)." Drawing upon a rich vocabulary, the prayer reiterates the familiar and initiates the new.

Third, the prayer fills a major gap in scene one, a gap of information between Yhwh's command (1:2) and Jonah's response (1:3). In explaining why Jonah "arose to-flee to-Tarshish," the prayer evokes a discussion among rhetorical criticism, poetics, and reader-response criticism. Sternberg declares the absence of an explanation between 1:2 and 1:3 "the only biblical instance where a surprise gap controls the reader's progress over a whole book."[28] He thinks that at first the reader would fill the gap with "the self-evident" reason that Jonah "is too tender-hearted to carry a message of doom to a great city." This hypothesis holds throughout scene one, which "fixes the image of the God of Wrath." By the beginning of scene two, "what began as a conjecture has hardened into certainty." Ideologically, then, the narrative "plays a dangerous game in misleading the reader almost to the end." The reversal in 3:10—4:3 (the sparing of Nineveh and Jonah's angry prayer) "shatters the entire model of the narrative world and world view . . ." to show that God is merciful and Jonah wrathful. In other words, the overturning (*hpk*) that happens within the story also happens between the story and the reader.

In the filling of gaps there is no end. What Sternberg deems "self-evident" another reader may not. Indeed, this reader fills the gap with other reasons. The first holds that Jonah arose to flee to Tarshish because he was scared. He fled because he feared that the messenger would suffer the doom of his message. The Ninevites would kill him.[29] The second reason turns Sternberg's reading upside down. Jonah fled because he was wrathful. He refused to announce doom upon Nineveh lest it not happen. But if he did nothing, doom would come. Early on his willingness to endanger innocent sailors challenges any idea of his tender-heartedness. By the same token, the hopeful words of the captain (1:9) and the sparing of the sailors (1:15) work against any "fixe[d] image of the God of Wrath," especially in reference to foreigners. In fact, through indirection these events prepare the reader for the possibility of divine mercy toward Nineveh.

Although these reasons counter Sternberg's filling of the gap, they accept his assumption that Jonah was commanded to "carry a message of doom" to Nineveh. Yet the unstable quality of the words "call to-her *kî*

---

28. Sternberg, *Poetics of Biblical Narrative*, 318–20.
29. Cf. Frye, who said that Jonah had "no taste for martyrdom" (*The Great Code*, 191).

has-come-up their-evil before-my-presence" (1:2) may mean that Jonah is to warn rather than doom Nineveh.[30] Such interpretation accords with the hypothesis of a hardhearted Jonah. He fled because he did not want to warn Nineveh; after all, it might repent and the doom not come. When in his prayer (4:2-3) hardhearted Jonah belatedly fills the gap, the reader is nevertheless appalled. Jonah accuses and condemns Yhwh for being Yhwh. He castigates divine mercy to justify himself. His anger attacks God's compassion. Thus he is far more "wrathful" than the reader suspected. His reason(s) for fleeing the command has to do, then, not with Nineveh itself, not with his views about foreigners, but with the very character of God.

As Jonah's prayer fills the gap, so it shifts the focus of the entire narrative. In effect it brackets all that has happened from the hurling of the great storm (1:4) through the deliverance of Nineveh (3:10) to engage the beginning of the story. The reference to "this my-word" opposes "the-word-of Yhwh" that started it all (1:1-2). The explanation "therefore I-hastened to-flee to-Tarshish" repeats the narrator's report at the beginning of scene one (1:3). Yet the repetition omits the telling phrase "from-the-presence-of Yhwh." The omission confirms what structure demonstrated: Jonah cannot flee from the presence of Yhwh. Hence, his prayer brings the story back to its beginning. The conversation not undertaken at that time commences *post facto*. Jonah has now confronted Yhwh.

c. Yhwh's Question (4:4)

Angry Jonah has launched his attack by asking Yhwh a rhetorical question (or by making an emphatic declaration): "Was-not this my-word . . .?" He has concluded by petitioning Yhwh for death, "And-now, Yhwh, take, please, my-*nepeš* from-me, for better my-death than-my-life" (4:2-3). Yhwh answers immediately by asking Jonah a question that evaluates and interprets the death wish. "And-said Yhwh, 'Is-it-good it-burns to-you?'" (4:4). The question belongs to the genre of disputation, a form-critical category that designates an argument between parties who hold differing points of view.[31] For Yhwh, Jonah's request to die manifests anger that is

---

30. Cf. the discussion in chapter 6. Note also that the second time around the words of Yhwh are even less suggestive of doom (3:2). They leave the substance of the message unclear. Cf. the discussion in chapter 8.

31. Cf. Long, *1 Kings*, FOTL, 248.

not good. The divine question plays off the narrated report, "And-it-was-evil to Jonah an-evil great and-it-burned to-him" (4:1). The two reliable witnesses, the narrator and Yhwh, encircle Jonah's prayer to identify the mode of being from which it comes. By countering Jonah, Yhwh seeks to persuade him to leave the circle of anger. But the rhetorical maneuver does not work.

2. Jonah Alone (4:5)

Jonah does not answer; instead, he walks away.

A	But-went-out Jonah from the-city
B	and-he-sat-down from-the-east to-the-city.
A'	And-he-made for-himself there a-booth
B'	and-he-sat-down under-it in the-shade
C	until ('ad 'ašer) he-should-see what would-happen in-the-city.

Four main clauses and a subordinate clause present Jonah's diversionary reaction to Yhwh's question. Parallel prepositional phrases about the city link the first two clauses and the last (A, B, C). The same verb, "and-he-sat-down" (*wayyēšeb*), begins the second and fourth clauses (B and B'). This verb of inactivity alternates with different verbs of activity in the first and third clauses: Jonah "went-out" (*wayyēṣē'*, A) and "he-made" (*wayya'aś*, A'). All these verbs deliver Jonah to the purposive verbs of the ending: "until he-should-see what would-happen."

Scholars propose three readings of the verse.[32] The first transposes 4:5 to follow 3:4, just after Jonah called to Nineveh. As rhetorical analysis has shown, external design supports the argument for transposition.[33] Vocabulary reinforces it. The word "city" clusters in 3:2, 3, 4 (cf. 1:2) and so draws 4:5 into its orbit. The second reading leaves 4:5 in place but interprets it as reporting on Jonah just after his announcement (3:4).[34] In translation the pluperfect tense may appear: "Now Jonah had gone out. . . ."[35]

---

32. Cf. Sasson, *Jonah*, 287–89.

33. See the discussion in chapters 5 and 8.

34. E.g., Wolff, *Obadiah and Jonah*, 159f, 163, who follows Lohfink in finding here "the flashback style"; Lohfink, "Jona ging zur Stadt hinaus (Jon 4,5)," 185–203; also Allen, *Books of Joel, Obadiah, Jonah and Micah*, 230f.

35. The proposal for the pluperfect tense is a relatively old one. Among Jews, cf., e.g., Radak, Rashi, and Ibn Ezra; among Christians, cf., e.g., Newcome, Rosenmüller, and Hitzig. On these critics and this matter see the commentaries.

Though accepting the logic of the argument for transposition, this interpretation holds fast to the final form of the text. It maintains that 4:5 fits
a tendency throughout the story to delay information (cf. 1:10 and 4:2).
The third reading both leaves the verse in place and interprets it in
place.[36] Jonah replies to Yhwh's question by walking away. He sits (sulks?)
in the shade of his booth outside the city to watch Nineveh. Thereby he
breaks off the conversation, sets distance, and shifts attention.

Vocabulary within 4:5 reaches out to set up a series of contrasts. The
noun in the prepositional phrase *miqqedem* (from-the-east) echoes the
sound *qiddamtî* (I-hastened, 4:2) and prepares for *qādîm* (east, 4:8).[37]
Once Jonah hastened to the west (the direction of Tarshish), but Yhwh
intercepted him. Now he locates in the east where God will appoint a
wind to attack him. The "shade" (*ṣēl*) he fashions for himself anticipates
the "shade" (*ṣēl*) that Yhwh will provide him (4:6). The verb "he-sat-
down" (*wayyēšeb*) parallels him to the king of Nineveh who "sat-down"
(*wayyēšeb*, 3:6). The king repents upon the ashes; Jonah rests in the
shade. The verb "and-he-made" (*wayya'aś*) reverberates with three deriv-
atives of the root 'śh (3:10): "their-deeds" (*ma'aśêhem*), "to-do" (*la'aśôt*),
and "and-not do" (*welō' 'āśâ*). Over against the work of Jonah stand the
deeds of the Ninevites and Yhwh. Moreover, the verb "he-should-see"
(*yir'eh*) contrasts him with the deity. When God "saw" (*wayyar'*) what the
Ninevites did, the deity repented of evil (3:10). With the same verb Jonah
looks at the city, but he "sees" differently. Whether he visualizes a relapse
by the Ninevites or their deliverance sustained, the narrator does not say.
Nevertheless, the depiction in 4:5 sets him in opposition to all that has
happened.

Jonah's behavior is ironically self-defeating. To go out from the city
leaves the place where the divine question was asked; yet previous geo-
graphical efforts to escape Yhwh's word have failed. To make a booth secures a shelter; yet in the past neither the innards of the vessel nor the
waters of the sea nor the belly of the fish has protected Jonah from Yhwh.
To sit down twice entrenches Jonah's position; yet other efforts at en-
trenchment have brought expulsion. To see what would happen in the
city resists what has already happened; yet from the beginning his resistance has not succeeded. Jonah's narrated response to Yhwh's direct question shows habitual defiance while hinting at inevitable defeat. Altogether,

36. E.g., Magonet, *Form and Meaning*, 58, 60; Limburg, *Hosea-Micah*, 154.
37. See Sasson, *Jonah*, 289.

verse 5 signals a major shift in the story; it moves the last episode out-side Nineveh.

B. EPISODE FOUR (4:6-11)

Episode four shifts the ground of the argument from the large to the small (*a maiori ad minus*), from Nineveh to Jonah. Five incidents unfold. The first three report appointments by Yhwh that eventually lead to speech by Jonah (4:6-8); the fourth presents a conversation between Yhwh and Jonah (4:9); the fifth poses a question by Yhwh to Jonah (4:10-11).

1. Yhwh's Appointments with Jonah (4:6-8)

Three tightly woven incidents show Yhwh using a circuitous rhetoric. It seeks to persuade Jonah through indirection.

And-appointed Yhwh God a-plant,

    and-it-grew-up from-upon (*mē'al*) to-Jonah

        to-be a-shade upon (*'al*) his-head

        to-deliver to-him from-his-evil,

    and-delighted Jonah upon (*'al*) the-plant a-delight great. (4:6)

And-appointed the-God a-worm,

        when-came-up the-dawn on-the-next-day,

    and-it-attacked the-plant

    and-it-withered. (4:7)

And-it-came-to-pass when-to-rise the-sun

    and-appointed God a-wind, east strong

    and-attacked the-sun upon (*'al*) the-head-of Jonah

    and-he-fainted

    and-he-asked his-*nepeš* (*napšô*) to-die and-he-said,

        "Better my-death than-my-life." (4:8)

Use of the verb "appoint" with the natural objects of plant, worm, and wind resonates with scene one where Yhwh "appointed" a great fish to swallow Jonah (2:1). Yet the contrast between one and three occurrences of the verb skews the symmetry to accent the longer passage. It gives three different formulations for the divine subject: "Yhwh God," "the-God," and "God." They collect all the divine references throughout the narrative, beginning with the distinctive name Yhwh in the hybrid appellative "Yhwh God" (cf. 1:1 and *passim;* also 1:9; 2:7) and moving to the demonstrative or emphatic "the-God" (cf. 1:6; 3:9, 10) and the simple generic "God" (cf. 3:5, 8).[38] To parallel these variant designations through the single verb "appoint" lends theological cohesion to the story. Other vocabulary strategically placed binds these incidents. "Jonah" and "head" appear in the first and third but not in the second incident. "Plant" appears in the first and second, but not in the third. "Attack" appears in the second and third but not in the first. Occupying the middle position, the clause "and-it-attacked the-plant" reaches forward and backward. A chart of the five words indicates their locations and relationships as it prepares for close readings to come.

4:6	4:7	4:8
appointed	appointed	appointed
	attacked	attacked
plant	plant	
Jonah		
head		head
Jonah		Jonah
plant		

Incidents one (4:6) and three (4:8) contain three parallel topics: divine appointment, the effect upon Jonah, and Jonah's reaction. Yhwh God appoints a plant; it shades Jonah; he delights in it (4:6). God appoints a wind; the sun causes Jonah to faint; he asks to die (4:8). The middle incident has but two of the topics. The-God appoints a worm; the plant withers (4:7). Missing altogether is Jonah's reaction to the withering. Thus in the center of these tightly woven incidents, the structure does not hold; in the center, the content does not hold. Like the plant on which it reports, incident two withers. Another chart outlines the interrelationship of the topics to expose the missing information and so prepare for close readings to come.[39]

38. For a literary analysis of the various designations for deity, see Magonet, *Form and Meaning,* 33–38.
39. Remember that topical or thematic arrangements depend for their validity upon structural analysis of the verbatim text. See the discussion in chapter 4, p. 104f.

4:6	4:7	4:8
divine appointment	divine appointment	divine appointment
effect on Jonah	effect on plant	effect on Jonah
Jonah's reaction		Jonah's reaction

a. Plant (4:6)

While Jonah waits outside Nineveh to see what will happen in the city, Yhwh God concentrates on him.

> And-appointed Yhwh God a-plant,
>> and-it-grew-up from-upon ($m\bar{e}'al$) to-Jonah
>>> x x x   x x x x x x
>>>   * * * * * * *
>
>> to-be a-shade upon ('al) his-head
>>> x x x x   x x x x x x
>> to-deliver to-him from-his-evil,
>> and-delighted Jonah upon ('al) the-plant a-delight great. (4:6)
>>> + + + + + + + + + + * * * * * x x x x   x x x x x x + + + + + + +

Besides the verb "appoint," three words evoke past events: "shade," "head," and "evil." The "shade" ($s\bar{e}l$) of the plant follows immediately upon the "shade" ($s\bar{e}l$) of the booth (4:5). Built by opposing characters, these shelters give Jonah double protection from opposite perspectives.[40] Under his booth Jonah sits; above "his-head" Yhwh appoints a plant.[41] In the belly of the fish weeds entwine to Jonah's "head" (2:6); now the plant shades "his-head" to deliver him "from-his-evil." The word "evil" has been associated variously with characters throughout the story, beginning with the Ninevites (1:2), moving to the sailors (1:7), returning to the Ninevites (3:10), coming to God (3:10; 4:2), and surrounding Jonah (4:1). Except in reference to Jonah, all the evil has been dispelled. Now the infinitive clause in which the word last appears seeks to remove its power over him: "to-deliver to-him from-his-evil."[42]

Sasson discerns a pattern in the four consecutive clauses that describe the appointment and purpose of the plant.[43] The first two are indepen-

40. Cf. Sasson's interpretation of directional opposites (*Jonah*, 298).
41. The word translated "plant" ($q\hat{i}q\bar{a}y\hat{o}n$) appears only here in the Bible, thereby rendering botanical identification virtually impossible.
42. Sasson wonders if the first and last occurrences of the noun "evil," each constructed with pronominal suffixes ("their-evil," 1:2 and "his-evil," 4:6), "can be labeled 'grammatical inclusio.'" They surround seven instances of the noun in the absolute form (*Jonah*, 755f).
43. Ibid., 290.

dent: "and-appointed Yhwh God a-plant"; "and-it-grew-up from-upon to-Jonah." The last two are infinitive clauses: "to-be a-shade upon his-head"; "to-deliver to-him from-his-evil." Charting the pattern as A a : b B, he finds contrasting forms joined to comparable subject matter. The outside sections report on God. The independent clause announces Yhwh's work, the appointment of the plant (A); the infinitive clause cites Yhwh's purpose, to deliver Jonah from his evil (B). The inside sections center on the plant. The independent clause describes its work, growing over Jonah (a); the infinitive clause cites its purpose, to shade his head (b). Rhetorical analysis observes further that in structure and content A and B contain and control a and b. The work and purpose of the plant on the inside take their meaning from the work and purpose of Yhwh on the outside.

Repetitions of vowels and consonants enhance the interplay among these clauses. On the insides (a and b) the sound *'al* reverberates three times and the Hebrew letter *lāmed* (l) appears in every word until the end:

> and-it-grew-up (*wayya'al*) from-upon (*mē'al*) to-Jonah (*leyônâ*)
> to-be (*liheyôt*) a-shade (*ṣēl*) upon (*'al*) his-head.

Lāmed also relates the two infinitive clauses (b and B). It occurs three times in each, excluding the last words:

> to-be (*liheyôt*) a-shade (*ṣēl*) upon (*'al*) his-head
> to-deliver (*lehaṣṣîl*) to-him (*lô*) from-his-evil.

Repetition of the combined Hebrew consonants *ṣādê* and *lāmed* (ṣ and l) produces a play between the noun "shade" in the first clause and the infinitive "to-deliver" in the second (*ṣēl . . . lehaṣṣîl*). "Shade" resonates with its purpose "to-deliver." In addition to consonants, the vowel sound "o" binds these clauses through rhyme artfully placed at the end of each:

> to-be a-shade upon his-head (*rō'šô*)
> to-deliver to-him (*lô*) from-his-evil (*mērā'ātô*).

The close associations between the infinitive clauses illustrate the rhetorical device asyndeton (literally, "unconnected"). It designates clauses set

210

side by side without a connecting conjunction: "to-be a-shade upon his-head to-deliver to-him from-his-evil." Without even the interruption of a connective (which itself brings disconnection) one infinitive clause merges with the other. The plant's purpose merges with Yhwh's purpose.

Throughout the consecutive clauses marked A a : b B, literary and rhetorical features accumulate emphases. They converge upon the last line in which the narrator gives Jonah's reaction to the appointing of the plant and its effect upon him:[44]

And-delighted Jonah upon the-plant a-delight great.

Structurally, delight envelops Jonah and the plant by the familiar construction of verb and cognate object (cf. 1:10, 16; 3:2; 4:1). Within the circle of delight, the words "Jonah" and "plant" relate inversely to the first two lines of the incident:

a
And-appointed Yhwh God a-plant,
b
and-it-grew-up from-upon to-Jonah

b' **a'**
And-delighted Jonah upon the-plant a-delight great.

Occupying the fourth position in the first and last lines, the references to "plant" enclose the references to Jonah. As in meaning so in structure, the plant shades him. But does it deliver him from evil? Though familiar as a syntactic arrangement, the delight that envelops him introduces verbal strangeness. The root *śmḥ* ("delight") occurs nowhere else in the book. Furthermore, the verb fails to confirm the intended purpose of the plant. It does not report that Jonah is delivered from his evil.

---

44. Note the principle of cause and effect operating in the incident.

b. Worm (4:7)

Time passes. A second incident happens.

And-appointed the-God a-worm,

> when-came-up the-dawn on-the-next-day,
> and-it-attacked the-plant
>
> and-it-withered. (4:7)

The report begins expansively with a complex construction of six words. It then shrinks to a simple clause of two words and again to a single word that may nonetheless serve several meanings. A worm advances the plot circuitously. Like the fish of the sea, the worm of the earth is God's instrument; unlike the fish, it does not relate to Jonah. Instead, "it-attacked the-plant." As first object of the verb "appointed" (*mnh*) and then subject of the verb "attacked" (*nkh*), the worm mediates between God and the plant. It shields the deity from directly perpetrating death. But the plant "withered." The sound of the verb form *wayyîbāš* (it-withered) echoes *hayyabbāšâ* (dry land) to evoke verbal association with the fish episode (2:11; cf. 1:9, 13). The purpose of the verb is to report the demise of the plant. By so doing, it adds nuances to the theme of death. In structure, syntax, and grammar "it-withered" is an exact parallel to "it-attacked." The association suggests that after doing its job, the worm, like the plant, died. For sure, the incident withers. It stops without reporting Jonah's reaction to the demise of the plant. Yet precisely for Jonah did the plant flourish.

c. Sun and Wind (4:8)

One thing leads to another; a third incident ensues.

> And-it-came-to-pass when-to-rise the-sun
>
> > and-appointed God a-wind, east strong
> > and-attacked the-sun upon ('al) the-head-of Jonah
>
> and-he-fainted
> and-he-asked his-*nepeš* to-die and-he-said,
> > "Better my-death than-my-life." (4:8)

The first four lines resemble the four lines of the preceding incident. Between the incidents lines one and two relate inversely:

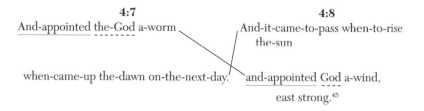

4:7
And-appointed the-God a-worm

4:8
And-it-came-to-pass when-to-rise
the-sun

when-came-up the-dawn on-the-next-day.

and-appointed God a-wind,
east strong.[45]

Acts by God, the appointing of a worm and a wind, interchange positions
with acts by nature, the coming up of the dawn (*haššaḥar*) and the rising
of the sun (*haššemeš*). Yet parallel relationships cut across the inversion.
Worm and sun endure; dawn and wind fade away. The third and fourth
lines report the endurance:

4:7
and-it-attacked the-plant
and-it-withered.

4:8
and-attacked the-sun upon the-head-of Jonah
and-he-fainted.

Parallel lines build on cause and effect. They share the verb "attack" and
then shrink to single verbs with corresponding meanings. The plant in its
withering ironically foreshades Jonah in his fainting.[46] Thanks to a killer
worm, protected Jonah has become exposed Jonah. The sun attacks
"upon-his-head" (cf. 4:6). So now he heads into another experience,
namely his reaction to it all.

The concluding lines of incident three contrast with the ending of incident one.

4:6
And-delighted Jonah upon the-plant
a-delight great.

4:8
and-he-asked his-*nepeš* to-die
and-he-said, "Better my-death
than-my-life."

From delight to death, Jonah reacts according to how events affect him.
On the first occasion, the narrator portrays him in a new light. On the

---

45. The description of the wind as "east-strong" relies on the common adjective
qādîm (east, cf. 4:5) and the unique term *ḥarîšît* whose meaning resists certainty. Cf. the
"great" (*gedôlâ*) wind that Yhwh hurled to the sea (1:4). Sasson suggests that *ḥarîšît* may
play off *gedôlâ* to connote strength (*Jonah*, 302–4).

46. Note also the association in sound in the external design between the verb *'tp*
(ebb-away, 2:8) and the verb *'lp* (fainted, 4:8). But the occasions of their use diverge sharply.
In the setting of the psalm Jonah seeks life; after the rising of the sun he seeks death.

second, Jonah portrays himself by repeating sentiments from the past (cf. 4:3). Neither plant nor worm nor wind nor sun has stayed him from his self-appointed round of seeking death.

2. Conversation between God and Jonah (4:9)

Jonah holds fast and God persists. In the fourth incident the deity initiates another disputatious conversation and on this occasion receives an answer (cf. 4:4-5).

> And-said God to Jonah,
> "Is-it-good it-burns to-you about the-plant?"
>
> And-he-said,
> "It-is-good it-burns to-me unto death." (4:9)

Once again God evaluates and interprets the death wish as an expression of anger. Jonah answers by turning the interrogative into the declarative. Divergent phrases at the endings of the question and the reply can be read both in sequence and in parallel. The first reading declares that burning "about the-plant" (a word Jonah himself never uses) is good "unto death." In other words, the phrase "unto death" follows from the incident "about the-plant." The second reading draws an analogy between the withered plant and desired death. In other words, the phrase "about the-plant" becomes a paradigm for the wish "unto death." In both cases, Jonah's affirmation repudiates God's intention. Good is anger unto death. The divine rhetoric has not worked.

This incident (4:9) repeats and diverges from the latter parts of episode three. A chart shows the relationships.[47]

4:3-5	4:8ef-9b
A *Jonah's Request to Yhwh for Death*	**A'** *Jonah's Inward Request for Death*
"And-now, Yhwh, take, please, my-*nepeš* from-me	And-he-asked his-*nepeš* to-die, and-he-said,
for better my-death than-my-life."	"Better my-death than-my-life."
(4:3)	(4:8ef)

---

47. Note the similarites and differences between this structure and the one proposed by Terence E. Fretheim, *The Message of Jonah* (Minneapolis: Augsburg Publishing House, 1977), 117.

214

B *Divine Question*

And-said Yhwh,
"Is-it-good it-burns to-you?" (4:4)

C *Jonah's Response*

But-went-out Jonah from-the-city
and-he-sat-down from-the-east to-
the-city.

And-he-made for-himself there a-
booth
and-he-sat-down under-it in-the-
shade until he-should-see what
would-happen in-the-city. (4:5)

B′ *Divine Question*

And-said God to Jonah,
"Is-it-good it-burns to-you about
the-plant?" (4:9a)

C′ *Jonah's Response*

And-he-said,
"It-is-good it-burns to-me unto-
death." (4:9b)

Structural, verbal, and thematic ties bind A and A′. Whether addressing Yhwh or himself, Jonah clings to his death wish. Structural, verbal, and thematic ties bind B and B′. Divine questions keep the heat on Jonah. Though the first does not specify the object of his anger (cf. 4:2), it forms an implied contrast with the second, which specifies the plant. The gravity of God counters the puniness of the plant to expose Jonah's problem as anger qua anger. Whatever happens contrary to his will leads him to choose death. The ties between A and A′ and B and B′ help to secure the structural and thematic correspondences between the divergent responses in C and C′. Jonah's narrated refusal to answer the first question (i.e., his exit) contrasts with his direct reply to the second. So he bridges distance but not defiance. "It-is-good it-burns to-me unto-death" are his very last words. They end, as his actions began, opposing Yhwh. But Jonah does not have the last word.

3. Yhwh's Question to Jonah (4:10-11)

In the last incident Yhwh poses another question.[48] It too fits the genre of disputation and follows a death wish by Jonah (4:3-4; 4:8-9). But

---

48. *Contra* Cooper who holds that the assumption of the interrogative (rather than the declarative) in 4:11 "flies in the face of the parallelism with 4:10" ("In Praise of Divine Caprice," 158–59). Instead, the contrast in grammar between the two verses produces the parallelism between Jonah and Yhwh. Moreover, Cooper's preference for the declarative "based on reading Jonah in light of Nahum" allows Nahum to control the meaning of Jonah. Another intertextual reading might just as easily reverse the relationship and the meaning. After all, *post hoc non est propter hoc.*

whereas the first two questions reflect in structure the two commands to Jonah (1:2 and 3:2), as parts reflect the whole, the third question stands apart. Whereas the first two balance each other in content and position, the third has no match. Whereas the first two engage the same subject of Jonah's death wish, the third shifts the argument. In various ways that cohere Yhwh plots a different rhetoric.

	4:10	4:11

And-said Yhwh

A "You, you-pitied for the-plant   **A'** And-I, (shall) not I-have-pity
                                                      ×××
                                                   for Nineveh the-city the-great.
                                                            ****

B which not you-planted it   **B'** which (is) in-it to-be-many
·······×××   ·······
and-not you-caused-it-to-be-great   more-than-two ten-of ten-
×××   ****   thousand human

C which-a-child-of the-night became   **C'** who not know between his-right-
······· +++++++++++++++   ·······×××
and-a-child-of the-night perished.   hand to-his-left
++++++++++++++++++++
                                        D and-animal(s) many?"

a. Internal Analysis

The disputation divides into two complex and complicated sentences. Each contains an independent clause and two relative clauses. At the start (A and A') independent personal pronouns emphasize Jonah and Yhwh: "You" (*'attâ*), "and-I" (*wa'anî*). Matching forms of the verb "pity" (*ḥûs*) build an analogy between them: "you-pitied"; "(shall) not I-have-pity." Prepositional phrases beginning with "for" (*'al*) pose the contrast: "for the-plant" and "for Nineveh the-city the-great." The relative clauses, introduced by the pronoun "which" or "who" (*'ašer* or the variant *še*), continue the analogy and the contrast. They relate in intricate ways. B and B' pair the great size of the plant and the large population of Nineveh. C and C' pair a child-plant and an ignorant population. Another pattern operates. Negative statements in B and C' (the adverb *lō'*, "not") crisscross with positive statements in C and B'.[49] The former pair Jonah's lack of power over the plant with the Ninevites' lack of knowledge. The latter pair the singularity and ephemerality of the plant with the plurality and gravity of the Ninevites. The coda (D) at the close of verse 11 extends the description of the city to its animals. Syntax implicates them in the ignorance of the humans; the adjective "many" (*rabbâ*) parallels them to the size of the city with its "many (*harbēh*) more-than."

Between these complicated sentences balance and imbalance contend. The sixteen words of the declarative give the premise for the twenty-three words of the interrogative. As the number of words, so goes the weight of the argument. It moves from the small to the great (*a minori ad maius*), from Jonah and the plant to Yhwh and Nineveh.[50] Yet because Yhwh concludes the second sentence with a question, rather than an imperative or a declarative, Jonah holds over the divine argument the power of an answer.

Vocabulary within the relative clauses lends familiarity, strangeness, and emphasis to the disputation. The verb "to-be-great" elevates the plant even while preparing for its diminishment in contrast to the "great" city.[51] The unique description "a-child-of-the-night" plays off the previous references to the dawn and the sun (4:7, 8). The verb "became" (*hāyâ*) gives life; it recalls the growing up of the plant (4:6). The verb "perished" (*'ābād*) brings death; it recalls the withering (4:7).[52] Unusual constructions depict Nineveh. Belabored counting stresses its size: "to-be-many more-than-two ten-of ten-thousand human." The city's population of more than one hundred twenty thousand plays off its spatial dimensions of "a-walk-of three days" (3:3). With the consonants *rēš* (r) and *bêt* (b), the verb *harbēh* (to-be-many) evokes the word *ribbô* (ten-thousand). In turn, *ribbô* resounds in *rabbâ* (many), the last word of the book.[53] The collective term *'ādām* (human) and the collective word *ûbhēmâ* (and-animal) pick up on

---

49. For a similar arrangement of two parallel independent clauses followed by relative clauses arranged chiastically, cf. 4:7-8.

50. Another Latin phrase describing this argument is *a fortiori* (all the more). In Hebrew the comparable term is *qal wāḥōmer;* see L. Jacobs, "The *Qal Va-homer* Argument in the Old Testament," *BSOAS* 35 (1972): 221–27; also Sasson, *Jonah*, 307–8. Cf. the reversal of this movement (*a maiori ad minus*) at the beginning of the episode (4:6-8).

51. Note that Yhwh and the narrator, in contrast to Jonah (3:4), have steadfastly retained the appositive "great" for Nineveh (1:2; 3:2, 3, 4, 5, 6, 7; 4:10).

52. Note that this occurrence of *'bd* completes its fourfold appearance (1:6, 14; 3:9; 4:10); cf. the comments in chapter 5.

53. See K. Almbladh, *Studies in the Book of Jonah*, Studia Semitica Upsaliensis 7 (Stockholm: Almqvist & Wiksell International, 1986), 40.

their identical pairing in the royal edict: *hāʾādām wehabbēhemâ* (3:7, 8). The phrase not knowing "between his-right-hand to-his-left" is unique in the Bible. Across centuries its precise meaning has eluded commentators.[54]

The verb *ḥûs* (have-pity or compassion) in the independent clauses is new to the story. The concept it conveys fits well Yhwh, who has repented toward Nineveh (3:10) but seems altogether inappropriate for Jonah. Nowhere in the narrative has he shown pity, for the plant or anything else. (Self-pity is another matter.) Yet on Yhwh's attribution of the verb to Jonah hinges the validity of Yhwh's argument. *Ḥûs* controls the premise and the conclusion. The integrity of the narrative ending as an artistic and theological statement depends on it. Of course, one might reason that because the reliable witness Yhwh says Jonah pitied the plant, then it is true. But such reasoning only begs the point.

Samplings of exegesis attest the problem. One treatment evades it by repeating rather than explaining the text.[55] A second obscures the issue by giving to *ḥûs* the indeterminate meaning "show concern."[56] How the verb acquires such versatility and how this meaning makes a valid analogy are not cogently argued. A third treatment proposes that Yhwh gives Jonah "the benefit of the doubt by attributing his second round of hot anger to his 'pity'" for the withered plant.[57] But this second round does not come after the withering of the plant; it comes only after the sun beats on Jonah's head. Moreover, if his anger comes from his pity, then, contrary to Yhwh's implied view, Jonah would be right after all. It would be "good" it angers him "unto death." A fourth treatment resorts to irony. Yhwh's ascription of pity to Jonah conveys the opposite of its true meaning, which applies only to Yhwh.[58] In other words, the one verb *ḥûs* signifies two different things. But how the text indicates this difference remains unclear. Unstable irony seldom convinces.[59] A fifth treatment rejects this ironic solution but nonetheless (ironically) assigns the verb two different meanings, "fret" and "have compassion."[60] The argument makes the

---

54. On the elusive description, see Sasson, *Jonah,* 314–15.

55. E.g., Limburg, *Hosea-Micah,* 155.

56. E.g., Allen, *Books of Joel, Obadiah, Jonah and Micah,* 230–34.

57. See Ackerman, "Satire and Symbolism in the Song of Jonah," 242–43.

58. See Wolff, *Obadiah and Jonah,* 173; cf. Good, "Jonah: The Absurdity of God," 53.

59. Cf. Wayne C. Booth, *A Rhetoric of Irony* (Chicago: University of Chicago Press, 1974), esp. 1–31.

60. See Sasson, *Jonah,* 300, 309–10, who follows Jerome.

dubious claim that because the plant, unlike the people of Nineveh, is nonhuman, it cannot be the object of pity. How the text indicates the difference again remains unclear. Like unstable irony, shifting meaning hardly convinces. The problem of *ḥûs* persists, threatening the validity of Yhwh's argument.

b. External Analysis

In seeking a solution to the problem of *ḥûs*, rhetorical analysis relies upon its guiding rubric. Structures in episodes three and four provide clues for validating Yhwh's claim that Jonah pitied the plant. The first structure pivots on four occurrences of the verb "burn" (4:1, 4, 9a, 9b). The first occurrence comes in a declarative statement by the narrator (A); the middle two come within questions that Yhwh asks (B and B'); the last comes in a declarative statement by Jonah (A'). Every voice in the episodes, from the most to the least reliable, speaks about the "burning" of Jonah.

4:1 and 4	4:9a and 9b
A *Narrator about Jonah* ". . . and-it-burned to-him."	B' *Yhwh to Jonah* "Is-it-good it-burns to-you about the-plant?"
B *Yhwh to Jonah* "Is-it-good it-burns to-you?"	A' *Jonah about Jonah* "It-is-good it-burns to-me unto death."

The arrangement shows both the extent and the limit of Jonah's anger. It spreads from the first incident of episode three (4:1) through the fourth incident of episode four (4:9b), but it stops short of the fifth incident (4:10-11). By thus containing the anger, the structure separates it from Jonah's pity to supply a negative clue for understanding *ḥûs*.[61] The verb does not pertain to Jonah's anger about the plant.

Other structures contain positive clues for validating Yhwh's attribution of the verb *ḥûs* to Jonah. To trace them requires a return to passages that have received close readings. As Yhwh takes a circuitous route to bring Jonah to the final question, so the rhetorical critic emulates the process in seeking to understand the question. A topical chart outlines the way. It begins with Jonah's first death wish.

---

61. This containment of Jonah's anger joins other structures that isolate 4:10-11; cf. above the discussion of it as the third question.

A

4:3-5

a Jonah's request to Yhwh for death

b Divine question about anger

c Jonah's response: exit

B

4:6-8f

d divine appointment *plant*

  effect on Jonah *shade and deliver*

  Jonah's reaction *delight*

e divine appointment *worm*

  effect on plant *attack and wither*

f divine appointment *wind (and sun)*

  effect on Jonah *faint*

  Jonah's reaction *death wish*

A'

4:8ef-9

a' Jonah's inward request for death

b' Divine question about anger

c' Jonah's response: words

C

4:10-11

x Jonah's pity on the plant

y Yhwh's pity on Nineveh

Three sections within A (a, b, c) correspond in content and placement to three sections within A' (a', b', c'). The center B contains its own three sections (d, e, f). The first and last of them (d and f) match completely, thereby throwing into bold relief the gap in the middle (e). Following A, B, A', the ending C has two internally related sections (x, y). Given the many symmetries, the gap at the center (e) of the center (B) calls attention to itself. Its prominence in the structure bespeaks its prominence in the lack of content. On the one side (d), the narrator reports Jonah's reaction of delight to the plant growing upon his head. On the other (f), the narrator and Jonah report his reaction of despair to the sun beating upon his head after the demise of the plant. But no one tells of Jonah's reaction to the withered plant itself. Having exposed the gap, rhetorical analysis struggles with its meaning. The struggle takes place within the text and between the text and the reader. Rather than appeal to extraneous possibilities, the reader tries to fill the gap from within the story.

Other rhetorical observations assist the struggle. After the demise of the plant, the next reference to it comes when God asks Jonah if it is good for him to burn about the plant (A', b'). The question interprets Jonah's death wish, a wish that comes only after he faints from the sun attacking his head. The double function of the wish in the structure as the ending of B, f and the beginning of A', a' underscores that God's question results from what has happened to Jonah in the searing sun and not from what Jonah felt about the withering of the plant. In other words, the anger about the plant cited in the question does not fill the gap.

By contrast, when Yhwh refers a second time to Jonah and the plant, the deity gives the reader new information. Speaking to Jonah, Yhwh declares, "You-pitied the plant." Distinct in vocabulary, location, and message (C, x), the information serves two purposes. The obvious purpose is to form, for the incident in which it occurs, the premise of the argument. The subtle purpose is to supply, for the incident about the withered plant, the missing report about Jonah's reaction. Hence, this reference to the activity of pity fills the gap. Subject matter (Jonah and the plant) and point of view (pity rather than anger or self-pity) argue for the reading back into B, e of the information given in C, x. In the process the subtle purpose validates the obvious purpose. It validates the premise of Yhwh's argument that Jonah pitied the withered plant qua withered plant. He pitied it in and for itself.

When read back into verse 7 (B, e), the information about Jonah pitying the plant comes between his reaction to its growth above his head and his reaction to the attack of the sun upon his head. While the first and last reactions swing from one self-confirmatory emotional extreme to the other, from great delight to despair unto death,[62] the middle reaction lifts Jonah out of himself. The narrator supplies the first reaction; Yhwh, the middle; Jonah, the last. The reader envisions the pattern:

4:6	4:7; cf. 4:10a	4:8
And-delighted Jonah	[and-pitied Jonah	and-he-asked his-*nepeš* to-die
upon the-plant	the-plant, said Yhwh.]	and-he-said,
a-delight great.		"Better my-death than-my-life."

The verbs "delight" and "pity" expand the character of Jonah beyond the one-dimensional portrayal of his being angry (4:1). In using them, the reliable witnesses, the narrator and Yhwh, suggest that there is more to Jonah than Jonah himself discloses when he asks to die. And yet the reliable witnesses present different Jonahs. His delight for the plant (like his anger) is self-serving. The plant shades him and saves him. His pity, on the other hand, is disinterested compassion. It extends to the withered plant apart from the effect of the withering upon him. Though Jonah abandons this mode of being as soon as he suffers from the beating sun, Yhwh claims it to instruct him and the reader.

The reading back of 4:10a into 4:7 does not mean that the former verse has been misplaced or that a version of it was once a part of 4:7. To the contrary. The incident of the worm and the plant never included the reaction of Jonah. Instead, the storyteller deliberately withheld the information until the closing argument. Matching moves elsewhere in the plot (cf. 1:14; 4:2), the strategy of delayed information strengthens the rhetoric through surprise. It requires the reader to reread: to read backward as well as forward. Having discerned and filled the gap through the clues in structure and content, the reader then interprets the last incident with new understanding. No longer does the analogy between Jonah and Yhwh appear suspect. Jonah's showing of pity becomes a valid premise from which to argue for Yhwh's showing of pity.

As Yhwh's argument discloses a different Jonah, so it reveals a different Yhwh. The change emerges through comparison with the divine portrayal at the end of episode two in the scene. There the narrator reports that God adopts a theology of repentance toward Nineveh. The deity works on a *quid pro quo* basis, an equal exchange between God and Nineveh.

---

62. Cf. Limburg, *Hosea – Micah*, 154–55.

"And-saw the-God their-deeds, that they-turned from-their-way-of the-evil, and-repented the-God about the-evil that he-worded to-do to-them and-not he-did" (3:10). But at the end of episode four Yhwh says nothing at all about mutual repentance between the deity and Nineveh. Instead, Yhwh shifts to a theology of pity (rather than of reciprocity). The shift leads in turn to a different perception of Nineveh: not according to their evil, their deeds, or their repentance of evil but according to their size, their ignorance, and their animals. Juxtaposed at the end of their respective episodes, two theologies account for the salvation of Nineveh: the theology of repentance and the theology of pity.

The change in Yhwh from repenting to pitying comes in still another way. By supplying Jonah's missing response to the withered plant, the deity uses it to reinterpret the divine response to Nineveh. Ironically, Jonah becomes the model for Yhwh free of self-interest, free even of the requirement for repentance. An ecology of pity becomes the paradigm for a theology of pity. That theology embraces plant and animal, perhaps even a worm.

4. Overview

At the beginning of episode three Jonah's prayer (4:2-3) fills a gap in content (but not in structure) that derives from the opening verses of the story (1:1-3). In explaining why he arose to flee to Tarshish, the prayer includes the ancient confession of divine attributes that resonates with a theology of repentance and a theology of pity. It contains thirty-nine words. At the end of episode four Yhwh's disputation (4:10-11) fills a gap in content and structure that derives from within the episode itself (4:7). The disputation relates that Jonah pitied the withered plant and then argues by analogy for Yhwh's pity of Nineveh. It also contains thirty-nine words. Balanced in their respective locations, subject matter, use of direct discourse, contrast of speakers, and number of words, the two passages counter each other as angry Jonah berates Yhwh and merciful Yhwh seeks to persuade Jonah. Both passages surprise the reader; the rhetoric of gap filling discloses the unexpected in Jonah.

The passages contribute to another structure with yet more meanings. Building on word balance, Sasson discovered a well-plotted symmetry in the allocation of direct discourse throughout the episodes.[63]

---

63. Sasson, *Jonah*, 317.

4:2-3	Jonah's monologue	39 words
4:4	God's query (unanswered)	3 words
4:8	Jonah's query (sotto voce)	3 words
4:9	dialogue: God	5 words
	dialogue: Jonah	5 words
4:10-11	God's monologue	39 words

The impressive symmetry suggests that Jonah and Yhwh are evenly matched and that each emulates the other. Initiator and respondent interchange roles to produce the irresolute ending of the book. Yhwh seemingly has the last word, but because it is a question, Jonah has the power of an answer. So the last question moves the story beyond its confines. There is no closure.[64]

Summary. In the irresolute ending, Yhwh shapes a different rhetoric. To mix form critical and classical categories, the genre of disputation finds its *Sitz im Leben* in judicial and deliberative speech.[65] The concern with justice for Nineveh (and for Jonah) befits a legal setting.[66] Through "artful words" Yhwh seeks to persuade Jonah, judge and complainant, to make a right decision about past events. Speech becomes paramount. At the same time, the disputation reaches out to a public assembly. Through "artful words" Yhwh seeks to persuade the hearers (or readers) about the rightness of what the deity does and will do. Their response becomes paramount. In shaping the rhetoric Yhwh appropriates the five skills of the classical orator. The deity chooses material suitable for the occasion (*inventio*). The deity arranges the material so that the parts effectively compose the whole (*dispositio*). The deity selects words appropriate for the content (*elocutio*). The deity fashions a mnemonic system to aid the retention of the content (*memoria*). The deity adeptly delivers the disputation (*pronunciatio*). In short, Yhwh uses all available means of persuasion to argue for the activity of pity toward Jonah, Nineveh—and the reader.[67] Rhetorical eloquence is theological eloquence.

---

64. Cf. the reflections on time and closure in apocalyptic thinking in Frank Kermode, *The Sense of an Ending* (New York: Oxford University Press, 1967).

65. Cf. chapter 1 on types of classical rhetoric.

66. Cf. Terence E. Fretheim, "Jonah and Theodicy," *ZAW* 90 (1978): 227–37.

67. Observe the rhetorical device of anaphora in the five preceding sentences. Each begins with the same words, namely "the deity." The deliberate repetition strives for clarity, parallelism, and emphasis. It also serves as a mnemonic device.

✧   ✧   ✧   ✧   ✧   ✧   ✧

As the closing question opens the narrative beyond its confines, the long journey through external design and internal structure stops though it does not end. The riches of the text signal other possibilities. But this study is sufficient for learning the method of rhetorical criticism under the guiding rubric that appropriate articulation of form-content yields appropriate articulation of meaning. In teaching rhetoric as the art of composition, the book of Jonah unfolds rhetoric as the art of persuasion. What more can the reader want?

10
Guidelines for Continuing

By stopping with a question, the book of Jonah remains open-ended. By stopping with a question, the rhetorical analysis of Jonah remains open-ended. Though the reader may want no more, the writer carries on. In classical rhetoric the faculty of *dispositio*, the arrangement of material in an ordered whole best suited for subject and occasion, moves from the introduction (*exordium*) through stages to the conclusion (*peroratio*).[1] The Greek term for conclusion is *epilogos* (epilogue), deriving from the verb "to say in addition."[2] Adopting the concept but not the specifics, chapter 10 adds words to form an *inclusio* with chapter 4. Both chapters talk about guidelines. Yet even as they correspond, they diverge. Guidelines for beginning are elementary, practical, and detailed. They give the novice techniques for how to do (and not to do) rhetorical analysis. Guidelines for continuing take up advanced issues. They give the student initial reflections on interpretation theory and suggest expanding horizons.

Two observations illuminate the discussion. First, the issues raised emerge from questions asked over many years. In other words, audience-

1. Aristotle recognized between introduction and conclusion only two stages, the statement of the case and of the proof (Aristotle, *"Art" of Rhetoric*, LCL, "Analysis," xiii; also Book III, xiii–xix). Other rhetoricians identified four stages: the statement of the case (*narratio*), the outline of the steps in the argument (*partitio* or *divisio*), the proof of the case (*confirmatio*), and the refutation of opposing arguments (*refutatio*). Cf. *Ad Herennium*, Book I, iii; Cicero, *De Inventione* I, xiv, 19.
2. Aristotle cited four functions for the epilogue: to convince the audience of one's persuasion over against the adversary, to amplify and depreciate, to incite appropriate emotions, and to summarize the case (*Rhetoric*, III, xviii.6—xix.6). Cicero cited three functions: to sum up, to arouse ill will against the opponent, and to arouse the pity (*misericordia*) of the audience (*De Inventione* I, lii.98—lvi.109).

227

response criticism informs the text. The audience is friendly, if not persuaded. Hence, one facet of the classical epilogue has no place: to incite ill will against an adversary in order to win an argument. Second, the answers offered are evocative, not exhaustive. Guidelines cannot conclude the subject, for audiences assure that the work is never finished.[3] So the classical meaning of "epilogue" comes into play. Adding words keeps the discussion open.

A. INTENTIONALITY

The first additional word returns to a favorite topic of readers who ask about authors: intentionality. Frequently comes the question, "Did the author intend the literary structures and meanings that you have presented?"[4] The forthright, if simplistic and dissatisfying, answer is, "I do not know." But the matter does not rest. The word "author" needs clarification. If it means the historical flesh and blood individual(s) who composed Jonah, then little can be said because we lack information about the author's identity, date, place, setting, and intention.[5] If the word means the implied author (the core of norms and choices within the text), then more can be said.[6] The preponderance of literary structures and meanings throughout the book attests to authorial intentionality. This answer to the question comes not from external verification but through textual analysis. It receives support from other texts whose particularities likewise argue for intentional structures and meanings.[7]

Intentionality is tricky business. In writing this book, I have stated the overall intention: to teach rhetorical criticism. I have also stated specific intention: e.g., the structuring of Part One as an *inclusio*, of chapter 2 as a chiasm, and of Part Two as an *inclusio*. Further, I have stated intention in the use of rhetorical devices such as anaphora, hyperbaton, irony, litotes, and pun. All these features the reader can identify as authorial

---

3. Cf. Lentricchia, "In Place of an Afterword—Someone Reading," *Critical Terms for Literary Study*, 321–38.

4. Note the use of question and answer as a teaching device. Cf. the Socratic method; in recent biblical studies, see, e.g., Raymond E. Brown, *Responses to 101 Questions on the Bible* (New York: Paulist Press, 1990).

5. Scholars nevertheless speculate about the author; see the commentaries. But note the rule of Ludwig Wittgenstein: "Of that of which nothing is known nothing can be said." See *Tractatus Logico-Philosophicus* (London: Routledge & Kegan Paul, 1961), 4.461; 5.6, 7.

6. Cf. the discussion of the implied author in chapter 3, p. 68.

7. Cf. the samplings given in chapter 2, pp. 33–40.

intention because I the author have told you the reader. But what about features not so identified? Can you assume that I intend them? The answer is yes for some instances and no for others. Numerous devices are deliberately unidentified for the sake of a pleasing text and with the hope that you are "catching on." Yet other devices, small and large, occur apart from intention. For example, I did not intend the rhyme in the phrase "the test of the best,"[8] nor the alliteration in the phrase "seals the structure and the stress."[9] A reader pointed them out. I did not intend use of the device anastrophe in the sentence "These oppositions deconstruction seeks to reverse and displace,"[10] nor a play on the noun "reflections" and the verb "illuminate" as a link between the first two paragraphs in this chapter. Upon a rereading of "my" text, I discovered these and other features.

A striking example of unintended structure and meaning unfolded as I prepared an early draft of this very discussion. First occurred the thought that I had reached the last chapter, number ten. Then occurred the thought that in the Bible this number functions as a defining concept for completion.[11] Next occurred the thought that ten comprises two other sacred numbers, three and seven. Voilá. The present study contains three chapters in Part One and seven chapters in Part Two for a total of ten. Observing so perfect a correspondence between the biblical rhetoric of numbers and the arrangement of the book, a reader might conclude that the author intended the artifice. Not so. I did not intend the structure and the meaning, though I am delighted to have found them and now wish to claim them.[12] By the same token, you the reader may have found meanings in my writing of which I am unaware—including some I may wish to repudiate. Similarly, the rhetorical critic can find structures and meanings in the biblical text apart from the intention of the implied, much less the real, author.[13] The lesson is that, for weal or woe, a text carries meanings its author never intended.

8. See chapter 2, pp. 46.
9. See chapter 6, pp. 142.
10. See chapter 3, p. 71.
11. See M. H. Pope, "Number, Numbering, Numbers," *IDB* 3 (K-Q), 565f., and the biblical references cited therein.
12. Psychological analysis would no doubt talk about conscious, subconscious, and unconscious faculties at work here.
13. Cf. Craven on her rhetorical analysis of Judith: ". . . I would not want to argue that the author intended all the moments in the story which give me pleasure" (*Artistry and Faith*, 121).

The concept of intentionality holds possibilities and pitfalls. We do not know the intention of the flesh-and-blood author of Jonah, but we can discern signals of intentionality in the text. Whether they come from the actual author, the implied author, the implied reader, or interaction between the text and the actual reader remains a moot proposition. For example, the withholding until 4:2-3 of the reason for Jonah's flight in 1:3 appears deliberate.[14] Structure, style, and content support the idea, though external verification is wanting. But who knows if the author intended through contrasts between the sailors and the Ninevites to disallow stereotypical thinking about foreigners? Who knows if the author intended by use of the verb *hpk* (overturn) to hold in tension the opposite meanings of destruction and deliverance (3:4)? Who knows if the author intended the disappearance of the word "evil" in the last line of 3:10 to mirror the decision of God not to do it?[15] Without explicit documentation, authorial intentionality cannot be assured. And even if it be known, it cannot control interpretation of the text. My own writing teaches me so. But the lesson disavows the claim that all interpretations are equally valid. (More on the subject later.)

Aphorisms enliven the answer as they round it off. "By their fruits [not by their intentions] you shall know them" (cf. Matt. 7:16). The appropriation of this biblical injunction about false prophets shifts emphasis away from intentionality to text and reader. In turn, Jesus' words inspire a reappropriation of Alonso-Schökel's: "By the sweat of your brow [including your intentions] you shall produce fruit; share the fruit, not the sweat." At the boundary of text and reader, where sharing takes place, the intentionality of an author (ancient or contemporary) meets confirmation, challenge, and uncertainty.[16]

B. SUBJECTIVITY

The second additional word is like unto the first: "Isn't rhetorical analysis subjective?" The question assumes a total divide between objectivity and subjectivity. Objectivity constitutes the only valid model for scholarly

---

14. See chapter 9, pp. 203–04.

15. In using the words "who knows," I had no intention of imitating the king of Nineveh (3:9). Only when I read the paragraph aloud to a friend did I hear the allusion.

16. Cf. Annabel Patterson, "Intention," *Critical Terms for Literary Study*, 135–46.

pursuit.[17] Subjectivity threatens critical research by allowing any and all interpretations to be imposed upon the text. Within literary critical scholarship, the debate often pits so-called objective theories against reader-response criticism or deconstruction. Within biblical scholarship, the debate often pits historical criticism against literary criticism. Round and round go the debates with each side committing transgressions it finds in the other.

To the extent that the words "objective" and "subjective" are useful, one must allow for both in scholarly endeavors. Each corrects and is corrected by the other; neither gains ascendancy. So a straightforward answer to the question posed accepts the label "subjective" but rejects the assumptions. The answer continues by observing that subjectivity characterizes all biblical methods. Subjects (i.e., scholars) devise methods, subjects use methods, and subjects draw different conclusions from the use of methods. Research on Jonah anchors the point.[18] Historical critics offer a range of dates for the book, stretching from the seventh to the second centuries B.C.E. Form critics offer an array of genres with no consensus beyond the category of fiction. Source critics offer equally persuasive arguments for and against the presence of the psalm as integral to the story. Similarly, rhetorical critics offer different analyses of literary divisions and structures. Devised and used by subjects, methods do not produce "objective" findings. Like all other biblical disciplines, rhetorical criticism participates in subjectivity.

The label "subjective" need not mean that all interpretations are equally valid or even valid. No, the text itself sets limits to subjectivity. Evaluation of four literary analyses of Jonah 1:3-16 has already demonstrated the principle.[19] The chiasm that introduces the passage advances the argument.

---

17. For recent attempts to redefine "objectivity" and "subjectivity," cf. Lorraine Code, *What Can She Know? Feminist Theory and the Construction of Knowledge* (Ithaca, N.Y.: Cornell University Press, 1991), 31–55; Thomas L. Haskell, "Objectivity is not Neutrality: Rhetoric vs. Practice in Peter Novick's *That Noble Dream*," *History and Theory* 29/2 (1990): 129–57.

18. See the discussion *passim* in chapters 5 through 9; also check the commentaries.

19. See the excursus at the end of chapter 6.

A And/but-arose Jonah to-flee to-Tarshish from-the-presence-of Yhwh

   B and-he-went-down to-Joppa

   　C and-he-found a-ship

   　　D returning (to) Tarshish

   　C′ and-he-paid her-fare

   B′ and-he-went-down in-it

A′ to-return with-them to-Tarshish from-the-presence-of Yhwh. (1:3)

A first reading might suggest that both the repetition and the placement of the phrases "to-Tarshish" and "from-the-presence-of Yhwh" confirm the message of flight. Structure and content stress Tarshish as Jonah's destination away from Yhwh. What they say is what happens. But the interpretation flounders as the story develops and the reader learns that Jonah cannot escape Yhwh. So the reader looks again at the verse and this time sees the irony of its structure and meaning: that the presence of Yhwh surrounds Jonah's flight to Tarshish from Yhwh. Accordingly, the story undermines the first reading and validates the second.[20] Verse 3 figures also in another illustration of interpretive limits. It gives no reason for Jonah's flight from Yhwh's imperative. Readers seek to fill the gap by declaring that Jonah is tenderhearted (Sternberg) or that he fears martyrdom (Frye).[21] But as the story continues, structure and content discredit these interpretations. Jonah gives the reason: his antipathy to the loving character of Yhwh. Whatever subjective ideas the gap in 1:3 inspires, the information in 4:2-3 undercuts. The text constricts interpretation.

For gaps that are never filled, subjective responses (as distinguished from the subjectivity of methods) may produce outlandish readings. The failure to explain why the Ninevites readily believed in God has led to the idea that Jonah's ghastly flesh (contaminated by the gastric juices of the fish) convinced them.[22] No method supports such unbridled fantasy. Yet even a respectable (itself a subjective word) reading of an unfilled gap can encounter trouble. The silence in the text about how the Ninevites responded to their deliverance from evil has led to the claim that they became Yhwh worshipers. At several places the text restrains the

20. See the discussion in chapter 6, pp. 129–31.
21. Cf. chapter 9.
22. See the discussion in chapter 8, p. 182.

speculation: the silence about the Ninevites versus the report about the sailors worshiping Yhwh (1:14, 16); the use of only the generic term "God" ('*elohîm*), never the name Yhwh, throughout the account of the Ninevites (3:5-10); and the failure of Yhwh to cite their conversion in justifying divine pity upon the city (4:10-11). Narrator and characters, silence and speech argue against filling the gap with a subjective hypothesis about Yhwh worship.

If rhetorical criticism does not shrink from the label "subjective," neither does it embrace all sorts and conditions of readings.[23] Proper or appropriate (themselves subjective words) articulation of form-content limits meaning. Within the limits varieties flourish, but they need not hold equal validity.

C. ARTISTRY AND THEOLOGY

The third additional word returns to artistry and theology. After being shown how these concerns interweave, some hearers still harbor skepticism. Those who reside in biblical studies worry that artistry may diminish, replace, or vitiate theology. "Isn't rhetorical analysis so enamored of style that it neglects theology?"[24] they tactfully ask. The question echoes the ancient, yet ever-present, debate about ethics and eloquence.[25] It also harks back to the discussion about aesthetics and the Muilenburg mode.[26] My answer but recalls two analyses that bind artistry and theology.

In replying to the sailors' questions, Jonah proclaims:

> And-Yhwh, God-of the-heavens,
> I (am) fearing
> who made the-sea and-the-dry-land. (1:9b)

The words abound with theological language. Yhwh is God of the cosmos: the heavens, sea, and dry land. Using merism, Jonah underscores

---

23. Another way of stating this view is that all exegesis is eisegesis but not all eisegesis is exegesis.

24. The question borrows from Brueggemann, whose concern was with the neglect of the political in rhetorical analysis; see chapter 2, p. 52. For comparable concerns, see Clifford, *Fair Spoken and Persuading*, 35–36; Childs, *Old Testament Books for Pastor and Teacher,* 73. An artist may well ask the contrasting question, "Isn't rhetorical analysis so enamored of theology that it devalues art?"

25. Cf. chapter 1, pp. 6–7.

26. Cf. chapter 2, p. 51.

transcendence and immanence. By itself the formula presents a compelling portrait of the deity, and yet the particular construction skews the meaning. Practicing hyperbaton, Jonah splits the formula by inserting the words "I (am) fearing." This device achieves double irony. Jonah makes himself the pivot of a proclamation about Yhwh and surrounds himself with the God he is fearing. Yhwh pursues the runaway Jonah; Jonah cooperates by occupying the center of the divine orbit. The structure of the sentence mirrors the meaning; the meaning mirrors the structure. In explicating form-content, rhetorical analysis shows the interweaving of art and theology.

At the end of the story Yhwh says to Jonah: "You, you-pitied (*ḥûs*) for the-plant" (4:10a). The verb "pity" and the information it gives is new to the story. Nowhere has the reader been told that Jonah pitied the plant. Yet on this declaration rests the validity of Yhwh's argument for divine pity: "And-I, (shall) not I-have-pity (*ḥûs*) for Nineveh. . . ?" (4:11a). After sampling attempts to secure "pity" as a suitable verb for Jonah, rhetorical analysis turned to its guiding rubric with the hope, but not the guarantee, that appropriate articulation of form-content might yield appropriate articulation of meaning. For a long time (so I testify) no insights emerged. Indeed, earlier drafts of this book said that rhetorical criticism, like other biblical disciplines, cannot solve the problem raised by use of the verb "pity." Then upon a day an answer began to surface. The specifics are set forth in chapter 9. Suffice it to recall the chart that outlines 4:3-11.[27] In reference to appointments by Yhwh, their effect, and Jonah's reaction (4:6, 7, 8), the structure showed a gap at the center of the center: the omission of Jonah's reaction to the withering of the plant qua plant (4:7). Pondering the omission brought the realization that the principle of delayed information operating elsewhere (e.g., 1:10 and 4:2-3) was also at work here. The information given by Yhwh in 4:10a about Jonah's pity for the plant fills the gap in 4:7. There Jonah responded with disinterested compassion to the withering of the plant. Reported only later, that response validates the premise of Yhwh's argument for divine pity upon Nineveh. All in all, rhetorical analysis illuminates and secures the theological vocabulary of "pity." In the process and its outcome artistry and theology intertwine.

---

27. See above p. 220.

No matter how one answers the question about artistry and theology, it will probably never go away.[28] Definitions, interests, and fears differ from theologian to theologian. Not everyone hears with the same ears and sees with the same eyes. But enough. For rhetorical critics, like literary artists over the centuries, "Poetry is a revelation in words by means of the words."[29] For rhetorical critics, like biblical exegetes throughout the ages, "God dwells in the details."[30] From both perspectives, not a jot, not a tittle, passes away. Like steadfast love and faithfulness, artistry and theology meet; like righteousness and peace, they kiss (cf. Ps 85:10).

∘ ∘ ∘ ∘ ∘ ∘ ∘

Additional words never cease. They come from every tongue and from the confusion of tongues. They want to know, for example, if rhetorical criticism can be applied to all sorts and conditions of texts (yes), if it would not be desirable to formulate a program of procedures more specific than the guiding rubric (no), if the process cannot be made easier (no), and if the fruit is worth the sweat (yes).[31] Still other tongues ask about philosophical underpinnings, about the intersection of rhetorical and social-scientific analysis, about rhetorical criticism and intertextual studies, and about rhetorical criticism and interdisciplinary endeavors. To hear all these tongues and to speak oneself is to engage hermeneutics, the art of understanding.[32] The engagement is no easy task, and the reader of the text may well resist. In that case, let the book of Jonah perform its hermeneutical duty. Though the rhetorical critic may arise to flee from the

---

28. For sympathetic treatments, see Timothy Polk, "In the Image: Aesthetics and Ethics through the Glass of Scripture," *HBT* 8 (1986): 27–59; Craven, *Artistry and Faith in the Book of Judith*, 34–43.

29. See Wallace Stevens, "The Noble Rider and the Sound of Words," *The Necessary Angel: Essays on Reality and the Imagination* (New York: Vintage Books, 1951), 33.

30. The sentence "God dwells in the details" plays on the saying "God is in the details." The latter has been variously attributed to the novelist Gustave Flaubert, the critic Aby Warburg, the architect Mies van der Rohe, and the ever-present woman Anonymous.

31. Cf. the counsel that Elizabeth Bishop wrote to an aspiring poet: "It can't be done, apparently, by willpower and study alone—or by being 'with it'—but I really don't know *how* poetry gets to be written. There is a mystery & a surprise, and after that a great deal of hard work." See Elizabeth Bishop, "To Miss Pierson" [28 May 1975], *One Art: Letters, Selected and Edited by Robert Giroux* (New York: Farrar, Straus, Giroux, 1994), 596.

32. For an introduction, see Bernard C. Lategan, "Hermeneutics," *ABD* 3, 149–54 and the bibliography cited there; cf. Sandra M. Schneiders, *The Revelatory Text: Interpreting the New Testament as Sacred Scripture* (San Francisco: Harper, 1991), 110–79.

imperative of interpretation, it will pursue her on sea and dry land: in the words of strangers and the deeds of foreigners; in the belly of the fish, the shelter of the booth, and the shade of the plant; in her own words spoken and unspoken; and in the persistent questioning of the Divine Interpreter. Epilogue becomes prologue; rhetoric does not rest; the book continues as it concludes.[33]

33. On the rhetoric of this sentence, cf. Aristotle: "to the conclusion of the speech the most appropriate style is that which has no connecting particles, in order that it may be a peroration, but not an oration: 'I have spoken; you have heard; you know the facts; now give your decision'" (*Rhetoric,* III, xix, 6). On the idea, cf. Virginia Woolf. "For books continue each other, in spite of our habit of judging them separately" (*A Room of One's Own* [New York: Harcourt, Brace & World, Inc., 1957], 84).

Appendix A

THE BOOK OF JONAH: A STUDY IN STRUCTURE

This appendix assembles the text of Jonah according to the literary divisions and rhetorical structures presented in chapters 6 through 9. For consistency and clarity, the underlinings and markings follow the pattern used above. They pertain to the individual rhetorical structures within incidents and are not coordinated across larger literary divisions.

Scene One

Episode One (1:1-3)

And-was the-word-of Yhwh to Jonah, son-of Amittai, saying:
"Arise
    go to Nineveh the-city the-great
    and-call to-her because has-come-up their-evil before-my-presence."
                                (1:1-2)

A   And/but-arose Jonah to-flee to-Tarshish from-the-presence-of Yhwh

    B   and-he-went-down to-Joppa

        C   and-he-found a-ship

            D   returning (to) Tarshish
               × × × × × × ×

        C'   and-he-paid her-fare

    B'   and-he-went-down in-it

A'   to-return with-them to-Tarshish from-the-presence-of Yhwh. (1:3)
    × × × × × × × ×

Episode Two (1:4-6)

But-Yhwh hurled a-wind <u>great</u> <u>to the-sea</u>,

 and-there-was a-tempest <u>great</u> <u>in-the-sea</u>,

 and-the-ship thought to-break-up. (1:4)

And-feared the-sailors,

 and-they-cried, each-man to his-god(s),

 and-they-hurled the-wares that (were) in-the-ship <u>to the-sea</u>

 to-lighten from-upon-them.

But-Jonah went-down to-the-innards-of the-vessel,

 and-he-lay-down,

 and-he-slept. (1:5)

And-drew-near to-him the-captain-of the-mariners,

 and-he-said to-him:

 "What to-you, sleeping!

 Arise, call to-your-god.

 Perhaps will-favor the-god to-us so-not we-perish." (1:6)

Episode Three (1:7-16)

And-they-said, each-man to his-neighbor:

 "Come <u>and-let-us-cast lots</u>

 and-let-us-know

 <u>on-whose-account</u> the-evil the-this (is) to-us." ××××

<u>And-they-cast lots</u>

 and-cast the-lot upon Jonah. (1:7)

And-they-said to-him:

 A "Tell, please, to-us
     ××××

   <u>on-whose</u> account the-evil the-this (is) to-us? ××××

  B What (is) your-occupation
       ****

      and-from-where have-you-come?
       +++++++++++

    What (is) your-land
     ****

      and-where from-this people (are) you?"
       +++++++++++++++++++

And-he-said to-them:

  B′ "A-Hebrew (am) I.

 A′ And-Yhwh, God-of the-heavens,

   I (am) fearing

   who made the-sea and-the-dry-land." (1:8-9)

And-were-afraid the-men a-fear great.

And-they-said to-him:
"What (is) this you-have-done!"

For (*kî*) knew the-men

that (*kî*) from-the-presence-of Yhwh he (was) fleeing

for (*kî*) he-told to-them. (1:10)

And-they-said to-him:
"What shall-we-do to-you

and-may-be-quiet the-sea from-upon-us?"
× ×
Indeed (*kî*) the-sea (was) going and-storming. (1:11)
- - - - - - - *
And-he-said to-them:
"Pick-up-me and-hurl-me to the-sea

and-may-be-quiet the-sea from-upon-you,
× ×
for (*kî*) knowing (am) I

that (*kî*) on-account-of-me

the-storm the-great the-this (is) upon-you." (1:12)

And-digged the-men to-return to the-dry-land,
and-not were-they-able.
Indeed (*kî*) the-sea (was) going and-storming upon-them. (1:13)
- - - - - - - *
And-they-called to Yhwh and they said:

Invocation:	"Ah! Yhwh,
Petition:	Not, pray, let-us-perish
	for-the-life-of (*nepeš*) the-man the-this;
	and-not give upon-us blood innocent.
Motivation:	For (*kî*) you, Yhwh,
	as you-wish you-do." (1:14).

A ⎡ And-they-picked-up Jonah
    B ⎡ and-they-hurled-him to the-sea
        ⎣ and-ceased the-sea from-its-raging. (1:15)

    B′ ⎡ And-feared the-men a-fear great (of) Yhwh
         ⎣ and-they-sacrificed a-sacrifice to-Yhwh
A′ ⎣ and-they-vowed vows. (1:16)

Episode Four (2:1-11)

A   And-appointed Yhwh a-fish great to-swallow Jonah,

           a   **b**   **c**

B   and-was Jonah in-the-belly-of the-fish three days and-three nights.

           a′   **d**   **b′**

B′   And-prayed Jonah to Yhwh his-God from-the-belly-of the-fish. (2:1-2).

And-he-said:

A

> "I-call from-the-distress to-me
>   to Yhwh and-he-answers-me.
>
> From-the-womb-of sheol I-cry.
>   You-hear my-voice. (2:3)

B

> You-cast-me toward-the-depths,
>   into-the-heart-of the-sea,
>   and-the-current surrounds-me.
>
> All your-waves and-your-breakers
>   over-me pass. (2:4)
>
> But-I, I-said, 'I-have-been-driven-out
>   from-before your-eyes,'
> Nevertheless I-continue to-look
>   to-the-temple-of your-holiness. (2:5)

B′

> Enclosed-me waters up-to the-neck (*nepeš*);
>   * * * * * * *
>   deep surrounds-me.
>
> Weeds entwine to-my-head
>   to-the-roots-of the-mountains I-go-down.
> The-earth [netherworld], its-bars about-me forever. (2:6-7b)
>
> But-you-bring-up from-the-grave my-life,
>   Yhwh my-God.
> When-ebbing-away to-me myself (*napšî*)
>   * * * * * *
>   Yhwh I-remember.
> And-comes to-you my-prayer
>   to-the-temple-of your-holiness. (2:7c-8)

$\mathbf{A'}$ ⎡ Those-obeying idols empty
their-loyalty forsake.
But-I with-a-voice-of thanksgiving,
I-shall-sacrifice to-you.
What I-vow I-shall-pay.
Deliverance to-Yhwh!" (2:9-10)

A' And-said Yhwh to-the-fish and-it-vomited Jonah to the-dry-land. (2:11)

Scene Two

Episode One (3:1-4)

And-was the-word-of Yhwh to Jonah a-second-time, saying:

"Arise
go to Nineveh the-city the-great
×××××××× ******
and-call to-her the-calling that I (am) wording-to-you." (3:1-2)

a
And-arose Jonah
     b
 and-he-went [walked] to Nineveh according-to-the-word-of Yhwh.
··············· ××××××××

  b' **c**   **d**   **e**
And-Nineveh was a-city great to-god, a-walk -of three days,
×××××××××× *****   ············ +‡+

   a'   **c'** **d'** **e'**
And-began Jonah to-enter into-the-city a-walk-of day one. (3:3-4a)
       ****** ············++‡
And-he-called and-he-said:
"Yet forty day(s) and-Nineveh will-be-overturned
+‡++ ××××××××× [or] overturns." (3:4b)

Episode Two (3:5-10)

And-believed the-people-of Nineveh in-God,
and-they-called a-fast,
and-they-put-on sackcloth, from-their-great and-to their-small. (3:5)

And-reached the-word to the-king-of Nineveh. (3:6a)
 A And-he-arose from-his-throne
  B and-he-removed his-robe from-upon-him
  B' and-he-covered-himself [with] sackcloth
 A' and-he-sat upon the-ashes. (3:6b)

241

And-he-cried and-he-said:

Authorization   In-Nineveh
                  By-the-authority-of the-king and-his-great-ones,
                       to-say,

Salutation   The-human and-the-animal,
                  The-herd and-the-flock

Corpus
  Negative   Let-not them-taste anything;
  instructions   Let-not them-graze;
                  And-water let-not them-drink.

  Positive   But-let-them-cover-themselves (in) sackcloth,
  instructions   the-human and-the-animal,
                  And-let-them-call to God with-strength,
                  And-let-them-turn, each-one,
                       from-his-way-of the-evil
                       from the-violence that (is) in-their-hands.

Conclusion   Who knows,
                  May-return
                  And-may-repent the-God
                  And-may-turn from-the-burning-of his-nostrils,
                  And-not we-perish. (3:7-9)

a

And-saw the-God their-deeds,

b

kî they-turned from-their-way-of the-evil,

b'

and-repented the-God about the-evil

a'

that (*'ašer*) he-worded to-do to-them,

a"

and-not he-did. (3:10)

Episode Three (4:1-4 and 5)

And-it-was-evil to Jonah an-evil great and-it-burned to-him. (4:1)
And-he-prayed to Yhwh and-he-said:

Invocation   "Ah, Yhwh!

Corpus

Rebuke   Was-not this my-word
         while I-was in my-homeland?

Justification Therefore I-hastened to-flee to-Tarshish

Motivation because I-knew that (*kî yādaʿtî kî*)
            You God (are)
               gracious and-merciful
               long-of nostrils
               and-abundant-of faithfulness
               and-repenting about the-evil.

Conclusion

Petition   And-now, Yhwh,

            take, please, my-*nepeš* from-me,

Reason   for (*kî*) better my-death than-my-life." (4:2-3)

And-said Yhwh: "Is-it-good it-burns to-you?" (4:4)

A   But-went-out Jonah from the-city
  B   and-he-sat-down from-the-east to-the-city.
A' And-he-made for-himself there a-booth
  B' and-he-sat-down under-it in-the-shade
    C   until he-should-see what would-happen in-the-city. (4:5)

Episode Four (4:6-11)

And-appointed Yhwh God a-plant,
   and-it-grew-up from-upon to-Jonah
         ×××××××××××
              *****
         to-be a-shade upon his-head
            ×××××××××××
         to-deliver to-him from-his-evil,
      and-delighted Jonah upon the-plant a-delight great. (4:6)
      + + + + + + + + + ***** ············ + + + + +
                  ×××××××××××

And-appointed the-God a-worm,

       when-came-up the-dawn on-the-next-day,
and-it-attacked the-plant

and-it-withered. (4:7)
And-it-came-to-pass when-to-rise the-sun

    and-appointed God a-wind, east strong

    and-attacked the-sun upon the-head-of Jonah

    and-he-fainted
    and-he-asked his-*nepeš* to-die and-he-said:

    "Better my-death than-my-life." (4:8)

And-said God to Jonah:

    "Is-it-good it-burns to-you about the-plant?"

And-he-said:

    "It-is-good it-burns to-me unto death." (4:9)

And-said Yhwh:

  A "You, you-pitied for the-plant,

    B which not you-planted it

      and- not you-caused-it-to-be-great,

      C which-a-child-of the-night became,

        and-a-child-of the-night perished.

  A' And-I, (shall) not I-have-pity for Nineveh the-city the-great,

    B' which (is) in-it to-be-many

      more-than-two ten-of ten-thousand human
      C' who not know

        between his-right-hand to-his-left,

      D and-animal(s) many?" (4:10-11)

244

Appendix B

Prepared by Sarah Ryan

This book has sought to do what it teaches. Among its instruction is the use of various literary and rhetorical devices. Sometimes they have been identified; other times they have not. Now the time has come to test your awareness and knowledge. After all, no teaching situation is complete without examination.

Below in the left hand column is a list of devices used throughout the book; in the right hand column, grouped by letters of the alphabet, are numbers of pages where examples of these devices can be found. Read the page or pages in each group and identify one device they exhibit in common. Match the identification with the device listed by writing the corresponding letter of the alphabet in the space provided. The first entry is done as an example. The answers are on the pages following. (Have fun. No cheating!)

F	alliteration	A.	pp. 161–62, 186, 192, 202, 234
___	allusion, biblical	B.	p. 236
___	allusion, non-biblical	C.	pp. 182, 191–92, 195, 216
___	*anacephalaeosis*	D.	pp. 49, 95, 108
___	anadiplosis	E.	pp. 182, 202–03
___	anaphora	F.	pp. 25, 28, 40, 98, 184

245

___ anastrophe	G. pp. 105, 145, 172, 173, 178
___ antanaclasis	H. p. 161
___ antithesis	I. p. 180
___ asyndeton	J. p. 190
___ chiasm	K. pp. 82, 94 and 191, 170, 175, 208, 214
___ ellipsis	L. p. 12
___ hysteron proteron	M. pp. ix, 73, 161, 172, 235
___ *inclusio*	N. p. 225
___ leitmotif	O. pp. 42, 121, 157
___ litotes	P. pp. 60, 192–93
___ merism	Q. pp. 31, 39, 105
___ paronomasia	R. pp. 230, 235
___ pun	S. pp. 48, 53, 213
___ rhetorical question	T. pp. 23, 47–48, 83–84, 190–91, 201–02
___ syllepsis	U. p. 1 and *passim*

Answers

Note: For the definitions given here, see Corbett, *Classical Rhetoric for the Modern Student;* Holman and Harmon, *A Handbook to Literature;* Lanham, *A Handlist of Literary Terms.*

 F alliteration: recurrence of an initial consonant sound
     p. 25 - program, proposal, practice
     p. 28 - Practice precedes proposal.
     p. 40 - samples, subject, suffice
     p. 98 - structure, style, substance
     p. 184 - dwelling, dress, dignity

 M allusion, biblical: indirect reference to or appropriation of a biblical text (from the Latin *allusio*, a playing with)
     p. ix - "When I was a child. . ."; cf. 1 Cor. 13:11
     p. 73 - "a new thing in the land"; cf. Jer. 31:22
     p. 161 - "Round and round. . ."; cf. Eccl. 1:6
     p. 172 - "Much labor becomes a weariness of the mind"; cf. Eccl. 12:12
     p. 235 - "jots and tittles"; cf. Matt. 5:18

 K allusion, non-biblical: indirect reference to or appropriation of a well-known historical or literary figure, event, idea, or text
     p. 82 - "The judgment of impending death was exaggerated." Cf. Mark Twain: "The report of my death was an exaggeration" (note to London correspondent of the *New York Journal,* June 1, 1897).
     pp. 94 and 191 - ". . . no text is an island unto itself." Cf. John Donne: "No man is an island, entire of itself" ("Devotions upon Emergent Occasions," Meditation XVII).
     p. 170 - "The verse that heads stanza four (2:9) lies uneasy in the psalm." Cf. William Shakespeare: "Uneasy lies the head that wears the crown" (*Henry IV, Part II,* Act III, Scene 1).
     p. 175 - "With remembrance of things past. . . ." Cf. Marcel Proust, *Remembrance of Things Past.*
     p. 208 - "Thus in the center . . . the structure does not hold; . . . the content does not hold." Cf. William Butler Yeats:

"Things fall apart; the center cannot hold . . ." ("The Second Coming," *The Collected Poems of W. B. Yeats*).
    p. 214 - "Neither plant nor worm . . . self-appointed round . . ." Cf. the motto carved above the columns of the U.S. General Post Office in New York City: "Neither snow nor rain nor heat nor gloom of night stays these couriers from the swift completion of their appointed rounds." The motto adapts a saying by the Greek historian Herodotus.

T   *anacephalaeosis:* summary or recapitulation that is intended to refresh the hearer's or reader's memory
    p. 23 - the last paragraph, beginning "Biblical rhetorical criticism . . ."
    pp. 47–48 - *Summary* and the first paragraph of A'
    pp. 83–84 - *Summary of Part One*
    pp. 190–91 - *Summary*
    pp. 201–02 - *Summary*

A   anadiplosis: repetition of the last word of one line or clause to begin the next
    pp. 161–62 - ". . . dissonance. Dissonance. . . ."
    p. 186 - ". . . the conclusion. The conclusion. . . ."
    p. 192 - ". . . acts of penance. Penitential acts. . . ."
    p. 202 - ". . . Jonah; Jonah. . . ."
    p. 234 - ". . . the meaning; the meaning. . . ."

C   anaphora: repetition of the same word at the beginning of successive clauses
    p. 182 - three sentences beginning "Unlike the sailors . . ."
    pp. 191–92 - four sentences beginning "When . . ."
    p. 195 - four sentences beginning "In the first . . .", with second clauses beginning "in the second . . ."
    p. 216 - three sentences beginning "Whereas the first two . . ."

__Q__ anastrophe: unusual arrangement of words or clauses within a sentence
> p. 31 - "Commented Muilenburg . . .": Verb precedes subject.
> p. 39 - ". . . the Hebrew verb '*mr* he translated in 17:34 . . ." (note 39): Object precedes subject and verb.
> p. 105 - "The double task of description and interpretation you may intertwine or treat sequentially": Object precedes subject and verb.

__J__ *antanaclasis:* one word that is used in two contrasting, usually comic, senses
> p. 190 - "Immediately they . . . put on sackcloth. Their king follows *suit.*"

__S__ antithesis: conjoining of contrasting ideas
> p. 48 - "To credit or criticize . . . ."
> p. 53 - "The four elements balance . . . ; they diverge . . ." (note 2).
> p. 213 - "Jonah seeks life; . . . he seeks death" (note 46).

__B__ asyndeton: omission of conjunctions between words, phrases, or clauses
> p. 236 - the last sentence, beginning "Epilogue becomes . . ."

__R__ chiasm: inverted correspondences between words, phrases, sentences, or larger units
> p. 230 - "the actual author, the implied author, the implied reader, . . . the actual reader"
> p. 235 - the parenthetical answers "yes, no, no, yes" in the last paragraph

__D__ ellipsis: omission of a word that is easily supplied
> p. 49 - "The former interprets a text through the history of its composition and the latter [interprets a text] exclusively in its final form."
> p. 95 - "Articulation of form-content remains primary; environment, [remains] secondary."
> p. 108 - "Some proposals reflect disagreements about the book; others [reflect] disagreements about nomenclature for genres" (note 2).

__P__   *hysteron proteron:* syntax or sense that is out of normal, logical, or temporal order

        p. 60 - "The latter is only . . .; the former . . ."

        pp. 192–93 - five sentences *passim* in which "Jonah 3" precedes "Jonah 1"

__E__   *inclusio:* parallelism of words, phrases, or sentences between the beginning and ending of a unit

        p. 182 - the paragraph that begins and ends with sentences starting with the word "Why"

        pp. 202–03 - the paragraph beginning and ending with the words "the prayer" and "vocabulary"

__U__   leitmotif: thematic passage or dominant theme

        p. 1 and *passim* - ". . . tongues and the confusion of tongues": The phrase is also a biblical illusion; cf. Gen. 11:6-9 and Acts 2:3-4.

__O__   litotes: denial of the contrary; understatement that intensifies

        p. 42 - "Though Muilenburg did not use these categories, his observations are *not incompatible* with them."

        p. 121 - ". . . the work *does not get easier* the more one does it."

        p. 157 - ". . . a matter of *no small consequence.*"

__L__   merism: division of the whole into its parts

        p. 12 - ". . . expresses the author's own *mind, heart, and soul. . . .*"

__H__   paronomasia: type of pun that plays on similarly sounding words

        p. 161 - "But the matter does not *rest* there because rhetorical analysis must always *wrestle* with the final form."

__G__   pun: generic term for a play on words

        p. 105 - a play between "clear prose" and "this prosaic undertaking" (guideline 9)

        p. 145 - the verb "harbors" and the marine imagery of sea and sailors (paragraph f)

        p. 172 - the description "nauseous effect" and the verb "it vomited"

        p. 172 - the play between chasm and chiasm (note 44)

        p. 173 - the phrase "casts its lot" and Jonah 1:7

        p. 178 - the words "the last two clauses walk away" and the word "walk" in Jonah 3:3-4a

 N rhetorical question: question that implies the answer it asserts or denies

      p. 225 - the last sentence, "What more can the reader want?"

 I syllepsis: type of pun whereby a word is understood differently in relation to two or more other words that it modifies or governs

      p. 180 - "They *invite* characters and readers to exploit meanings."

Indexes

AUTHORS AND EDITORS

HEBREW WORDS

SCRIPTURE*

*Verse by verse references to Jonah are not listed.

SUBJECTS